Dear ?

MW00532928

The Miracle of
Organic Vitamins
for
Better Health

The Miracle of Organic Vitamins for Better Health

CARLSON WADE

Foreword by William S. Keezer, M.D.

Parker Publishing Company, Inc.   West Nyack, N.Y.

© 1974, by

PARKER PUBLISHING COMPANY, INC.

West Nyack, N.Y.

Reward Edition . . . . . June 1976

Library of Congress Cataloging in Publication Data

Wade, Carlson.
    The miracle of organic vitamins for better health.

    Includes bibliographical references.
    1. Vitamin therapy. 2. Vitamin metabolism.
3. Vitamin in human nutrition. I. Title.
[DNLM: 1. Nutrition--Popular works. 2. Vitamins--
Popular works. QU160 W119m 1974]
RM259.W3   615'.854   74-7255

Printed in the United States of America

Dedication

To Nature Who Created Perfect Vitamin Healers

Foreword
by a Doctor of Medicine

This book is a masterpiece of the secrets for partaking of the best that Nature has to offer in the way of youth, life and health. It is one of the most complete guidebooks on natural rejuvenation that is currently available. It offers hope for natural healing by using healthful foods in a simple, yet powerfully effective method. This book offers you a treasure of secrets from the Garden of Nature. It is the one book everyone, who seeks perpetual youth, should have in his possession.

Carlson Wade, a highly respected writer-reporter on medical topics, tells how vitamins in everyday foods can be used as natural healers for almost all popular ailments from head to toe. He tells you how fresh fruits, vegetables, grains, seeds and nuts, as well as oils and many common, everyday foods from the animal world can do more than just satisfy your taste and appetite. He tells you how they can help heal your skin, how they can improve your eyesight; how they can give you rich, throbbing blood; how they can act as natural tranquilizers.

This leading medical researcher offers you documented programs showing how to make some simple eating adjustments and enjoy youthful mentality. Even arthritis can be soothed by corrective vitaminized programs as outlined herein. Carlson Wade, then, tells you how you can use vitamins in foods to build natural antibodies, resist colds, then use these same foods to rebuild your internal organs.

His book shows you how simple foods have cholesterol-washing vitamins and how some foods can heal nervous disorders. He taps the little-known secrets of using plant vitamins for healing your body and supercharging your organism with the joy of youthful health. In chapter after chapter, the noted Carlson Wade shows how everyday foods can be your natural medicines, and how you can use vitamin-containing foods to help feed your glands to give you the digestive energy of a youngster, to awaken your circulation and to make life very beautiful, indeed.

The programs are amazingly simple and just as amazingly effective. In easy step-by-step outline, you are shown how to improve your eating methods and put vitamin-power into everyday foods. Some of these programs call for a few moments of time. Many of them cost just a few pennies. The foods are available in almost any local market. Many are probably right in your own pantry. With this arrangement, you can use Carlson Wade's books as a guideline for better health of your body and your mind, too.

Wade has written a highly recommended book that is fully researched, very well documented. It is helpful to almost everyone. His many case histories are vivid proof that natural vitamins found in foods can (and do) promote better health and youthful alertness.

This book offers you hope for looking youthful and for feeling supercharged with vitality. It shows you how to tap the Fountain of Youth in foods and drink the vitamins of Nature for a forever healthy life. This may well be the most thorough book on health that you will ever need.

William S. Keezer, M.D.

What This Book Will Do for You

Ever since the discovery of vitamins, there has been a growing search for more and more ways in which these medicines of Nature could be used to heal the body and the mind. For many decades, scientists the world over have compounded endless documents and research reports on the miracle of using vitamins for healing. This has given rise to the increased use of vitamins as supplements. In our desire for reaching as many folks as possible needful for vitamins in as short a time as possible, we have been able to manufacture synthetic vitamins in mass production by the hundreds of millions. Yet, there is an ever-growing awareness of the need for *natural* vitamins as *created by Nature in foods.* Many scientists who cheer the health-building powers of vitamins have reported that healing success is much more assured when *organic vitamins in foods* are used in the program for daily living.

Indeed, the key to youthful health may lie in this simple secret — *let food support your vitamin program.* With this objective in mind, I have made personal contacts with biologists, researchers, laboratory scientists, food technologists, physicians, surgeons, psychiatrists and asked them to help me prepare a book that will fill this basic need for natural or organic vitamins. That is, to show how selected simple, wholesome and everyday foods can be a storehouse of natural vitamins. The benefit here is that since you are a child of Nature, you are nourished and sustained by the foods of Nature, placed here for your health, vitality and youthful well-being. The selected foods that contain organic vitamins can help give you the feeling of youthful health as well as maintain it. This is the basic theme of this book.

The secrets of using foods as medicinal vitamins were shared with me by medical people the world over. How to use foods for healing of the body from head to toe; from the inside to the outside; how to use foods to send vitalic vitamins to nourish every part of your body and your mind, are just some of the secrets that were given to me in the preparation of this book. The benefit is that *organic vitamins* in wholesome foods are perfect health builders as created by Nature. Selected foods can become Nature's all-purpose organic vitamin supplements. Foods can be used as "vitamin" healers, in a wide range of health conditions. This book will show you how you can use foods so that they become a "miracle" of organic vitamin healing.

This book is unique because it shows you how you can very easily use simple, everyday foods to supercharge your body with healing *vitaminization*. This book will open up a brand new world of youthful vitality and longevity. This is the promise given to you by Nature in her medicinal foods that contain all-natural vitamins. By using these natural vitamins in very simple programs, you can help give yourself that extension of life and vitality you always sought.

In easy step-by-step programs, you tap the hidden secrets of many civilizations and countries the world over. You learn how you can use simple foods to vitaminize your body and enjoy the miracle of youthful health. You learn how you can use supplements—in the form of foods. This is Nature's plan for giving you years in your lifetime and life in your years! With a simple food vitaminization program, you will radiate and glow with the throbbing vitality of youthful health.

An outstanding, unique and exclusive feature of this book is the ORGAN-O-MATIC VITAMIN FINDER. If you want to locate any information concerning an organic vitamin, consult this quick locator index set up in the back of the book. It is set up in alphabetical order by various adverse health symptoms to ascertain the particular vitamin to cope with a given health situation. You can use this ORGAN-O-MATIC VITAMIN FINDER for instant reference and daily guidance as to the suggested organic food vitamin and its sources.

Nature has a plan for giving you a lifetime of more healthful and youthful daily living. The secret of this renewed healthfulness and youthfulness is in the selection of certain organic vita-min-bearing foods. All this is set out in this book's programs and case histories of those people who have secured desired health benefits in following the guidance in this book.

Carlson Wade

Other Books by the Author

Contents

1

The "Miracle 13" Vitamins
for Youthful Health

Your health is a product of the foods that you eat. Your body from head to toe, from the inside to the outside, your emotional health and your youthful vitality all rely upon the types of foods that you eat. More important is your ability to assimilate and metabolize certain Nature-created "health feeders" in the foods that can send a powerhouse of dynamic vitality throughout your body. These "health feeders" are known as _vitamins_. These are all-natural "spark plugs" that alert and activate your metabolic processes to give you health and vigor of your body and mind. When you eat healthful foods with these Nature-created organic vitamins, you energize your powers of assimilation and metabolism so that these "health feeders" can then be sent to all parts of your body to give you the appearance and feeling of healthful youth.

Nature's Miracle Source of Health

Vitamins are Nature-created miracles that perform as catalysts. That is, they help speed up health building processes in your body. For example, they lend a hand to enzymes (also catalysts) in their crucial job of transforming carbohydrates into energy. Vitamins work with minerals, proteins, fats and other

17

substances to build and sustain your health from top to bottom. Organic vitamins in foods are a vital link in the chain of events that convert crude materials in your body to the cells and tissues that make up your skin, bones, eyes, hair and teeth.

Organic vitamins are "Miracle Sparks" which are vital to the proper metabolism of food by your body. Just suppose you had a stove or a furnace, all set up with oil or coal or gas, and you had *no* match to light it . . . you could perish of cold despite all the fuel in the world.

Organic vitamins are "Miracle Sparks" which ignite the fuel to then work upon ingested food to metabolize them and extract the needed ingredients that work to keep you looking and feeling youthfully fit.

The "Miracle 13" Vitamins Tip the Scales for Healthful Balance

Organic vitamins work together as links in a chain. The absence of one vitamin can upset the delicate body balance and the end result is a decline in your health. Each and every organic vitamin performs a different and necessary function in your body. If any vitamin is lacking, it means that the scales of health are upset. This deficiency can weaken or halt many of the vital metabolic processes in your cells. The biological reactions which are essential for your life and health now become slowed up or come to a grinding halt. Your health declines. Nature has created "Miracle 13" vitamins. *All* are needed in order to help balance and slightly tip the scales in your favor. To enjoy better and better health, you need these "Miracle 13" health feeders every single day. Here is a listing of these "health feeders" and how you can "plant" them in your body so that they can blossom forth and create those metabolic processes that help give you the spark of life and energy to make life a joyful experience.

#1 — MIRACLE VITAMIN A

What It Does for Your Body: Stored in your liver, kidneys, lungs, adrenal glands and body fat. Helps create healthy skin, eyes, hair, teeth, gums and many glands. Influences the metabolism of fats and essential fatty acids. Promotes a "dark adaptation" of the eyes so that they can adjust when moving from bright light to dim lighting or to darkness. Helps moisten the skin to keep it soft and smooth.]

Good Food Sources: Milk, butter, eggs, liver, kidney, fish liver oils, cheddar cheese, carrots.

Official U. S. Government Recommendation: Professors Ernestine B. McCollum and Elmer V. McCollum, in *Food, Yearbook of Agriculture* say, "A deficiency of Vitamin A injures the epithelial tissues throughout the body. These cells form the outer layer of the skin and the mucous membranes that line the mouth and the digestive, respiratory and genito-urinary tracts. The secretory glands, such as the tear glands and digestive glands are composed of specialized epithelial cells which dry and flatten and slough off when Vitamin A is lacking. The cells, instead of being soft and moist, become hard and dry like the scales of dry skin.

"The mucous membranes are barriers against many kinds of bacterial invasion. Impairment of their structure and function, when Vitamin A is deficient, lowers resistance to respiratory and other infections. Severe infections of the eyes, genito-urinary tract and mouth may occur."

The official government recommendation is for a minimum of 5000 units of Vitamin A daily. The official Yearbook says, "The recommended allowance for Vitamin A can be met by including yellow and green, leafy vegetables such as collards, turnip greens, kale, carrots, squash and sweet potatoes in the diet everyday. Yellow peaches, apricots, cantaloupes and papayas are also good sources. Liver of all animals is an excellent source. [A 2-ounce serving of cooked beef liver provides more than 30 thousand units of the vitamin]"

Your Vitamin A Health Feeder

Daily, eat a large helping of a variety of the government recommended vegetables and fruits. For a powerhouse of cell-feeding Vitamin A, enjoy a cup of grated raw carrots with a plate of broiled liver. You will be giving your system a treasure of rejuvenating Vitamin A.

#2 — MIRACLE VITAMIN B₁ (Thiamine)

What It Does for Your Body: Works within your living cells as an essential part of carbohydrate metabolism. Aids your appetite and digestion, also improves the health of your nerves and promotes good muscle tone. A deficiency of the vitamin means that not all the carbohydrate is used and this may lead to metabolic disorder.

Good Food Sources: Whole grain cereals, breads, dried yeast, wheat germ, nuts, soybeans, brown rice, fish, lean meats, liver, poultry.

Official U.S. Government Recommendation: Grace A. Goldsmith, M.D., in *Food, Yearbook of Agriculture*, says, "Thiamine is present in many natural foods but is abundant in few. Dry beans and peas, certain of the organ meats and some nuts furnish sizable amounts. Whole wheat cereals and bread are dependable sources. They can contribute valuable amounts to the diet. The small amounts provided by other foods, such as milk, eggs, other meat, fruit and vegetables, add up and represent a worthwhile contribution to the diet.

"Effects of a moderate shortage of thiamine include fatigability, apathy, loss of appetite, nausea, such psychic and personality disturbances as moodiness, irritability and depression; a sensation of numbness in the legs and abnormalities of the electrocardiogram.

"Advanced deficiency of thiamine, or beriberi is characterized by peripheral neuritis, heart disease and edema. Peripheral neuritis is a disease of the nerves of the extremities; usually both legs are affected and sometimes the arms as well. The symptoms include loss of sensation, muscle weakness and paralysis.

"A deficiency of thiamine can also cause damage to the brain which may be manifested by confusion, delirium and paralysis of the muscles that move the eyeballs. This condition is called Wernicke's syndrome."

The official government recommendation is for a minimum of 1.5 (or 1 1/2) milligrams daily.

Your Vitamin B₁ (Thiamine) Health Feeder

Sprinkle raw wheat germ flakes over a whole grain cereal and eat as a dynamic source of nerve-feeding Vitamin B$_1$. Feature brown rice with chopped nuts for a source of super-Vitamin B$_1$. Delicious and nutritious, too.

#3 — MIRACLE VITAMIN B₂ (Riboflavin)

What It Does for Your Body: A vital part of Nature's chain of reactions to transport metabolized carbohydrates to energy-producing sites in your body. Vitamin B$_2$ is a constituent of many enzyme systems and is intimately connected with many life and health-producing processes. Also helps your body use proteins and fats. Helps prevent eye sensitivity to light. Aids in the assimilation of iron, promotes better digestive processes and soothes the nervous system.

Good Food Sources: Eggs, whole grain breads and cereals, leafy green vegetables, lean meats, liver, dried yeast, milk, fish, peanuts.

Official U.S. Government Recommendation: Grace A. Goldsmith, M.D., in *Food, Yearbook of Agriculture,* says, "Among the best sources of riboflavin are milk and variety of meats like liver, heart and kidney. Other lean meat, cheese, eggs and many of the leafy, green vegetables also furnish valuable amounts. Whole grain cereals and bread contribute important amounts of riboflavin to the diet.

"Research (has) disclosed riboflavin to be an essential human nutrient, which is combined with protein in the body to form a number of important enzymes. These flavoproteins function in the respiration of tissue and act closely with enzymes containing niacin, another B vitamin. Some flavoproteins are known as oxidases since they catalyze the oxidation of various chemical substances.

"Deficiency of either (riboflavin or niacin) may result in soreness and redness of the tongue and lips, atrophy of papillae on the surface of the tongue, and cracks at angles of the mouth. In riboflavin deficiency, dermatitis of the greasy type often involves the scrotum, and may affect the face and ears."

The official government recommendation is for a minimum of 1.7 (nearly 2) milligrams daily.

Your Vitamin B₂ (Riboflavin) Health Feeder

Drink one glass of freshly prepared raw *green* vegetable juice for a treasure of many nutrients, especially riboflavin. Daily, eat an assortment of seasonal raw green vegetables as a salad. This gives you much-needed enzymes with riboflavin for double-barreled power within your system.

#4 — MIRACLE VITAMIN B₆ (Pyridoxine)

What It Does for Your Body: Helps in the formation of certain proteins and also assists in the metabolism of fat. Aids in the formation of needed red blood cells. Also influences the utilization of amino enzymes. It helps maintain a healthful and youthful central nervous system.

Good Food Sources: Wheat germ, vegetables, Brewer's yeast, meat, whole grain breads, cereals, liver, kidney, soybeans, peanuts.

Official U.S. Government Recommendation: Grace A. Goldsmith, M.D., in *Food, Yearbook of Agriculture,* says, "The best sources of Vitamin B₆ (pyridoxine) are muscle meats, liver, vegetables and whole grain cereals. The bran from the cereal grains has especially large amounts.

"Vitamin B₆ may also function in the metabolism of essential fatty acids. A deficiency (revealed) symptoms including irritability, depression and sleepiness. Other findings were a seborrheic (greasy) type of dermatitis, skin lesions that resembled pellagra, soreness of the tongue and lips, conjunctivitis and peripheral neuritis. These abnormalities resemble those seen in deficiency of riboflavin, niacin and thiamine and attest the close metabolic relationship of these vitamins of the B complex."

Dr. Goldsmith says that while "the exact requirement of Vitamin B₆ has not been determined, probably 1 to 2 milligrams daily should be enough for an adult."

Your Vitamin B₆ (Pyridoxine)
Health Feeder

A bowl of healthful nuts and seeds, good for munching and snacking, will give you a balanced amount of the B-complex vitamins that are recommended. For super-plus pyridoxine, sprinkle wheat germ into chopped liver and broil in a bit of oil. You will be feeding yourself a juicy good source of this healthful vitamin with many other essential nutrients.

#5 — MIRACLE VITAMIN B₁₂

What It Does for Your Body: Helps in the building of genetic substances for the cell nucleus and in the formation of red blood cells. Also helps in soothing and protecting the nervous system. It is especially valuable in protecting you against anemia and enriching your bloodstream.

Good Food Sources: Liver, kidney, milk, salt water fish, lean meats, whole grain breads, cereals, eggs, soybeans, Brewer's yeast.

Official U. S. Government Recommendation: Grace A. Goldsmith, M.D., in *Food, Yearbook of Agriculture*, says, "The best sources are liver and kidney. Other sources are muscle meats, milk, cheese, fish and eggs. As far as we know, fruit and vegetables do not furnish any Vitamin B₁₂.

"It appears to be involved in the synthesis of nucleoproteins through the participation in the metabolism of purines and pyrimidines. Pernicious anemia is the most important human disease that is due to too little Vitamin B₁₂. Pernicious anemia is characterized by degenerative lesions in the spinal cord and peripheral nerves as well as by macrocytic (large cell) anemia . . . Soreness of the mouth and tongue, numbness and tingling of the hands, pains in the back, and (in one instance) combined degeneration of the spinal cord have been observed."

Although the exact requirement of Vitamin B₁₂ has not yet been established, Dr. Goldsmith says, "A normal diet is estimated to contain 8 to 15 micrograms" of this miracle vitamin.

Your Vitamin B₁₂ Health Feeder

A glass of milk is a good source of this healthful vitamin. Liver is a top-notch source. For folks who dislike the taste of liver, try broiling it with lemon juice. The tangy taste of the lemon juice will "cut through" the usually disliked liver taste and you'll find it to be delicious when later sprinkled with simple wheat germ. Meatless sources include Brewer's yeast as well as soybeans. Salt water fish will also give you appreciable amounts of this blood-building miracle vitamin.

#6 — MIRACLE VITAMIN C (Ascorbic Acid)

What It Does for Your Body: Helps maintain the health of your bones and teeth, also blood vessels. Helps promote better skeletal structure. Helps form collagen, a protein that supports body structure, such as the skin, bones, tendons. Helps build resistance to respiratory ailments, such as the common cold.

Good Food Sources: All citrus fruits, berries, tomatoes, cabbages, cantaloupes, strawberries, green vegetables, green peppers, watercress, potatoes.

Official U. S. Government Recommendation: Dr. Mary L. Dodds in *Food, Yearbook of Agriculture*, says, "Anemia has been associated with a lack of Vitamin C. The dietary abuse that results in a lack of Vitamin C is likely to produce other deficiencies. An anemia can be expected when loss of blood by persistent small hemorrhages occurs and both iron and Vitamin C therapy will be beneficial.

"Other data, however, indicate a direct relationship between low intakes of Vitamin C and low hemoglobin levels, a measure of one kind of anemia.

"A deficiency of Vitamin C carries with it liability to infections. A suggestion has been made that activity of white blood cells can be stimulated by ascorbic acid. The white blood cells are able to destroy harmful materials as disease organisms.

"The theory that the formation of new cells, as antibodies, and the replacement of impaired body tissue depend on the presence of Vitamin C is a reasonable one. The failure of wounds to heal in scorbutic (scurvy or Vitamin C deficient) persons indicates a need for new building material.

"The higher concentration of Vitamin C in young tissue than in old and the high concentration in actively multiplying cells and tissue indicate that Vitamin C must be present where tissue is formed or regenerated."

It is also believed that protein builders must be present if new tissue is to be formed. This suggests the need for protein and Vitamin C for a natural interrelationship. Vitamin C influences "the formation of intracellular cementing substances," says Dr. Dodds, "for both soft and bony tissues, which make possible an orderly but infinitely diverse and patterned alinement of the cells . . . The aim in providing ourselves with the necessary Vitamin C is to promote and protect a continuing biological function."

The official government recommendation is for a minimum of 60 milligrams daily.

Your Vitamin C (Ascorbic Acid) Health Feeder

Just one glass of fresh whole orange juice will give you about 125 milligrams of Vitamin C, as well as other vitamins, minerals and enzymes. You may also feature raw fruit salads made from berries, melon slices, orange wedges, grapefruit wedges, tangerines. Sprinkle with lemon juice and you'll have a juicy good source of tissue-building Vitamin C. Potatoes and sweet potatoes are additional sources of Vitamin C along with green and yellow vegetables. Be sure to eat or drink these fruits and vegetables daily to nourish the trillions of body cells and tissues with "cement" building Vitamin C.

#7 — MIRACLE VITAMIN D

What It Does for Your Body: Necessary for teeth and bones. Helps prevent or protect against bone deformities. Also helps in the normal utilization of such minerals as calcium and phosphorus.

Good Food Sources: Vitamin D fortified milk, cod liver oil, salmon, tuna, egg yolk, liver, sunflower seeds, almonds, coconut.

Official U. S. Government Recommendation: Drs. Ernestine B. McCollum and Elmer V. McCollum in *Food, Yearbook of Agriculture*, say, "Vitamin D promotes the absorption of calcium from the digestive tract" and appears to lessen the amount of waste. "By improving the absorption of calcium and phosphorus and by aiding in the maintenance of the normal blood levels of these two essential blood builders, Vitamin D makes both available in a concentration that is suitable for the formation and growth of bones."

This government source also says that good sources of Vitamin D include cod liver oil and halibut liver oil.

Drs. Ernestine B. McCollum and Elmer V. McCollum explain, "Salt water fish generally contain large amounts of Vitamin D. Herring, mackerel and canned salmon and sardines are good sources. Vitamin D is present in the body oil as well as in the fat of the liver. Egg yolk and liver (beef, chicken) contain the vitamin.

"Most evaporated milk and much of the dried whole milk contain enough Vitamin D to give 400 units per quart after reconstitution with the recommended amount of water. Milk contains calcium and phosphorus in amounts and ratios conducive to their absorption, retention and utilization. The addition of Vitamin D to milk further promotes this relationship."

The official government recommendation is for a minimum of 400 units daily.

Your Vitamin D Health Feeder

Mix two tablespoons of cod liver oil or halibut liver oil in a glass of fresh raw vegetable juice. Stir vigorously. Drink daily for a tremendous source of natural Vitamin D. Several times weekly enjoy salmon and sardines on a "bed" of raw vegetables or salad leaves. You'll be giving yourself a naturally balanced amount of vitamins, minerals, enzymes, and proteins together with

Vitamin D. This is a healthful balance of the scales of Nature that tip in your health favor.

#8 — MIRACLE VITAMIN E

What It Does for Your Body: Helps form normal red blood cells, muscle and other tissues. Protects fat in the body tissues from abnormal breakdown. Acts as an antioxidant (prevents rancidity) to help keep your metabolic processes in a natural balance.

Good Food Sources: All non-processed oils made from vegetables, seeds and nuts, wheat germ, whole grain breads, whole grain cereals, seeds, nuts, peanuts, walnuts.

Official U. S. Government Recommendation: Originally isolated in 1922 and labelled Vitamin E, it was in 1972 that it was recognized as having a definite value in building health. The recommended daily amount is for 30 units.

Drs. Ernestine B. McCollum and Elmer V. McCollum in *Food, Yearbook of Agriculture*, say, "The red blood corpuscles of adults on rations low in Vitamin E are abnormally susceptible to destruction by an oxidizing agent like hydrogen peroxide. Vitamin E is an antioxidant — that is, it unites with oxygen both within and outside the body." This guards against oxidation, a process that makes fat rancid and destroys Vitamin A. "This property," say Drs. McCollum, "is probably responsible for the protection of the red blood cells in the presence of hydrogen peroxide as well as the protection of Vitamin A and carotene in food and in the body."

"The stores of Vitamin A are depleted in the livers of (subjects) deficient in Vitamin E and are increased when Vitamin E is provided." Vitamin E affords protection to the red blood cells in the presence of a blood-destroying agent like hydrogen peroxide.

It is believed that Vitamin E helps "open up" blocked channels, combats cholesterol within the blood system and makes the arteries and veins more flexible and "clean" to permit normal passage of oxygen and blood. This is believed to protect against disorders of the heart and vascular systems throughout the body.

The official government recommendation is for a minimum of 30 units daily.

Your Vitamin E Health Feeder

Use non-processed or cold-pressed vegetable or seed oils as a salad dressing daily. Take several tablespoons of this oil mixed with vegetable juice for a tremendous supply of this miracle vitamin. Use unbleached grains and flours. Fortify with raw wheat germ. You will be fortifying your body with this needed vitamin.

#9 — MIRACLE VITAMIN K

What It Does for Your Body: This vitamin manufactures, in the liver, a substance which causes blood to coagulate normally. Without Vitamin K, a person could bleed to death. In addition to helping promote normal blood clotting, it is essential for good circulation and acts as a natural anti-hemorrhage agent. Strokes, for example, are hemorrhages of blood vessels and it is possible that a deficiency of Vitamin K may be partially responsible. This vitamin helps maintain a healthful blood circulation balance in the system and protects against vascular tightening or choking.

Good Food Sources: Green leafy vegetables, oats, alfalfa sprouts, whole wheat and rye breads, cabbage, nuts and seeds and their cold-pressed oils.

Official U. S. Government Recommendation: Drs. Ernestine B. McCollum and Elmer V. McCollum in *Food, Yearbook of Agriculture*, say, "Of the many green leaves studied, those of the alfalfa plant proved to be exceptionally rich in the new factor ... because it corrected the clotting or coagulating time of the blood.

"Vitamin K is essential for normal formation of the liver and for the formation of prothrombin by the liver. Prothrombin is a normal constituent of blood. It is one of the several components that react together to form a blood clot. When Vitamin K is deficient, the prothrombin content of the blood falls and clotting time is prolonged. The capillaries must also become fragile, since extensive hemorrhage accompanies the reduction of prothrombin.

"The administration of the vitamin causes a prompt response of the body with the formation of prothrombin, and the blood returns to its normal composition and physical properties. Fibrin is one of the chief constituents of a blood clot. Prothrombin is required for its formation.

"The green leafy vegetables, tomatoes, cauliflower, egg yolk, soybean oil and liver of all kinds are good sources. Since it is insoluble in water, there is no loss in ordinary cooking procedures."

Drs. McCollum add, "Although it is clear that human beings must have Vitamin K, no requirements have been established and no allowances have been set up."

Your Vitamin K Health Feeder

Daily, eat a raw vegetable salad emphasizing tomatoes and lettuce. Sprinkle with a mixture of soybean oil as well as lemon juice for a tangy taste. Broiled liver is another good source. A top-notch "dynamite" source of Vitamin K is in the alfalfa plant. Use alfalfa tea and grains (sold in health stores and special diet shops). Juice your raw vegetables and sprinkle raw wheat germ and raw wheat bran for a triple-headed powerhouse of Vitamin K.

#10 — MIRACLE FOLIC ACID

What It Does for Your Body: Aids in the formation of certain body proteins and genetic materials for cell nucleus. Aids in cell formation, especially red blood cells. Helps guard against some forms of anemia.

Good Food Sources: Leafy green vegetables, Brewer's yeast, whole grain breads, cereals, eggs, liver, seeds and nuts and their cold-pressed oils.

Official U. S. Government Recommendation: Grace A. Goldsmith, M.D., in *Food, Yearbook of Agriculture*, says, "Folic acid . . . is necessary for the formation of blood cells. The best sources include liver, dry beans, lentils, cowpeas, asparagus, broccoli, spinach, collards. Other good sources include kidney, peanuts, filberts, walnuts, immature or young lima beans, cabbage, sweet corn, chard, turnip greens, lettuce, beet greens and whole wheat products.

"Folic acid stimulates the formation of blood cells in certain anemias, which are characterized by oversized red cells and the accumulation in the bone marrow of immature red blood cells, called megaloblasts. The bone marrow is the organ that manufactures red blood cells. It cannot complete the process in the absence of folic acid." Some symptoms that may suggest folic acid deficiency include glossitis (a sore, red, smooth tongue), diarrhea, gastro-intestinal lesions, anemia. Sprue may improve with the addition of folic acid. Sprue is an ailment in which absorption of food from the intestinal tract is seriously impaired and the stools contain large amounts of fat. Folic acid," says Dr. Goldsmith, "may improve absorption in this condition."

The requirement of folic acid has not been established, but Dr. Goldsmith, writing in the U. S. government publication, says, "Available evidence suggests that approximately 0.1 to 0.2 milligrams daily may suffice." A tiny amount . . . but a tiny deficiency can create havoc!

Your Folic Acid Health Feeder

Broiled liver with a plate of beans and lentils will give you a powerhouse of folic acid. You can also fortify yourself with folic acid by eating whole wheat products, an assortment of nuts and seeds and their cold-pressed oils as a salad dressing.

#11 — MIRACLE PANTOTHENIC ACID

What It Does for Your Body: Essential for metabolism of carbohydrates, fats and proteins into the molecular form needed by the body. It is intimately involved with many processes so that a deficiency may cause such symptoms as apathy, depression, instability of heart action, stomach pains, susceptibility to infections, malfunctioning of the adrenal glands which reduces the response to stress; this may lead to nerve disorders which produce muscle weakness and "pins and needles" in your hands and legs.

Good Food Sources: Eggs, broccoli, liver, nuts, Brewer's yeast, peanuts, seeds, soybeans.

Official U. S. Government Recommendation: Grace A. Goldsmith, M.D., in *Food, Yearbook of Agriculture*, says, "Pantothenic acid is needed by man . . . it is widely distributed in foods. Liver and eggs are particularly good sources. Broccoli, cauliflower, lean beef, skim milk, white potatoes and sweet potatoes, tomatoes and molasses are quite high in pantothenic acid."

Dr. Goldsmith explains that pantothenic acid creates a miracle metabolic process in the formation and breakdown of fatty acids and in the entry of fat and carbohydrate into the biological reactions that give you energy, health and life, itself!

A deficiency may cause "numerous physical and biochemical disturbances," says Dr. Goldsmith. "The subjects became quarrelsome, sullen and petulant. Some of them developed pains and disturbances of sensation in the arms and legs. Others noted loss of appetite, indigestion and nausea. Fainting attacks were common. The pulse tended to be unduly rapid. There seemed to be an increase in susceptibility to infection.

"A deficiency of pantothenic acid may be responsible for the 'burning foot syndrome,' which is encountered in places where other deficiencies are common. This condition has been reported to respond to doses of pantothenic acid."

The requirement of pantothenic acid has not been established, but Dr. Grace A. Goldsmith, writing in the U. S. government publication, suggests approximately 5 milligrams daily.

Your Pantothenic Acid Health Feeder

A glass of boiled water into which two tablespoons of blackstrap or unsulphured molasses (sold at health stores and most supermarkets) has been dissolved, will give you a tremendous source of pantothenic acid and other vitamins and minerals, too. Daily, eat available tomatoes and potatoes as well as broccoli as a raw and partially cooked salad.

#12 — MIRACLE NIACIN

What It Does for Your Body: Involved in energy-producing reactions in the cells. Helps protect against pellagra. Also works with enzymes to convert carbohydrates into energy. Needed for normal growth. Helps the nervous system.

Good Food Sources: Lean meats, liver, Brewer's yeast, eggs, whole grain breads, cereals, poultry, fish, green vegetables, peanuts, soybeans.

Official U. S. Government Recommendation: Grace A. Goldsmith, M.D., in *Food, Yearbook of Agriculture*, says: "Lean meat and poultry are good sources of niacin. Among plant sources, peanuts are outstanding in niacin . . . other plants include beans, peas, other legumes, most nuts and several whole grain cereal products. Oatmeal is low in niacin."

"Niacin deficiency is characterized by dermatitis, particularly in areas of the skin which are exposed to light or injury; inflammation of mucous membranes, including the entire gastrointestinal tract, which results in a red, swollen, sore tongue and mouth, diarrhea and rectal irritation; and psychic changes such as irritability, anxiety, depression and (in advanced pellagra) delirium, hallucinations, confusion, disorientation and stupor. . . . A deficiency of riboflavin often accompanies a deficiency of niacin. Thiamine deficiency may also be present at times." This indicates how vitamins are so interrelated that a deficiency of one may reduce the efficiency of others. Like links in a chain, remove one link and the entire chain (your body) falls apart.

The official government recommendation is for a minimum of 18 milligrams of niacin daily.

Your Niacin Health Feeder

Eat raw peanuts as often as possible. Also sprinkle chopped or pulverized peanuts over salads. Peanut oil sold almost everywhere in food markets, offers a tremendous source of niacin and other vitamins, too. Use peanut oil with a bit of honey and lemon juice for a natural powerhouse of niacin and other essential helpful vitamins, minerals, enzymes.

#13 — MIRACLE BIOTIN

What It Does for Your Body: A coenzyme (helper) in the formation of certain fat-like substances and other reactions involving carbon dioxide. Helps in carbohydrate metabolism and fatty acid synthesis.

Good Food Sources: Liver, kidney, eggs, vegetables, Brewer's yeast, whole grain breads and cereals, soybeans, seeds and nuts and their cold-pressed oils used as salad dressings or in cooking.

Official U. S. Government Recommendation: Grace A. Goldsmith, M.D., in *Food, Yearbook of Agriculture*, says, "Biotin is presumably essential for man. Liver, milk, meat, nuts, egg yolk, most vegetables and a number of fruits (bananas, grapefruit, tomatoes, watermelon and strawberries) contain significant amounts of biotin.

"Biotin seems to be an essential component of a coenzyme in carbon dioxide fixation, an important reaction in intermediary metabolism." Dr. Goldsmith refers to symptoms traced to biotin deficiency as including dry, scaly dermatitis, changes in the color of the skin, nervous symptoms, tongue lesions and abnormalities in the electrocardiogram. "Findings similar to those produced by deficiency of other vitamins of the B-complex," says the doctor. This emphasizes the need for a well-balanced supply of all vitamins to maintain good health of body and mind.

The requirement of biotin has not been established, but the official *Recommended Dietary Allowances*[1] suggests a daily amount of approximately 150 to 300 micrograms of biotin.

Your Biotin Health Feeder

Sprinkle Brewer's yeast over your whole grain cereals for a tremendous supply of biotin with many other vitamins and minerals. Eat whole grain breads and cereals. Stir a tablespoon of

---

[1]*Recommended Dietary Allowances*, 7th edition, 1968, Publication 1694. Published by the National Academy of Sciences — National Research Council, Washington, D. C. 20418.

wheat germ into a glass of milk. Warm slightly for a delicious and healthful nightcap.

The preceding list of the "Miracle 13" is your guide to better health through organic vitamins as they are found in food. While a small quantity of each vitamin may be required each day, no one vitamin can substitute for another. A balance is needed to give your body the balanced amount of working materials that will give you youthful life and health from head to toe, from the inside to the outside. Better health can become super health — with organic vitamins!

CHAPTER HIGHLIGHTS

1. The health and well-being of every part of your body (your mind, too) depend upon a balance of the "Miracle 13" vitamins outlined.
2. Organic vitamins as found in the listed foods can help regenerate body tissues and cells, produce youthful energy, boost metabolism, protect against infections, guard against nervous disorders, promote more rapid healing, improve glandular function, and contribute to overall well-being.
3. Each of the listed "Miracle 13" vitamins carries an all-natural "Health Feeder" which is a do-it-yourself supplement that you can make in your own kitchen; in most cases, you need just everyday foods that may cost just pennies per portion . . . for a million dollar feeling of good health.

2

How to Feed Rejuvenating Vitamins to Your Skin and Hair

Part One: YOUR SKIN

Nature has endowed you with the youthful birthright of firm, vibrant, glowing skin. This is a gift of Nature that needs to be cherished and maintained properly. Carelessness or vitamin deficiency may deplete and destroy that precious gift of perpetual youth. Nature has a treasure of skin feeding vitamins that will help you protect the gift of a youthful texture and glowing health of your body envelope. These organic vitamins, found in everyday foods, can help nourish your skin, inside and outside, and help feed rejuvenation to the cells and tissues so that you will be admired for your youthful appearance. Let us see how these Nature-created organic vitamins in everyday foods can help feed youth to your skin.

THE MIRACLE VITAMIN THAT REBUILDS AGING SKIN CELLS

A physician[1] has discovered that the key to perpetually young skin is the nourishment of the cells. Specifically, each living cell includes a quantity of *nucleic acids*. One type, DNA

[1]Benjamin Frank, M.D., *Nucleic Acid Therapy in Aging and Degenerative Disease*, 1969, New York: Psychological Library.

(deoxyribonucleic acid) is enclosed in the central nucleus of the cell. The other, RNA (ribonucleic acid) is more widely distributed. By feeding vitamins to these *nucleic acids*, it is possible to help "plump up" and "prime" the decaying and degenerating cells and thereby help reverse the aging process. In effect, *the vitamins have the power of being able to recharge the spark plugs of your worn out cells, giving them a renewed ability to create the process of rebuilding and rejuvenating your skin.*

Secret Rejuvenating Benefit

The vitamins nourish the nucleic acids (DNA and RNA) which are the cellular components which influence tissue regeneration and repair. These vitamins give a strange power to the cells so that they now have the ability to reproduce. This helps build new cells to replace those that have deteriorated with the passage of years. Yet this self-regenerative process requires vitamins in order to function adequately and repair your skin from within. The vitamins needed by the nucleic acids are the B-complex group.

The Vitamin Food That Promotes Cellular Rejuvenation

Benjamin Frank, M.D. administered *Brewer's yeast* to his test patients who had problems of premature aging of the body as well as skin deterioration. Dr. Frank reports that Brewer's yeast is about 15 per cent of *natural* nucleic acid. But it is also a treasure of the B-complex vitamins needed by the skin cells for nourishment and self-rejuvenation. Dr. Frank gave his patients desiccated liver, sardines, sweetbreads as well as B-complex vitamins as supplements.

Miracle Food

The most important food is Brewer's yeast because just 200 milligrams a day would give some 30 milligrams of natural nucleic acid, the ingredient that nourishes the skin. Just one tablespoon of Brewer's yeast flakes taken in a glass of fresh vegetable juice will give you a treasure of the natural nucleic acid needed as a "magic" food for nourishment of these cells. Simple, but effective.

Immediate Rejuvenation

Dr. Frank notes that this simple program produced immediate effective rejuvenation. Just two or three days, and the folks enjoyed increased energy and well-being. But most important, their skins become healthier and rosier looking. Gradually, the wrinkles decreased. There was better tightness of the skin. There was an increased moisture which is the key to youthful skin. (These are some of the coveted benefits of costly facial creams.)

Additional Benefits of Brewer's Yeast

Dr. Frank says that when the B-complex program extended over several weeks, the folks noted that there was an improvement in the skin of the elbows and other joints where there was roughness. In a "vast majority" of those taking the simple B-complex food, Brewer's yeast, the backs of their hands showed smoother skin and less wrinkling. When Brewer's yeast was reduced or eliminated from the food program, the aging symptoms returned. This encouraged the doctor to report that vitamins can help create youthfulness when they nourish the DNA and RNA nucleic acids.

How to Take This Miracle Rejuvenation Food

Most health stores and special diet shops as well as herbal pharmacists carry Brewer's yeast. This is a grain product available in powdered or "flaked" form. It is a treasure of the valuable cell-feeding B-complex vitamins as well as nearly all other "Miracle 13" vitamins. Just take one tablespoon daily, mixed with fruit or vegetable juice for added enzyme boosting. You may use Brewer's yeast as a "filler" in baking meat loaf, in casseroles, in soups and stews. Sprinkle some Brewer's yeast over a bowl of whole grain cereal. Try it in a cup of yogurt. It is the all-natural miracle vitamin food that helps rebuild the nucleus of your skin cells. It helps keep you looking and feeling youthful.

HOW OCEAN-CREATED VITAMINS PROVIDE "BUILT-IN" SKIN MOISTURE

Elsa T. is reluctant to tell her age. She says that her skin is so youthful, friends will think she had a facelift. In reality, Elsa T. is in her middle 50's, yet looks in her early 30's. As a travel agent, she learned the secret of youthful skin from some Pacific co-workers who visited her New York office. She was told that the secret of youthful skin among so many Pacific peoples is that they know how to keep their cells *moisturized*. Elsa T. was told that if she could maintain the natural reservoir of "oils" beneath the surface of the skin, she could help protect herself against wrinkles and enjoy a youthful skin.

Two Ocean-Created Vitamins Provide Youthful Moisture

Elsa T. was told that two vitamins, A and D, as found in *fish oils* are miracles of moisture. The cod liver oil and halibut liver oil are treasures of these two vitamins. Any fish oil is a superior source of these two vitamins because the oceans are a natural source of virtually all known vitamins and minerals. The fish are born in the ocean and are nourished by these nutrients in the depths of the ocean. Their prepared oils are about the most natural sources of Vitamins A and D that are available. Fish oils are used by countless many as a means of giving their skins the needed natural moisture.

How Elsa T. Uses Fish Oils for Youthful Skin

Once a day, Elsa T. mixes two tablespoons of cod liver oil (or halibut liver oil) in a glass of *chilled* orange juice. She stirs vigorously. Then she sips it slowly. It is this simple beverage that helps moisturize her skin so that she looks decades younger.

Why Moisture Is Key to Perpetual Youth

Beneath the skin surface lie tiny "wells" in the form of small honeycomb like cells. These "wells" need moisture to help plump up and firm up the skin surface. The dewy fresh glow of youth may diminish as early as in the early 20's because of changes in hormone secretions; this means a decline in the amount of moisture in the honeycomb cells. You need to give Nature a helping hand by supplementing with natural moisture to the tiny "wells" beneath your skin.

Fish oils are prime sources of Vitamins A and D. These two vitamins act as transports by sending vaporous moisture to the honeycomb cells. The two vitamins thereby spark the action of *hydrolysis* whereby the "wells" receive supplementary moisture. This is Nature's protection against dehydration, the forerunner of wrinkling and aging.

THE PLANT VITAMIN THAT REBUILDS AND RESTORES YOUTHFUL SKIN

A cross-section view of your skin would show the *dermis,* composed of elastic connective tissue with a rich network of blood vessels and nerves; and the *epidermis,* a protective outer covering with a deep layer of growing cells and a covering of dead cells that are constantly shed and replaced from the growing layer. The aging process begins when the cells die at a faster rate than they are replaced. Even if the cellular restoration is slowed up (and this occurs in a gradual process) there is a slow decline in the youthful health of the skin. Unless the *dermis* and *epidermis* receive adequate nourishment, they cannot maintain cellular repair and restoration. The key to correction is in "feeding" vitamins to your skin. In particular, one vitamin stands out as a miracle of "cell food" and self-rejuvenation.

How Vitamin C Helps Maintain Cellular Rejuvenation

Vitamin C helps nourish the structure of the ground substance of the connective tissue. When you eat a citrus or plant food containing this miraculous organic vitamin, here is how it helps rebuild your skin:

Vitamin C acts as a "starter" in enabling your body to produce a skin rejuvenating substance known as collagen. This is a protein-like material which acts as a cement-like substance. It binds together the broken and fragmented cells and tissues. Vitamin C propels collagen throughout the dermis and epidermis to form the intercellular substance of dentin, cartilage and bone. Vitamin C also sends collagen to maintain the youthful health of the non-epithelial tissue such as the bones, body organs, blood vessels. Vitamin C is the "food" used by cells for self-rejuvenation. Vitamin C is a miracle of natural skin nourishment. Without Vitamin C, the entire skin structure dries up. The cells of the body would die. The less Vitamin C available, the less youthfulness of the skin. Nature has created Vitamin C and made it readily available for body nourishment and for helping your skin self-perpetuate its youth.

HOW TO FEED THE REJUVENATION VITAMIN C TO YOUR SKIN

Michael L. was careless about his food program. As a traveling salesman, he was always "on the go" and had little time or desire to plan a healthful meal pattern. He paid the penalty in the form of sagging, "crepe like" skin, a sallow complexion, dark blotches. He was given a rude (but beneficial) awakening when a buyer on his sales route asked if his company had many "old men" such as himself. At age 43, Michael L. chafed at being considered old. When he looked at himself closely, he saw how "tired" his entire skin looked. Indeed, he could certainly pass for an "old man." He set upon a simple program as outlined by a youthful looking manager:

1. Every morning, start with a large glass of freshly prepared orange juice. If unable to squeeze it yourself, then obtain pure and natural bottled orange juice. This gives a powerhouse of Vitamin C (at least 125 milligrams).
2. Begin each meal with a raw citrus fruit salad. These could include oranges, grapefruits, peaches, pineapple, berries, watermelon. For added Vitamin C, sprinkle a bit of lemon juice over the salad.

3. As a nightcap, drink a glass of pure orange juice into which has been dissolved one tablespoon or one envelope of unflavored gelatin. The benefit here is that the Vitamin C of the orange juice takes up the protein of the gelatin and uses it for the building and rebuilding of age-causing damaged cells and tissues.

Looks and Feels Younger in One Week

Michael L. used this simple 3-step program for replenishing his stores of Vitamin C as well as other vitamins, minerals, enzymes and proteins. Within one week, his skin firmed up, his complexion brightened, his blotches gave way to a youthful color. Now the salesman felt young and was no longer considered an "old man" thanks to the vitamin power of simple but powerfully rejuvenating plant foods — citrus fruits.

THE GOLDEN FRUIT THAT OFFERS A MILLION DOLLAR FACE REJUVENATION

A golden fruit — *the lemon* — holds Nature's secret for a million dollar face rejuvenation. This fruit is a rich treasure of vitamins that can nourish your skin cells and tissues. But more important, it has a natural acid that can replenish the decaying tissues and help restore a little-known moisture to your skin surface. This secret is known as the acid mantle which the lemon will restore along with the picture of golden youth.

How Lemon Juice Vitamins Rejuvenate the Skin

When ordinary lemon juice is applied to the skin surface, the vitamins help the natural "flaking" process of skin cells which have outgrown their usefulness. The lemon juice vitamins and enzymes soothingly lift up the decaying and skin-dulling particles of "crepe skin flakes" and enable new cells to take their place. This helps promote a clear and more youthful complexion.

Vitamins Restore Acid Mantle

The skin surface is normally acid. Most soaps are alkaline. When you wash your face, the alkaline soaps strip away the protective acid mantle covering placed on your skin by Nature, and "denuding" your skin of this needed covering. This can cause premature or unnecessary aging. But Nature has given you simple lemon juice as a vitamin source for restoration of the acid mantle.

Youthful, smooth and healthy skin should be acid-balanced within the pH (acidity) range of 4.5 to 5.5. Washing, scrubbing will remove this protective mantle; along with removal is the problem of a loss of moisture balance. The skin begins to dry and flake. Lines appear and the skin takes on an aging look. To counteract this problem, along with overexposure to the sun, wind, pollution, your skin needs lemon juice as a natural "vitamin wash" that helps restore the acid mantle.

How Gloria V. Uses Golden Lemons for Natural Face-lifting

Gloria V. boasts that her beauty shelf has a "million dollar" formula that is perfectly created for her skin. That formula is lemon juice squeezed from an always available golden lemon on her beauty shelf.

After each soap and water face washing, Gloria V. squeezes lemon juice into the palms of her hands and splashes it all over her face. She also rubs it over her hands so they will also enjoy restoration of the protective acid mantle.

The lemon juice is a prime source of Vitamin C as well as enzymes that join forces to replenish the washed away acid mantle covering of her skin.

Gloria V. also splashes lemon juice over her throat so that it stimulates her circulation, relaxes the muscles of her face and neck and helps alert her skin into sparkling freshness.

Gloria V. knows that the vitamins in the lemon juice help "melt out" clogging grime and impurities. Once the balance of the pH acid mantle is restored (lemon juice reportedly is able to restore it to a youthful range of 5.5), her skin glows with the fresh faced beauty of a country maiden. Gloria is 59! She proudly says that this simple vitamin-enzyme fruit juice is her secret of "natural face-lifting." She looks it!

20 WAYS TO USE PLANT FOODS FOR SKIN YOUTHIFYING

Fresh fruits and vegetables are prime sources of Vitamins A, C, E as well as minerals, enzymes, some protein. When used as natural beauty treatment, these plant foods can give you that fresh-faced flow you've always wanted . . . and help you keep it, thanks to the vitamin-ization of your skin. Here are 20 secrets for using plant foods as "vitamin treatments" for better skin:

1. *Facial Cleanser.*   Mix the mashed half of a ripe peeled avocado with the beaten yolk of an egg and one half cup of milk. When as thin as a lotion, apply on cotton squares all over your skin. Just keep rubbing and then wash off with contrasting warm and cool water. The benefit here is that these food vitamins, minerals and enzymes go deep into the pores of your skin and help cleanse out pollutants and city grime. Once the pores are open, they can aerate your skin and keep it looking and feeling better.

2. *Fruit Wash.*   Mash one-half peeled avocado. Mix with a one-half cup of fine ground cornmeal. Now, wash your face, then apply this Fruit Wash to all troubled spots. Gently rub into your face. Let remain up to 30 minutes so vitamins and enzymes can help loosen blemishes and help remove dirt and grime. Then remove with a damp washcloth. Finish with a cold splash of witch hazel or lemon juice.

3. *Overnight Facelift.*   Work a piece of avocado (about the size of a strawberry) in your palm until buttery. Now mix in a small amount of any ordinary face cream. Blend together. Now apply this cream to your face and throat and massage deeply. Apply it at bedtime. The vitamins in the avocado work by supplying to the epidermis layer of your skin a synthesis of the natural ingredient that provides youthful moisture to give you smoothness and freshness. The vitamins spark the change overnight so that the rehydration of the epidermis is accomplished while you sleep. Many say that in the morning, the skin is so refreshingly youthful, it looks as if this cream created an "overnight facelift."

4. *Skin Smoother.*   Use the rind of any citrus fruit. Lemon, orange or grapefruit inner rind is good because it offers a vital source of Vitamin C. Rub this inside on your face, your feet, your back, your hands, just about anywhere that you are troubled with rough skin. The vitamins and oils in the inside of the fruit rind will help sluff off dead cells. You get double-benefits because the natural oil of the fruit rind will restore the acid mantle and help lubricate your skin.

5. *Firming Up Neck and Throatlines.*   Purée one half of an avocado. Stir into it one tablespoon fresh wheat germ oil. You now have a miracle mixture of nearly all known vitamins together with Vitamin E. Now rub this cream into your neck and throatline areas. Use firm strokes. When most of this cream has been absorbed, remove excess and leave on the residue an hour or overnight. The vitamins here help firm up flabby jawlines, crepey neck and sagging muscles. Use nightly for best results.

6. *Dry Skin Masque.*   Beat an egg yolk until light and frothy. Add the mashed pulp of one-half avocado. Now cleanse your face and neck thoroughly. Apply this Dry Skin Masque over your face and neck evenly. Lie down and relax up to 60 minutes. Then remove with clear, tepid water, then a splash of cold water and a lemon juice splash. The vitamins in the Masque have helped rehydrate dry skin and offer needed moisture to help boost skin texture.

7. *Oily Skin Masque.*   In a blender, mix one egg white, one teaspoon of lemon juice and the mashed pulp of one-half avocado. You have a green mixture. Have your face and throat very clean. Apply this Oily Skin Masque evenly. Lie down and rest up to 60 minutes. Then remove with tepid water, a splash of cold water and a lemon juice wash. You might also try a very cold lemon juice wash for helping to wash away excess oils and maintain normal skin equilibrium.

8. *Vitamin E Masque.*   Add 1 tablespoon of hot water or milk to one-half cup ordinary oatmeal. Now combine with the puréed pulp of a half avocado. When well blended, apply to your freshly scrubbed face. Lie down and rest up to 60 minutes while it dries on your face. Then sponge off with warm water and several clear water rinsings. Finish with a lemon juice splash. The

benefit here is that the oxygen in Vitamin E will help repair damaged cells and help tired skin look fresher almost at once.

9. *Natural Skin Color.*   Put a splash of color in your tired skin by just splashing on chilled watermelon juice. Let the juice remain about 5 minutes, then splash off. The vitamins in the watermelon juice have a skin-stimulating effect that perk up the tired look that may make you appear older than you are.

10. *Satin Smooth Skin Secret.*   Stand in a tub or shower. Rub ordinary table salt all over your body with emphasis upon those trouble spots. Use a lot of friction. Now apply the peeled rind of any fruit. The vitamins will now help sluff off dead skin in a truly miraculous way, particularly on your feet, knees, elbows. Then shower off. You should have a satin smooth skin.

11. *Erasing Blackheads.*   Blend one tomato (include seeds, pulp and skin which offer a treasure of vitamins and enzymes) with one ripe peeled avocado. Apply on your skin, rubbing into regions covered with blackheads. The vitamins and enzymes "dig deep" and help get the dirt out of the pores. The Vitamin C in both the tomato and avocado is especially good in helping to cleanse away accumulated grime. Let this masque remain up to 30 minutes. Finish with a clear water rinse, then a lemon juice wash. Also helps sooth and heal acne and pimples.

12. *Skin Blemishes.*   Lighten skin blemishes and freckles, by coating them with a mixture of equal portions of lemon juice and baby oil. Let remain up to an hour or more, if possible. The vitamins and enzymes help lighten the blemishes. The oil helps keep the skin soft.

13. *Potato Pulp.*   After cleansing your face, apply raw potato pulp all over your skin. Let it remain up to 60 minutes and then wash off with cold water. It helps correct problems of oily skin. The Vitamin C in the potato also helps restore a normal acid mantle that protects against oiliness.

14. *Skin Refresher.*   Just rub half of a chilled tomato over your face. Let the juice dry. Then rinse with tepid and cool water. The vitamins in the tomato help perk up your sluggish skin cells and make you look and feel refreshed.

15. *Rough Elbows.*   Bleach and smooth elbows with a few drops of wheat germ oil in the bottoms of two empty lemon

halves. Bend your arms, stick lemons on your elbows and straighten arms. Leave lemon "cups" in place for 30 minutes. Vitamin C and Vitamin E with the enzymes do much to smooth out rough elbows.

16. *Rosy Glow.*   Have everything ice cold: sour cream and an avocado. Mash one-half peeled avocado. Blend into one-half cup of sour cream. Mix together. Apply to your clean face and relax about 60 minutes. The vitamins and enzymes and minerals help refine your pores and give your face a rosy glow. Splash off with tepid and then cold water and finish with a lemon juice splash.

17. *Nu-Skin Cream.*   Mix a cake of yeast (do *not* use dried yeast or Brewer's yeast) until it dissolves in about a tablespoon of whole milk. Now add the puréed meat of one-quarter of an avocado. Blend well. Apply evenly to your clean face and throat. Let remain up to 60 minutes. The benefit here is that the vitamins in the yeast will draw all impurities from your skin; your avocado vitamins will moisturize your skin and the nutrients in the milk will help give you a "new skin" appearance. Remove with a sponge or washcloth and warm water. Finish with a cold water splash and lemon juice rinse.

18. *Three Way Skin Aid.*   Mix one-half mashed avocado, one tablespoon honey and one-quarter cup milk. Be sure all ingredients are at room temperature and blend evenly. Now apply this Skin Aid to your freshly washed skin. Lie down, relax for 30 minutes. The ingredients will work to help "scrub" impurities from your pores, send vitamins into your skin, provide your "wells" with needed lubrication and moisture. Wash off with tepid water. Finish with a brisk patting of ice water. Your skin should glow with youthful alertness.

19. *Cabbage Juice Facial.*   Juice a few green leaves of a cabbage. (Use a juice extractor or grate the leaves until you have a half cup of cabbage juice.) Now pat onto your freshly washed skin, let remain as long as possible or overnight for good results. The vitamins in the cabbage take up its sulphur and chlorine and help cleanse and purify. The enzymes are sent by the vitamins through your skin pores to help tighten up your skin, pull sagging tissues together, giving you an overall youthful appearance.

20. *Baby Smooth Face*.   To help rejuvenate that crepe-like appearance, combine one egg yolk with one tablespoon wheat germ, one tablespoon apricot juice. Beat together. Now apply to your face. It should dry like a "coat." Keep applying a second and third "coat" or as many as needed. Now lie down and rest for 60 minutes. The vitamins in the egg yolk join with Vitamin E in the wheat germ, then the Vitamin C in the apricot juice and penetrate "thirsty" skin to promote a moisture saturation that helps "plump" up dry furrows and smooth them out. This helps create a baby smooth face. After 60 minutes, wash off with tepid and then cold water. Finish with a lemon juice splash.

Nature has prepared a garden of foods that are delicious to eat and prime sources of vitamins that help nourish from the inside, and can also help nourish you from the outside. Your skin is the mirror of health. Use food vitamins to help give you glowing youthful health . . . inside and outside.

Part Two: YOUR HAIR

Healthy hair is a product of good nutrition. Nature gave you a head of hair to be used for protection rather than just self-expression or decoration. A thick or healthy head of hair offers you protection against dirt and pollution, helps provide some insulation against the sun and also helps keep your head warm when going out in cold or windy weather. Hair is the reflection of your health. Your hair is a "plant" that grows because your bloodstream feeds it essential vitamins through the connected follicles. If your diet contains an ample amount of vitamins, your hair can be adequately nourished. If you are vitamin deficient, then your hair can lose health just as the rest of your body. To begin, you need to nourish your hair through your body. This calls for wholesome foods that emphasize vitamins.

HOW ORGANIC VITAMINS HELP FEED
YOUR SCALP AND HAIR

Organic vitamins in wholesome foods can help feed your scalp and hair through your bloodsteam. Here are ways in which everyday foods can nourish your hair-growing processes:

Fresh Fish: A prime source of ocean-created vitamins in a healthful balance together with minerals and protein that offer you good amounts of Vitamins A, B-complex, C and D as well as E for good nourishment of the roots that help promote healthful hair.

Whole Grains: A prime source of essential fatty acids that are used with Vitamin E to help lubricate and moisturize the shafts of the follicles through which hair should grow healthfully. Use whole grains such as oatmeal, buckwheat, natural brown rice, wheat germ, bran.

Fresh Fruits: Excellent sources of Vitamins A and C that nourish the skin and your scalp and help detoxify your follicles against infectious bacteria.

Fresh Vegetables: A prime source of Vitamins A, C and E that help stimulate the processes that nourish the walls of the hair growing follicles.

Seeds and Nuts: A treasure of many minerals, protein, polyunsaturated fats and Vitamins A, B-complex, C, D and E that work together to give your hair the needed elasticity and shimmering glow needed for youthful appearance.

THE SIMPLE PLANT OIL THAT NOURISHES YOUR HAIR ROOTS

Jean B. was troubled with stringy, dry and lifeless hair. She had tried one popular advertised hair cream after another with negligible results. When one advertisement boasted that the product contained pure vegetable oil that was known for nourishing the hair root, Jean B. decided to go one better. That is, instead of a synthetic preparation with a few drops of vegetable oil, she would try pure oil. Here is Jean's program for helping to nourish your scalp:

1. Each day, she would eat a salad of raw vegetables. She would lace it generously with any cold-pressed seed or nut oil and a bit of apple cider vinegar. This would give her a treasure of Vitamin E a little-known but powerful hair health restorative — The "EFA" Factor. Namely, the oils she used were prime sources of three essential fatty acids — arachidonic acid, linoleic acid, linolenic acid. These three essential fatty acids cannot be

made by the body. They must come from cold-pressed seed or nut oils available in almost every food market and health store.

Benefit: Vitamin E in the oils took up these three natural acids from the same oils, then sent them via the bloodsteam to all parts of the body, especially to the surface of the skin. Vitamin E used these natural acids to moisturize and nourish the hair shafts and thereby improve the health and lubrication of the hair. This is the all-natural but powerful "EFA" Factor that helps promote healthier hair growth.

2. Each and every day, Jean B. would mix two tablespoons of ordinary cold-pressed vegetable oil in a glass of fresh fruit or vegetable juice. She would drink this "Hair Growing Cocktail" every day. The benefit here is that the enzymes and vitamins take up the essential fatty acids and propel them throughout the body to nourish and replenish the dried follicles. This promotes better skin care. Your scalp is skin, too, and it benefits from this all-natural "EFA" Factor in moisturizing the follicles. Jean B. found that this "Hair Growing Cocktail" did much to help lubricate her dry scalp.

3. Jean B. used cold-pressed oils as a replacement and substitution in recipes calling for "hard" fats such as butter or animal fats. This gave her more vitamins and essential fatty acids so that she could give her metabolism the working materials needed to lubricate her arteries and send natural moisture to her "parched" follicles.

Hair Grows with Shimmering Glow

After just 7 days of this simple program, Jean B. noted that her hair looked fuller and thicker. The dryness was gone. Her scalp was tingling with alertness. Her hair glowed with natural youthful moisture, thanks to the use of plant oils. It is the natural way to help nourish your scalp so that your hair responds with youthful aliveness.

10 STEPS TO BOOST VITAMIN ACTION FOR HEALTH OF YOUR HAIR

To help improve the health of your hair, you need to improve the health of your body. Vitamins can function better if you refrain from interfering in their health-building activities. Here is a simple program that can do much to boost body health and hair health, too:

1. *Gentle Brushing.*   Use a natural bristle brush. Avoid excessive vigorous brushing with harsh nylon bristles which can tear the scalp shaft and cause abrasive injury to the scalp.

2. *Sun Shield.*   When going out under the warm or hot sun, protect your scalp with a shield, such as a hat. Excessive heat can "burn" up the delicate scalp covering and injure the health of the hair. Vitamins can perish under the scorching sun and you'll have parchment-like scalp and hair.

3. *Body Health.*   Fevers and body infections such as colds or constipation can all drain out vitamin supplies. This can adversely effect your scalp and hair. So clear up body ailments. You'll feel better all over. Your scalp and hair will grow better, too, when they have adequate vitamins.

4. *Exercise Your Scalp.*   Free your scalp from congestion. Just place the balls of your ten fingers over your scalp and move it gently in all directions. Do this regularly. It liberates "congested" vitamins and "locked" nutrients and helps boost better vitamin-carrying circulatory systems.

5. *Relax.*   Nervous tension drains out much Vitamins B-complex and Vitamin C. This drain can deplete your scalp of needed nourishment. Relax and enjoy better health of your body and your scalp.

6. *Use Natural Hair Preparations.*   Chemicalized preparations in hair dyes or sprays or colorings and even shampoos can destroy vitamins in and on your scalp and hair. Use organic shampoos. Avoid chemicals because they are corrosive and destructive to body health and vitamins as well.

7. *Be Careful About Drugs.*   Your body may react to the invasion of careless use of patent medicines. This stepped up metabolism calls for the oxidation of more and more vitamins. Often, the body becomes weakened in fighting off harsh or unnecessary patent medicines which are antagonists to vitamins. Seek out natural ways to help enjoy better health.

8. *Organic Shampoos.*   These are preferable. A problem here with commercial or chemicalized shampoo is that those containing alkaline soaps will remove your scalp's protective

acid mantle. A shampoo containing detergent will "burn" your oil glands beneath your scalp. A dandruff-removing shampoo may be so volatile that it removes the skin along with the hair! Select herbal or organic shampoos available at most pharmacies, beauty supply outlets and health shoppes.

9. *Avoid Unnatural Hair Punishments.*   Vitamins are destroyed (along with other nutrients) when you punish your hair with harsh driers, hot air treatments, bleaches, chemical tints, long sessions in a chemicalized beauty parlor, chemicalized hair sprays. Avoid these vitamin destroyers and your scalp and hair will look better.

10. *Better Nutrition.*   To grow better hair, use better nutrition. Replace processed food with wholesome natural food. Emphasize vitamin high grains, raw fruit and vegetable salad, lots of seeds and nuts, lean meats, fish, occasional eggs. Feed your body well and your scalp will respond with better hair.

THE SIMPLE FOOD PROGRAM THAT HELPED CONTROL DANDRUFF

The pesky problem of dandruff may be solved by making a simple dietary adjustment. It calls for the *elimination of sugar and the replacement of natural sugar as found in fruits and vegetables*. In one reported situation[1], a physician, John Yudkin, M.D., treated a group of patients who were troubled with *seborrheic dermatitis* (a severe form of dandruff in which the scalp becomes inflamed) by telling them not to eat sugar. This refers solely to the refined or granulated sugar which is used in beverages as well as in processed foods and confections, sweets, pastries, and so forth.

Results?   The 8 folks who abstained from sugar were healed of seborrheic dermatitis and their pesky dandruff vanished. But . . . another set of 11 folks who were allowed all the sugar they wanted had *no* improvement of scalp inflammation or dandruff flakes. This led Dr. John Yudkin to suggest that by eliminating refined and processed sugar from the diet, the scalp could be made healthier and dandruff could be controlled.

[1]John Yudkin, M.D., "Scalp And Diet," *Nature*, London, England, September 22, 1972.

WHY A LOW-CARBOHYDRATE PROGRAM
IMPROVES SCALP HEALTH

Carbohydrates are forms of sugar and starch. They are linked to the formation of dandruff. Writing in a medical journal[2], A. P. Caspers, M.D., notes, "Many patients with *pityriasis capitis* (ordinary dandruff) or frank *seborrheic dermatitis* have low basal metabolic rates, who on questioning admit to consuming an excess of carbohydrates, fat or alcohol. In some instances, a deficiency of Vitamin B has also been noted. It is therefore my practice to supplement local treatment with general measures. Alcohol, chocolate and large amounts of cream, butter, milk and sweets are forbidden, and any suspected Vitamin B deficiency is rectified."

Why Sugar Restriction Helps Control Dandruff

To metabolize sugar and carbohydrates, your body must have a lot of B-complex vitamins. The metabolism will use up these needed vitamins. The more sugar you eat, the more B-complex vitamins are used up and burned up. This may cause a B-complex deficiency which leads to products of incomplete metabolism circulating in your bloodsteam. Such by-products as pyruvic acid and lactic acid cause skin distress. Since your scalp is skin, the earliest symptom is that of dandruff. Just as your face (made of skin) breaks out because of sugar intake, your scalp (made of skin) breaks out in dandruff. So the simple program is to restrict refined and processed sugar from your diet. Replace with healthful honey or natural maple syrup or blackstrap molasses. These are natural sweeteners with lots of vitamins, too.

How Fred M. Guards Against Scalp Starvation

Fred M. likes frequent sweets throughout the day. He "pays" for this compulsion with scalp lesions, breakouts, and excessive

[2]A. P. Caspers, M.D., "Dandruff," *Journal of the Canadian Medical Association*, July 15, 1968.

dandruff. But he is able to control his problem and guard against scalp starvation caused by the burning up of B-complex vitamins in sugar metabolism by following this program:

Each day, he uses Brewer's yeast in beverages or on a large raw vegetable salad. This gives him a powerhouse of needed scalp-feeding B-complex vitamins. He also uses whole grain breads and whole grain cereals. Granola is one such vitamin-powerhouse made up of whole grains and available in most health stores and many larger food markets. He uses Brewer's yeast on granola. He also uses wheat germ.

This simple "scalp feeding" program sends a stream of B-complex vitamins shooting throughout his bloodstream to help replace nutrients used up by sugar and carbohydrate metabolism.

Fred M. has controlled dandruff and it is not as severe as if he were completely "starved" for scalp feeding B-complex.

Of course, for better health, cut down on refined and processed sugar from the shaker and in foods. Give your scalp its needed amount of hair-feeding B-complex vitamins.

HOW TO FEED HAIR-GROWING VITAMINS TO YOUR SCALP

Your hair is *porous*. It is capable of absorbing nutrients. Your scalp is *porous*. It welcomes nourishment. Here are some ways to help feed your hair and your scalp, too.

1. *Natural Shampoo.* Use natural castile soap shampoo or any organic or herbal shampoo. Pour one-half cup into a blender; add one-half cup of warm water. Add the mashed pulp of one-half avocado. Blend on "high" for a few seconds. You should have a creamy, foamy pale green liquid. Wet your hair. Apply this shampoo to your scalp. Massage into your scalp and hair. Keep massaging. Work up a thick lather. The vitamins in the avocado will seep through your porous hair and scalp and feed them needed vitamins. After ten minutes, rinse with clear warm water. Then towel dry.

2. *Lemon Rinse.* Your scalp has an acid mantle that may be stripped away by alkaline soaps. After any shampoo, squeeze lemon juice over your hair and let it seep into your scalp.

The vitamins in the lemon juice help restore the healthful pH (acid mantle) to your scalp and offer better nourishment, too.

3. *Vitamin E Moisturizer*.   Apply ordinary wheat germ oil liberally to your hair. Massage in. Let remain up to an hour. Then wash off. Vitamin E in the wheat germ oil will help nourish your scalp, penetrate your hair shaft and lubricate your follicles. This helps moisturize your scalp and protect against dryness.

4. *Natural Glow*.   To help put a natural shine on your hair and add highlights, too, mix one-half cup of apple cider vinegar or the juice of a large lemon to the final rinse water after your shampoo. The vitamins will neutralize the alkali in the harsh, detergent shampoos that tend to dull hair.

5. *Natural Conditioner*.   Fluff out and "thicken" thin hair by giving yourself a mayonnaise massage. Mayonnaise is a prime source of vitamins from oils and eggs and will help nourish the starved hair and scalp. Massage into your scalp and let remain on your hair 30 minutes before shampooing.

6. *Hair Thickener*.   Beat one egg white with half a cup of water and let it soak on your hair. If possible, let it dry on your hair. Then brush vigorously. The vitamins in the egg white will help thicken your hair and you'll have a better appearance.

7. *Home Made Scalp Treatment*.   Heat any vegetable or seed oil. Then massage the oil into your hair and scalp. Wrap your hair in a terry cloth wrung out in water as warm as comfortable. Cover your hair and towel with heavy aluminum foil to seal in the heat. Remove when cool. This is beneficial because the warmth opens up the pores of your scalp and also helps enlarge the pores of your hair. The vitamins in the oil will now enter and moisturize the pores and keep them lubricated. When you remove the towel and foil, your hair and scalp have been "fed" with the vitamins in the oil. Now, you shampoo. It will give you a healthy and clean scalp and hair. Just as you feel good when nourished, so will your scalp and hair.

8. *Egg Yolk Treatment*.   Mix egg yolk with warm water. Then massage into your scalp. The vitamins in the egg yolk are activated by the warm water and take up the essential fatty acids from the yolk and send them through your porous scalp and hair. After a 30 minute massage and egg yolk treat-

ment, wash off. You'll note your nourished hair has youthful sheen; thicker hair is now free from dandruff.

9. *Brushing Alerts Vitamins*.   Use a natural bristle brush. Then brush gently. This brings up wastes that have been exuded and are clogging the lower portions of your hair strands and scalp. The stimulating action of daily brushing sends a stream of vitamin-carrying sebaceous gland oils to the ends of your hair to provide needed nourishment. Unless you brush daily, your vitamins remain clogged up and unable to feed your hair and scalp.

10. *Ocean Vitamins*.   Sea salt or kelp is an ocean treasure of vitamins and minerals. Mix two heaping tablespoons of sea salt (sold at most health stores and diet shoppes) in a quart of boiled water. Let it cool. Now rub a small amount of this *Ocean Vitamin Tonic* into your scalp daily. This sends a flood of ocean treasures of vitamins and minerals through your scalp and hair pores, feeding them needed nutrients.

11. *Onion Rub*.   A folklore remedy is to rub the sliced half of an onion into your scalp just before retiring. It is believed that Vitamins A and C from the onion replenish the scalp's store of nutrients and the hair is said to grow more abundantly. This vitamin rich onion juice seeping into your scalp helps to stimulate the sluggish scalp going down to the *roots* of the hair shaft for further invigoration and better nourishment. It is said to work overnight in helping to promote better hair and scalp care.

12. *Scalp Cleansing*.   A clean scalp does much to help grow healthy hair. Daily brushing and herbal shampoo should be followed by a lemon juice rinse. This helps maintain good health of your scalp and hair and also helps control dandruff.

13. *Hair Strengthener.*   Let warmed castor oil soak all parts of your scalp and hair. Vitamins will soak and penetrate your hair shaft. Afterwards, shampoo and finish with a rinse of apple cider vinegar. This vitamin treatment helps strengthen your hair, protect against dryness, against dandruff and lifelessness. It also nourishes your hair from end to end so that it protects against splitting.

14. *Dandruff Relief*.   One tablespoon of corn oil taken morning and evening with meals will cure dandruff within two

month's time[3], suggests D.C. Jarvis, M.D. It is believed that the vitamins in the oil are of more liquid type and help moisturize more effectively than vitamins from chewable foods.

To enjoy the youthful appearance of healthy hair, you need a healthy scalp. Feed your body the needed vitamins, follow the natural laws of healthful living, and you will be rewarded with the look and feel of exuberant youth from head to toe!

IN REVIEW

1. A doctor-prescribed food available almost anywhere is a powerhouse of B-complex vitamins that nourish the cellular components which help rejuvenate tissues to promote a more youthful skin.
2. Elsa T. used ocean-created vitamins via fish oils to give her skin needed moisture. She was able to help erase wrinkles with these vitamins in a simple food.
3. Vitamin C, the "plant vitamin," helped rejuvenate Michael L.'s skin so he no longer was called an "old man." A simple 3-step program made him look and feel younger in just one week.
4. Lemon juice is from a golden fruit that offers a "million dollar face rejuvenation." It holds the key to pH (acidity) of the skin which promotes youthful health.
5. Gloria V. uses golden lemons for natural face-lifting.
6. Take your choice of 20 easy ways to use plant foods for skin youthifying.
7. For a healthy scalp and hair, obtain organic vitamins from a wide assortment of everyday foods.
8. A simple plant oil helped put new life and youth into Jean B.'s hair.
9. Take your choice of 10 easy ways to boost vitamin action for hair health.
10. To control dandruff, just control your intake of refined carbohydrates. Doctors report that this helps maintain a needed amount of hair-feeding B-complex vitamins.

[3]D. C. Jarvis, M.D., *Folk Medicine*, Henry Holt & Co., Inc., New York, N.Y. 1958.

11. Fred M. protects himself against scalp starvation by using a simple B-complex food daily. He also uses whole grain breads and cereals to guard against deficiency. It gives him healthier hair and a dandruff relieved scalp.

12. Take your choice of 14 easy ways to help feed hair-growing vitamins to your scalp.

How to Improve Your Eye Health with "Vision Vitamins"

Everyday foods hold a miracle of healing substances that can help improve your eye health. These foods are prime sources of Nature's vitamins that are miracles of vision-improving power. When you nourish your body with these tasty foods, you send a stream of organic vitamins shooting through your bloodstream to give you better health and stronger organisms. Your eyes are organisms that need the miracle strengthening power of vitamins, just as your other body parts require this source of youthful vigor. When your sight-making organism is healthfully nourished, you are rewarded with better vision at any age. There is a recognized relationship between better eye health and "vision vitamins."

THE "VISION TONIC" THAT IMPROVES AND CORRECTS WEAK EYESIGHT

Stella C. is a statistical bookkeeper. She strains her eyes daily while poring over long columns of figures. She squints through eyeglasses as her fingers go over rows of adding machine keys. Stella C. has to be extra-cautious in verifying the tedious columns of numbers on the endless sheets of tapes. She found her eyesight growing dim. In addition to her daily work, she further strained her eyes reading newspapers and magazines. Nightly, straining at television took its toll of her eyesight. Clearly, if her vision was to improve or resist further decline, Stella C. would have to ease the strain. While she could refrain from some reading and some television watching, she could not eliminate or even reduce her eyestrain on her job as a statistical bookkeeper. Stella C. wanted to build resistance to weak eyesight. She wanted to strengthen the vision-making mechanism so that she could help correct her weak eyesight. She knew vitamins could improve vision. She prepared a simple "Vision Tonic" that gave her a powerhouse of vision vitamins.

"*Vision Tonic*." In one glass of fresh carrot juice, stir one tablespoon of desiccated liver. Add a sprinkle of lemon juice for a piquant taste. Stir vigorously. Drink this "Vision Tonic" in the morning. If possible, drink it at noontime again. Then drink a third "Vision Tonic" in the evening.

Miracle of Sight Saving

The secret miracle of this "Vision Tonic" is that carrot juice is a good source of Vitamin A which enters the bloodstream to synthesize the substance *rhodopsin* which then helps improve and maintain normal vision. When Stella C. read something, the bloodstream sent forth more *rhodopsin* which was consumed by the bright light whether from an electric bulb or daylight or even when looking at television. The key to better sight is that the bloodstream needs Vitamin A to make *rhodopsin* which is a self-protective element that nourishes the eyes to give them better health. In carrot juice, Vitamin A is made available in the form of carotene which the body then transforms into the miracle vitamin that provides sight-building *rhodopsin*.

The desiccated liver in the "Vision Tonic" is a dynamic source of all the B-complex vitamins. Desiccated liver is raw liver, dried at a low heat by a method which removes fat, water and connective tissues, but retains all the vital body and eye nourishing nutrients. It is available at almost all health stores. These vitamins enter into the cellular metabolism of the sight-producing mechanism. They strengthen the cells and tissues and work with Vitamin A to nourish the arterioles and cellular tissues to help produce better eyesight.

Stella C. Enjoys Stronger Vision Power

Taken three times a day, in conjunction with a wholesome food program that emphasized lots of leafy green and yellow vegetables, sun-dried apricots (a miracle source of sight-feeding Vitamin A) as well as fish liver oils, she was able to boost the health of her body and her eyes. Now Stella C. no longer needs to squint when laboring over long columns of numbers. Her fingers fly across the adding machine keys with enviable speed and accuracy. Her "Vision Tonic" helped "feed" her eyes and she can even look nightly at television with reduced eyestrain, thanks to the miracle of organic vitamins.

HOW WHOLE GRAIN FOODS OFFER A UNIQUE "EYE VITAMIN"

Whole grain foods are a rich source of riboflavin, the B-complex vitamin that is especially beneficial for sight health. When you sprinkle a whole grain cereal with raw wheat germ and Brewer's yeast, you have an "eye feast" that can strengthen and invigorate your sight-making mechanism and you can enjoy healthy sight for much of the day.

Secret Power of the "Eye Vitamin"

Whole grain foods offer you riboflavin so it can perform a unique sight-feeding function. The cornea of the eye does not normally contain any blood vessels. It gets nourishment from the lymph or the straw-colored portion of your bloodstream. The cornea must "breathe" and it is riboflavin that sends oxygen to every cell of this sight-giving portion of the eye. A deficiency of riboflavin means that tiny blood vessels are formed in an effort by the body to bring the blood into closer contact with the cornea. *Bloodshot eyes are characteristic of a riboflavin deficiency*. This can be corrected by eating whole grain cereals, breads and emphasizing the use of wheat germ and Brewer's yeast.

The Breakfast Food That Nourishes the Eyes

Daniel A. liked to stay up late at night. The problem was when he awakened early the next morning, his eyes itched and burned. Sometimes, Daniel A. would blink against the strong light when he drove to work on a sun-splashed highway. His eyes would also start watering. He feared loss of control of his car. When told that it could mean his riboflavin supplies were being depleted by his late hours, he was given a choice. Either go to bed early (which he refused to do) or else increase his riboflavin intake. He chose the latter. Here is his amazingly simple, yet just as amazingly effective eye-feeding program:

Each morning, Daniel A. would eat *whole grain granola*, a riboflavin rich cereal composed of oats, wheat, wheat germ, sesame seeds, honey, Brewer's yeast and other vitamin-high ingredients. (Granola is sold at almost all health stores and many supermarkets.) Mix a half cup of this vitamin-rich granola with milk or fruit juice, add some Brewer's yeast for increased B-complex fortification, some fresh fruit slices such as sun-dried apricots for needed Vitamin A. It is a wholesome breakfast. It is a breakfast food that is a veritable treasure of those vitamins needed for visual strength.

Enjoys Healthier Eyesight

Daniel A. finds that this natural B-complex fortification helps him see better in stronger light. His eyes no longer itch or burn. He sees much better generally speaking. Of course, his late hours still take their visual and health toll, but the whole grain *granola* breakfast helps him meet the challenge of eye stress and sight strain. Riboflavin is helping to nourish his eyes to control eyestrain.

HOW TO USE FRESH FRUITS TO IMPROVE EYESIGHT

When you eat a luscious juicy fruit, you are sending a supply of natural Vitamin C into your body. Vitamin C is needed for nourishment of the lens of your eye (that portion which may become cloudy in vitamin malnutrition).

How Fruits Nourish Eyes

Vitamin C from fruits sends a supply of needed oxygen to the eye lens, which has neither nerves or blood vessels. The lens is suspended in a structure called the *aqueous humor*. It must get its nourishment from this structure. Vitamin C is transported through this *aqueous humor* where it deposits oxygen and other elements needed for visual ability. Without Vitamin C, the lens starts to decline in power. Prolonged deficiency may even pre-dispose problems of cataract, uveitis, retinitis pigmentosa. But fresh fruits send Vitamin C to nourish the lens and give it needed transparency. It is the natural way to feed your lens and to help improve your eyesight.

Simple Eye Feeding Fruit Program

Each and every single day, plan to drink fresh citrus fruit juices that are prime sources of Vitamin C as well as many other vitamins, along with enzymes and minerals. Oranges, grapefruits, berries, tangerines, lemons are all good sources of this eye feeding vitamin. Plan to eat a large raw fruit salad each day. Because Vitamin C is water-soluble it is *not* stored in your body. You need a good supply everyday or else run the risk of a deficiency that may also cause sight disorders. It's simple to protect yourself with lots of fresh fruit juices and a fruit salad daily. Try a fruit salad for a dessert. Or when you feel thirsty, peel an orange, re-move the seeds, and eat the wedges. This will give you delicious Vitamin C that will be welcomed by your eyes.

PLANT FOODS NOURISH YOUR EYES

Fruits are good sources of Vitamin C which assist in the formation of collagen, the substance that makes up the eye cornea and the tissues and also helps nourish the liquids that bathe the eye.

Vegetables are good sources of Vitamin A which nourishes the retina to help protect the eye's response to light. The retina takes Vitamin A from vegetables and manufactures visual purple to protect you against night blindness and the "shock" of bright lights.

Both vitamins are used by the *aqueous humor* liquid that flows constantly over the front surface of the cornea. The liquid uses both of these vitamins to maintain the pressure inside the eyeball at a constant level. The liquid needs these vitamins to nourish the lens and the cornea.

Nature has given you a delicious assortment of fruits and vegetables containing these vitamins so that they can help build better eyesight. A daily intake of these vitamin-containing plant foods will help nourish your body and your eyes.

BUILD STRONGER EYESIGHT BY ELIMINATING SOFT DRINKS

Leonard J. noted his sight was getting dim. He had to squint hard to read an average newspaper. When he noted little "dark spots" floating before his eyes, he felt he was in serious trouble. When he caught a very bad cold and was confined to bed for a week, he made another discovery. His sight improved!

He attributed this to the fact that because he was bedridden with a cold, he could not imbibe his habitual soft drinks. Leonard J. was a "soda pop addict" because he was drinking the fizz beverages all the time. Could this have a relationship to his failing eyesight?

Soft Drinks Weaken Eyes

That was when he discovered that soda drinks can weaken the eyes. Soft drinks are high in sugar. The metabolism of the sugar drains out a supply of the B-complex vitamins so that the eyes suffer a shortage. But more serious is that the carbonic acid (the "fizz factor in all soft drinks) can weaken the eyes.

Carbonic acid is composed of carbon dioxide. This substance goes to every part of the body. In the eye, it produces a chronic water-logging of certain important structures. An abnormal amount of carbonic acid in the tissues of the white of the eye will cause a constriction of the vessels that traverse it and result in their congestion. The B-complex vitamins are rapidly used to help counteract this problem and this creates a vitamin deficiency. The end result is declining eyesight.

Leonard J. had to give up his soft drink habit for the sake of the health of his eyes. His vision improved noticeably. When he would sip several fruit juices throughout the day, the vitamins further rebuilt his eye-making mechanism. Soon, he could see clearly. The little "dark spots" faded away. He had sparkling clear eyes. Thanks to the fruit juice vitamins and, most important, the elimination of soft drinks, he could enjoy healthy eyesight.

10 STEPS TO BETTER EYE HEALTH

Strain drains out the B-complex and C vitamins. When strain is accompanied by vitamin deficiency, the eyes weaken. To help build better eye health, here are 10 steps. They are designed to strengthen the tine muscles of the eyes so that the eyeballs can then stretch and squeeze to see more clearly.

1. *Easy Eye Exercise.*   Relax in a chair. Move your eyes slowly in a wide circle, first several times in one direction, then several times in the other direction.

2. *Eye Improvement.*   Move your eyes very far to the right, then very far to the left. Repeat several times *without* moving your head.

3. *Up and Down.*   Move your eyes up and down. Move them far to the right top corner, then to the bottom left corner. Now move them far to the left top corner, then to the bottom right corner. Repeat several times *without* moving your head.

4. *Palming.*   Rub both of your palms together to produce a natural body electricity. Now just place your palms over your closed eyes. You should feel a stream of vitality shooting through your eyes.

5. *Knuckle Rub.*   To ease tired eyes, rub them with your knuckles, as a cat does. Be gentle.

6. *Distance Look.*   To help accommodate the different requirements of distance vision, avoid looking for prolonged amounts of time at a close object. Instead, keep changing your distance. Look far away, then suddenly very near to you at the tip of your nose. Now look far away again. This "contrast" between far and near is a healthful eye exercise.

7. *Blinking.*   Whenever you blink your eyes, you send a

natural washing that also helps feed nourishment to the various components of your sight-making mechanisms.

8. *Water Treatment.*   To help alert a sluggish circulation of the blood stream, give your eyes alternate hot and cold wet towel applications. If you have no towels, then just splash contrasting comfortably hot and comfortably cold water on your closed eyes. It helps spark the flood of nutrient-carrying blood to your eyes.

9. *Pleasant Scenes.*   Your eyes will feel relaxed and soothed if you look at pleasant scenes. The rolling fields of wheat, a forest of trees, a mountain, a clear or cloudy sky (avoid sun glare) or anything pleasant will make you (and your eyes) feel much healthier.

10. *Good Eye Care.*   Avoid eyestrain and do NOT stare at any object. Keep your eyes moving. Blink as often as possible. Relax your body and you relax your eyes to give them better health.

Extra Tip: Poor posture can cause a vitamin deficiency. When you are crouched, you have a curvature of your spine. There is a resulting pressure on the nerves coming out of the spine situated between the vertebrae. When the nerves are compressed by the narrowed spaces between the vertebrae, they are unable to send out sufficient nourishment to their nerve-endings in different parts of your body.

This may deprive your eyes of nourishment. Poor, cramped posture leads to a form of congestion which impedes the free flow of sight-feeding vitamins. So maintain good posture. Have a flexible spinal column. This helps liberate your nervous network. Vitamins can now be sent on a free lane to your eyes to build better visual health.

SIX EASY EXERCISES THAT HELP SEND VITAMINS TO YOUR EYES

To help release the "locked in" or "choked" vitamins from congested areas of your body, here are six easy exercises that should help promote better visual feeding health:

1. Sit upright. Stretch your right arm out in front of you.

Extend your index finger. Slowly, move your finger to the right. Now follow the fingertip with your eyes *without* moving your head. Next, slowly move your arm as far to the right as your vision will comfortably allow. Keep your eyes on your fingertip *without* moving your head. Repeat with your left arm. Do this several times.

2. Sit upright. Lift your arm as high as you can. Follow your arm with your eyes *without* moving your head. Repeat with your other arm. Do this exercise a few times a day.

3. Open your eyes wide. Visualize a clock with large numbers printed at the edge of your vision. Now focus upon 12 Noon on your visualized clock. Very slowly, *without* moving your head, let your eyes go from 12 Noon to 1 o'clock and downward, then all the way around until you have reached 12 o'clock again. *Next,* repeat this exercise but this time do it counterclockwise moving from 12 o'clock backwards until you come to 12 o'clock again. Do this several times.

4. Roll your head but *without* moving your shoulders. The benefit here is that this loosens up neck and upper body congestion. Once this occurs, there is an increased circulation to your optic nerves and nutrients can now go streaming to feed your eye apparatus. It also eases eyestrain. Repeat this as often as it is comfortable. It is the easy way to vitaminize your tissues.

5. Sit or stand. Keep your spine comfortably erect. Breathe deeply until you feel your stomach sucked in. Now very comfortably roll your head *in a circle.* The benefit here is that "tight" neck muscles start to loosen up and as you enjoy youthful suppleness in this region, vitamins can be more freely dispersed throughout your upper body, including your eyes. Repeat this regularly.

6. As you breathe deeply, in and out, roll your head from right to left, then from left to right but do *not* move your shoulders. Put the movement upon your neck so that the congestion can loosen. You should continue breathing. The combination of inhaled oxygen together with liberated tissues will send fresh vitamin-carrying blood through your system to nourish your eyes.

Suggestion: To help keep your eyes healthy, use them — but don't abuse them. Get sufficient sleep each night. Do not squint. Do not overuse your eyes. The aim is *not* to constrict your blood vessels. Avoid such artificial stimulants as coffee, tea, tobacco, alcohol, soft drinks. Replace with healthful herbal beverages and plant juices. Avoid excessive tensions and rushing. You will relax better if you protect yourself against noise which can drain out vitamins and deplete body and visual health. Fortify yourself with good nutrition.

BE GOOD TO YOUR EYES:
U. S. GOVERNMENT RECOMMENDATION

Good reading practices will help guard against eyestrain and nervous exhaustion. The official U. S. Government recommendation[1] for eye care calls for resting your eyes from continued close work. Close them for a minute, or look off at a distance.

Good reading habits enable you to use your eyes to best advantage and help prevent eyestrain and nervous exhaustion. Use a reading light of 100 watts, preferably placed about three feet back of you and to one side of the printed page.

You can also get good reading light from two shaded #100 watt pinup lights on each side of a desk or from a shielded desklight or from ample overhead lighting. To check whether you have enough working or reading light you can borrow a foot candle meter from a lighting company or a plant engineer.

Older people need more light on their work or reading. Avoid either glare or shadow. Avoid one lighted spot in an otherwise dark room; some general lighting gives eye comfort.

Do not read while riding in cars or during any kind of bumpy ride, as this puts an extra strain on your eyes. Children should be taught good reading habits early. They should be discouraged from reading while lying on the floor, as this usually brings the print too close to their eyes.

Basic Tips. When reading or doing close work, have adequate light and good reading conditions. Do not hold a book or paper nearer than 12 inches from your eyes when reading. Avoid reflections from book or paper. Also relax your eyes every 30 minutes or so when doing concentrated close work by briefly closing them or looking off into the distance. Protect your eyes from bright sunlight by wearing absorptive lenses during periods

[1] *Care of the Eyes,* Public Health Service Publication, No. 113, U. S. Department of Health, Education and Welfare, Washington, D.C.

of long exposure and especially at high altitudes. Never look directly at the sun.

ENJOY HEALTHIER EYESIGHT
WITH NATURAL LIGHTING

Wherever possible, use natural lighting. If you have to use indoor lighting, use an ordinary light bulb instead of the fluorescent variety which can be a vitamin antagonist.

Health Problem of Fluorescent Lights

The flickering light of a fluorescent bulb causes an increase in the body's metabolism and a speedy utilization of vitamins. Ordinarily, light enters the eye, strikes the nerve endings in the retina and stimulates electrical impulses that travel up the two stalks of the optic nerve to the brain. Vitamin A must be used to meet this challenge. But fluorescent lights provide very little long wave ultraviolet light and emit yellow and red radiations in a ratio quite different from ordinary lightbulbs. Prolonged exposure to this unnatural phototherapy can be a serious drain upon the body's store of Vitamins A and C. This is the consequence of what is known as distorted lighting from a fluorescent source. It also speeds up Vitamin D absorption to the extent that it may cause an excess utilization of this nutrient and lead to visual disturbances traced to a deficiency.

Select More Natural Lights

Wherever possible, use natural light for your daily activities. When indoors, during dark days, dark nights, use ordinary light bulbs. To help protect yourself against vision vitamin loss, boost your intake of lots of fresh yellow and green vegetables, broiled liver, egg yolk, lots of fresh fruits, raw vegetables and fruit juices, whole grain foods. This will help give your body more needed vitamins as a storehouse so that you will help protect your eyes against a shortage.

For better visual health, aim for total body harmony with healthful vitamins, better living programs and an alliance with Nature, the source of eternal health.

SUMMARY

1. Stella C. made a simple but nutritionally effective "Vision Tonic" that soothed her eyestrain, made reading easier, corrected difficulties. Just two ingredients but they add up to a goldmine of visual nourishment.
2. Daniel A. ate a special "eye feast" consisting of whole grain foods for B-complex nourishment. His eyes no longer itched, burned, watered. He could drive comfortably in the morning as he faced the early sunshine.
3. Fresh fruits contain a special vitamin that actually nourish the eyes.
4. Leonard J. gave up soft drinks and discovered his eyes improved. Dark spots faded away. He could see clearly.
5. To promote better eye health, soothe strain with the outlined ten steps.
6. Send a stream of vitamins to your eyes by following these six easy exercises that unlock congestion and open nutrient channels.
7. Be good to your eyes and follow the official U.S. Government recommendations for healthy vision. Enjoy healthier eyesight with natural lighting. Avoid fluorescent lights.

4

Blood Building for Health—
The Organic Vitamin Way

A rich, red bloodstream is a youthful river of life flowing within your body, bathing all internal organs and your billions of cells and tissues with health-building nutrients. To enjoy better health, your bloodstream must have adequate nutrition to help perform these youthful functions:

1. Your bloodstream takes vitamins from your digestive system and carries them to your billions of body cells and tissues.

2. Your bloodstream needs vitamins for energy to supply water and oxygen to your cells and transport the waste products produced by the cells' biological activity away from your body to be eliminated through various channels.

3. Your bloodstream uses vitamins for self-regulation of the normal water content in the tissue fluids.

4. Your bloodstream uses vitamins to "protect" the plasma proteins so that they help maintain a healthful acid base balance in your system.

5. Your bloodstream uses vitamins to combine proteins with water-insoluble fats to form complex molecules known as lipoproteins; the vitamins are used to transport the fats to their sites without coalescing (growing together) to form globules.

6. Your bloodstream uses vitamins to help carry oxygen from

the lungs to the cells and return carbon dioxide to the lungs for elimination from your body.

7. Your bloodstream uses vitamins to carry away from the cells those waste by-products such as urea, uric acid and phosphoric acid. Your bloodstream then uses vitamins to help eliminate these wastes through the urinary tract as well as through the kidneys. At the same time, your bloodstream uses vitamins to nourish these organs.

8. Your bloodstream uses vitamins in carrying away carbon dioxide from the cells, to partially combine this gas with body water to form carbonic acid; the remainder is combined with blood proteins. Blood vitamins help maintain a proper acidity and protect your body against the continuous formation of carbonic acid. This delicate balance requires adequate vitamin nourishment for functioning.

9. Your bloodstream needs vitamins to work with iron to create a blood protein known as hemoglobin. This is the red coloring matter of the blood and constitutes up to 17 percent of whole blood. A vitamin deficiency may mean a hemoglobin deficiency which is classified as anemia.

10. Your bloodstream needs vitamins for the creation of the red cells in your bloodstream. These red cells do not live forever. They break up after about 120 days and their hemoglobin is lost. Vitamins help in the formation of new hemoglobin-rich cells which are broken up and destroyed daily. Vitamins are needed to replace the quantity being broken down every single minute. Some 2,300,000 such red cells are destroyed *each second* and vitamins must be made available for their replacement.

A vitamin-enriched bloodstream adds up to a healthy and youth-building bloodstream. Nature has created an assortment of vitamins in plain, everyday foods. They are available to you and your bloodstream for better health.

THE VITAMIN THAT HELPS WAKE UP "TIRED BLOOD"

Clara R. was troubled with feelings of weakness. Her skin was pale. She could hardly do a half hour of simple housework without feeling exhaustion and having to lie down. Clara R. also experienced shortness of breath and occasional dizziness. When she bent over to pick up a fallen object on the floor, she would feel everything swerving so that she had to hold onto a chair for support, lest she collapse, losing her balance. Clara R. ate a wholesome diet, enjoyed good food, yet she felt chronic fatigue and weakness. She was told that while she had good iron supply, she needed a vitamin found in ordinary foods in which she was deficient. This vitamin would alert-awaken iron so that it could be metabolized and then perform the needed blood building process that would help correct her problems. In short, this vitamin would wake up her "tired blood." The vitamin was B_6, or *pyridoxine*.

How Clara R. Used Vitamin B_6 to Wake Up Her "Tired Blood"

Each *morning*, Clara R. would eat a whole grain cereal over which she would sprinkle Brewer's yeast. These two simple foods are organic sources of Vitamin B_6, along with a treasure of other nutrients.

Noontime.   Clara R. would have a slice of broiled fish together with a dish of soybeans. These two foods are prime sources of needed Vitamin B_6. She would also have a large raw fruit or vegetable salad to give herself a healthful balance of other vitamins, minerals and enzymes.

Dinnertime.   Clara R. would have a lean slice of broiled liver, the most effective source of Vitamin B_6 along with a score of other essential blood-building nutrients. She also had a raw salad.

Results: Within three weeks, Clara's bloodstream perked up. She was no longer so quickly fatigued. She had better balance. Gone were her headaches and the feeling of chronic tiredness. Vitamin B_6 had helped wake up her "tired blood" and now she could perform a full day's housework with youthful vigor, thanks to this simple nutritional program.

The Miracle Power of Blood-Building Vitamin B_6

This vitamin assists iron (which cannot properly function alone or without Vitamin B_6) in its making of needed red cells.

and increasing the amount of hemoglobin in the bloodstream. This helps nourish the bloodstream which can send a powerhouse of nutrition throughout the body. Vitamin B_6 acts as the body's "guardian" of iron to see that iron is properly metabolized and to protect against irregular amounts. You may have an appreciable supply of iron but you need Vitamin B_6 to metabolize that iron so it can nourish your bloodstream and protect it against sluggishness. Vitamin B_6 uses iron to wake up the tired bloodstream.

Sources of Blood-Building Vitamin B_6

The highest amounts are found in Brewer's yeast, liver, wheat germ and egg yolk. Fish, poultry and meats also contain beneficial amounts. While Vitamin B_6 remains quite stable, it is slightly weakened by prolonged heating during cooking. For better benefits, plan to eat Brewer's yeast raw by sprinkling it over salads or mixing with a fruit or vegetable juice as a healthful tonic. Broil liver just long enough to make it palatable. Sprinkle liver with wheat germ for a double-barreled Vitamin B_6 benefit. Two soft boiled eggs per week will also give you Vitamin B_6. Your blood will be enriched and you'll awaken from that sluggish feeling known as "tired blood."

THE VITAMIN THAT HELPS YOU FEEL "WARM AS SUNSHINE"

Lillian W. was troubled with cold fingers, cold feet and a chill that sunshine could not correct. Lillian W. was so weak and wan that she had little appetite. She walked with a shuffling gait, lost the sense of position of her feet and wanted just to lie in bed, huddled beneath the covers, even when the temperature was very warm. Lillian W. always felt cold! A concerned neighbor urged Lillian W. to "feed" her bloodstream with a special vitamin that could help correct her obvious problem. Lillian W. was running the risk of *anemia*. The blood-feeding nutrient was Vitamin B_{12}.

How Lillian W. Regained Youthful Warmth with Vitamin B_{12}

With the help of her neighbor, Lillian W. followed this simple program to boost her intake of Vitamin B_{12}:

1. *Blood Building Tonic.*   Three times a day, she drank a glass of vegetable juice into which was stirred one tablespoon of Brewer's yeast. This offers a rich supply of nearly all known B-complex vitamins but is especially potent in natural Vitamin B_{12}, needed for blood building.

2. *Grain Food for the Bloodstream.*   For breakfast each day, Lillian W. would have a whole grain cereal. The emphasis was on the raw germ or the complete kernel of the raw grain (such as wheat germ, rye, barley, oats, bran) which had the most potent source of Vitamin B_{12} in the plant kingdom. A cup of this raw grain food in a bowl of milk or fruit juice, sprinkled with wheat germ for still more blood food would give you a good supply of this needed nutrient.

3. *Mighty Blood Building Food.*   Three times a week, Lillian W. would have a small portion of lean broiled liver, a powerhouse of Vitamin B_{12}. Together with a raw vegetable salad offering vitamins, minerals and enzymes that "activated" Vitamin B_{12}, she was able to give her body a mighty blood building food.

4. *Powerhouse Potion.*   Early evening, Lillian W. would mix one tablespoon of desiccated liver (available at most health stores) in a glass of a raw vegetable juice. A sprinkle of lemon for a piquant taste. She would drink this Powerhouse Potion nightly. It was a most potent source of blood-building Vitamin B_{12} as well as iron and most of the other known B-complex nutrients.

Results: It took just nine days before Lillian W. felt so warm (and this was wintertime, too!) that she shed her heavy blankets, started doing her usual chores, and felt younger than ever. Her fingers and toes felt so warm that she thought she was bathed in sunshine. Her movements were agile and flexible. She had a youthful sense of balance. No matter how cold the winter became, Lillian W. said that she felt as "warm as sunshine" thanks to this simple program that emphasized Vitamin B_{12}.

The Miracle Power of Blood-Building Vitamin B_{12}

This vitamin functions as a coenzyme in important body enzyme systems to metabolize those substances which influence the health of the bloodstream. Vitamin B_{12} protects against such "cold blood" symptoms as numbness, tingling in the hands, back pains, soreness of the mouth and tongue. Vitamin B_{12} uses iron to permit better absorption into the bloodstream. Vitamin B_{12} uses iron to make hemoglobin which carries oxygen to the muscle cells. Vitamin B_{12} helps protect against premature death of the red cells so that they do not disintegrate so speedily. Putting it briefly, Vitamin B_{12} influences blood cell *longevity* as well as *quantity*. When you have trillions of trillions long-living red cells, your bloodstream surges throughout your body with warm youth!

Sources of Blood-Building
Vitamin B_{12}

The highest amounts are found in liver, kidney, then fish and eggs. These foods should be eaten regularly to help give your bloodstream the needed hemoglobin-making Vitamin B_{12}.

Plant Sources: Vegetarians can help protect against anemia or blood cell deficiency by eating *three* meatless foods containing this nutrient: Brewer's yeast, wheat germ, soybeans. While these three plant foods contain smaller amounts of Vitamin B_{12}, they should be eaten regularly for those folks who are on a meatless program.

THE VITAMIN THAT GIVES YOU
"YOUNGER THAN SPRINGTIME" BLOOD

Andrew N. caught one cold after another, even in summertime. He was vulnerable to whatever local virus happened to invade his community. His mouth and tongue always felt unusually sensitive and sore. He often had difficulty in keeping his eyelids open. Even after a night's sleep, Andrew N. was groggy and dizzy and would often doze off right after breakfast. He looked pale and much older than his 47 years of age. He was troubled with nervous temperament that made him grouchy and irritable upon the slightest provocation. His family, friends and co-workers started to drift away from him. With such moodiness, his appetite suffered. Soon, Andrew N.'s problems were compounded with malnutrition.

Routine Examination Alerts Need for
Enrichment of Bloodstream

His company-directed examination alerted Andrew N. to the need for using vitamins to help enrich his bloodstream. It was noted that the deficiency of one such vitamin was a contributing factor to his emotional and physical decline. The vitamin was a member of the B-complex family, or *folic acid.*

How Andrew N. Used Folic Acid to
Brighten Up His Bloodstream

The name of this vitamin is derived from the Latin word *folia* which means "leaves." Andrew N. started a program whereby he ate green leafy vegetables. This was the start of the program. He also would eat lean liver, unprocessed nuts and seeds, kidney and navy beans. These everyday foods were prime sources of folic acid that helped enrich the bloodstream of Andrew N. and make him feel "younger than Springtime."

Basic Program: Before each meal, every single day, Andrew N. would eat a salad of raw leafy vegetables. These include spinach, kale, endive, lettuce, cabbage. The benefit here is that *raw* leafy vegetables are prime sources of blood-rejuvenating folic acid, along with other vitamins.

The Oriental Secret of Healthful
Cooked Vegetables

Andrew N. liked cooked vegetables and was told of an Oriental secret for preserving much vitamin content even if cooked. Here's how — cut vegetables in shreds. Now heat a small amount of sesame, safflower or any polyunsaturated vegetable oil in a covered skillet. Quickly stir the vegetables in the hot oil. Cover. Cook *only* until tender-crisp. Then eat with luscious taste. The Orientals know this type of vegetable cookery is healthful. Andrew N. could now enjoy cooked asparagus, beet greens, endive, kale, turnip greens, potatoes which all offered him a tremendous source of this blood-building nutrient.

The Meat that Nourishes the Bloodstream

Liver is one of the best sources of folic acid. In particular, chicken liver is considered about the *highest* source of this blood-nourishing vitamin. All Andrew N. did was plan on eating broiled chicken liver with a large raw or Oriental-cooked vegetable salad and he quickly felt himself perk up. Nutrients in the liver immediately set about to nourish his bloodstream and body, too.

The Elixir that Gave "Instant" Blood Building

Once a day, Andrew N. made himself a Magic Elixir. He used fresh fruit juice, with one tablespoon of desiccated liver powder. He stirred quickly. Then he enjoyed this tasty drink. Within moments, Andrew N. felt his spirits surging. His bloodstream throbbed with youthful vitality. This Magic Elixir sent him an "instant" blood-building energy flow. The *secret benefit* here is that folic acid may often be weak in rebuilding the blood stream. Folic acid needs Vitamin C for functioning. Folic acid and Vitamin C then work to increase iron absorption and the rate of hemoglobin production. It is Vitamin C that changes folic acid into a form that can be used for iron rebuilding of the bloodstream. The Magic Elixir contained Vitamin C in the fruit juice and folic acid in the desiccated liver, together with iron. It was this triple-action that gave Andrew N. such a powerhouse of vitality. He often called it his "pep tonic" and said that if he took it in the morning, he was like a young racehorse!

Thanks to this folic acid and general vitaminization of his bloodstream, Andrew N. recovered from his setback. He was able to resist colds and respiratory ailments. His mouth and tongue healed up. His emotions were alert. He slept well. He awakened looking fresh and feeling energetic. His temperament became so even and smooth that he gained new friends and a promotion in his company. Small wonder he hails folic acid in wholesome foods as the vitamin that helped give him "younger than Springtime" blood.

The Miracle Power of Youthful Folic Acid

This vitamin works with Vitamin C and iron to help build body protein and other vital components of the blood cells. In particular, folic acid protects against anemia by nourishing the bone marrow in which red blood cells are made. It further nourishes the mucous membranes and linings throughout the body. Folic acid protects against such problems as weakness, poor appetite, diminished vigor and gastrointestinal weakness. In particular, folic acid increases the quality and power of the red blood cells so that they carry oxygen to all parts of the body via the bloodstream to nourish, regenerate and sustain. This organic vitamin is essential to just about every human life process. It is transported via the bloodstream to all body parts to put health and vigor into your very life. It is truly Nature's miracle blood-building vitamin.

Sources of Blood-Rejuvenating Folic Acid

Liver, kidneys, chicken liver and giblets, green leafy vegetables, Brewer's yeast, soybeans, kidney beans, navy beans, whole grain cereals and whole grain breads, nuts and some seeds. *Extra Tip:* Be sure to eat green leafy vegetables *raw* for top notch folic acid content. Plan on eating *fresh* vegetables since some folic acid is lost if they are kept at room temperature or in storage for a period of time. Keep vegetables refrigerated until use to preserve vitamin content.

It is important to get daily amounts of folic acid because since it is required for the manufacture of blood cells, it must be always available. Your bone marrow cannot perform its function of producing red blood cells without folic acid. Be sure to have lots of fresh fruits, too, because folic acid works with Vitamin C to help protect against a certain type of anemia known as megaloblastic. The two organic vitamins — folic acid and Vitamin C — cooperate to give you this protection and blood enrichment. All this, thanks to Nature.

THE MIRACLE VITAMIN
THAT IS FOOD FOR YOUR BLOODSTREAM

Mildred O. felt herself growing sluggish. She ate properly, was sure that her bloodstream was well-nourished, yet she was below par. Her memory appeared to have blank spots. She occasionally had difficulties in breathing. Sometimes she complained of "choking" sensations. There were nights when she would awaken from a troubled sleep, feeling choked. She would also have occasional coughing fits. She was told that while she was adequately nourished, she was deficient in one vitamin that is ordinarily overlooked in the quest for health. This one vitamin held the key to reviving her bloodstream and helping her enjoy the good health to which she was entitled. The "missing link" in her chain was *Vitamin E.*

How Mildred O. Used Vitamin E to Enjoy a Miracle Young Bloodstream

Every day, Mildred O. would take two tablespoons of polyunsaturated wheat germ oil in a cup of vegetable juice. She would also use the same oil as part of a salad dressing. She would combine it with equal parts of honey and a squeeze of fruit juice over a raw vegetable salad. This was her simple, yet miracle-like effective bloodstream rejuvenation program. She would also use *unbleached* flour and *unbleached* grains for her baking needs. All breads and cereals were whole grain and non-processed. This assured her of an increasing intake of this valuable life, health and bloodstream building nutrient.

The Youth-Preserving Power of Blood-Feeding Vitamin E

This vitamin preserves red cells and keeps them alert and healthy. In particular, when Mildred O. fortified herself with raw seed and nut oils, the Vitamin E protected her red cells against hemolysis (breakdown) by hydrogen peroxide. Vitamin E strengthened the walls of the red blood cells so that they would not so easily become fragile. Furthermore, Vitamin E helped maintain the integrity of her red blood cells and extend their survival.

Secret Power of Plant Oils

Vitamin E in plant oils act as a natural antioxidant in the body. That is, it helps protect the red blood cells by preventing or curtailing the formation of hydrogen peroxide. A deficiency means that oxygen may combine with the essential fatty acids to form this hydrogen peroxide which is a known destroyer of red blood cells. But with Vitamin E, made available in polyunsaturated plant oils, the red cells have stronger outer membranes; this helps protect against frequent breakage and the spilling of valuable hemoglobin. Vitamin E in plant oils takes up intracellular enzymes to boost membrane integrity of the red blood cells. Vitamin E thus helps red cells to survive and serve the bloodstream. Vitamin E is needed in the bloodstream to help bathe the erythrocytes (red blood cells) and protect them from oxidative damage and resultant hemolysis (breakdown) by hydrogen peroxide. This is the secret power of Vitamin E in plant oils.

How Vitamin E Rejuvenated
Mildred O's Bloodstream

Vitamin E helped protect Mildred's bloodstream from excessive viscosity or thickness. A problem is that a thick bloodstream slows down the circulation. It led to Mildred's problems of felling sluggish. But Vitamin E promoted the delivery of nutrients and sufficient oxygen to the blood cells and helped protect against premature aging.

Magic Power: Vitamin E has the magic-like power of preventing the oxidation of fatty acids in the bloodstream. It also increases the amount of oxygen to most body tissues. Vitamin E is Nature's magic food to maintaining an adequate oxygen supply without an overproduction of red blood cells.

Results: Mildred O. substituted "hard" fats with the more healthful "soft" fats such as polyunsaturated seed and nut oils, fruit and vegetable oils, sold almost everywhere in supermarkets, food stores, as well as specialized health food stores. Now her memory was sparklingly alert, she breathed easily, she could sleep the night through, and had no recurring feelings of being choked. Vitamin E gave her the "missing link" to promote better health through a healthier bloodstream.

The Easy Way to Self-Test Your Need
for Bloodstream Vitaminization

Here is how you can test yourself to see if your bloodstream is sluggish and in need of vitamin revitalization. Press your fingertips hard against a table top or windowsill or any desk. Are your nails red or a deep pink? Then it means your bloodstream is healthy and clean. But ... are your fingernails pale? Then it means your bloodstream may be sluggish and slowed down like a muddy river. It may also suggest that clogged or sluggish blood may predispose to blood clots. It means you need better vitaminization.

The Miracle Power of Blood Cleansing Vitamin E

This vitamin cleanses your bloodstream, helps clear away debris, helps transport oxygen from your lungs to your cells; carbon dioxide from your tissues back to your lungs to be given off with every exhalation. Vitamin E helps your bloodstream transport nutrients from your stomach and intestines through your liver to your body's trillions of tissues. Vitamin E further works to help your bloodstream take waste products from your tissues and send them to your excretory organs. Vitamin E helps your glands and all other compounds work in smooth balance.

Sources of Youth Restoring Vitamin E

Oils from the seeds of such plants as corn, wheat, soybeans, safflower, sunflower, peanut, are some of the best sources. Raw seeds and nuts are excellent sources, too. Be sure to obtain the non-processed and non-hydrogenated oils as well as seeds and nuts since the processing will cause a loss of perishable Vitamin E. Just use these oils wherever a "fat" is called for and you'll be feeding your bloodstream the needed amount of youth restoring Vitamin E.

Vitamins as found in wholesome good foods help maintain a delicate balance in red blood cell physiology. Vitamins also help protect against viscosity and oxygen loss. Vitamin E prevents the oxidation of fatty acids in the blood and automatically increases the amount of oxygen available to body tissues from head to toe. For this reason, miracle Vitamin E can be considered Nature's safest ticket to a youthful oxygen supply and a well-balanced production of red blood cells. All this is possible with cold-pressed, non-processed plant oils and whole grain foods. It is

Nature's "secret" for living young . . . with a "forever young" well-nourished bloodstream.

IN REVIEW:

1. For youthful health, maintain a well-nourished blood-stream. You receive at least ten youth-building benefits from vitamins in your bloodstream.
2. Four specific outlined vitamins have important functions in keeping your bloodstream (and you, too) in youthful health.
3. Clara R. used Vitamin B_6 to wake up her "tired blood."
4. Lillian W. used Vitamin B_{12} to make her feel "warm as sunshine."
5. Andrew N. used folic acid to brighten up his bloodstream.
6. Mildred O. used Vitamin E to rejuvenate and "clean up" her bloodstream.
7. Refresh-invigorate your bloodstream with the various potions, tonics, elixirs and wholesome foods that are brimming with miraculous vitamins.

How to Use Vitamins As Natural Tranquilizers

You can improve your moods with the miracle of organic vitamins in healthful foods. You can protect yourself against nervous tension, daily stress, emotional depression by making some very simple corrections in your food program. The foods you eat can act as natural tranquilizers and all-natural pain relievers. The foods you do *not* eat can help correct problems of emotional unrest and stressful tension. In particular, there are *two* non-foods that should be eliminated from your eating program if you want to enjoy youthful and healthful energy and freedom from nervous tension. These two non-foods are *sugar* and *salt*. By the simple action of eliminating them from your diet, you take the first step in enjoying "happy nerves" and protection against stress in daily living. Here are the nerve-healing benefits of eliminating sugar and salt.

HOW A SUGAR-FREE PROGRAM HELPS SOOTHE YOUR NERVOUS SYSTEM

Edna D. lived and worked under a constant barrage of tension. Her neighbors were noisy. Her family talked loud, played loud music, invited friends into the house which created more din and confusion. At work Edna D. could hardly endure the constant noise of office machinery, ringing telephones, grating voices of co-workers. Added to the distress was the screeching traffic noise on the highway where she commuted daily. Her nerves felt as raw and painful as if she had an open wound constantly being tortured. Edna D. thought she would collapse from the constant assault of tension on her nerves. Something had to be done or she would collapse.

Slimming Down Program Produces
Remarkable Peace of Mind

When someone suggested she lose weight so that she would feel better all over, Edna D. grasped at the suggestion like a desperate person seizes at straws. She eliminated calorie-high sugar from the shaker, from cooking and prepared foods without this man-made sweetener. As Edna D. slimmed down, she noted she began to feel better. But when she occasionally imbibed a sweet soft drink or pastry, she felt a "yank" at her nerves. She put two and two together and discovered that slimming down had made her feel better for an amazing reason — *the elimination of sugar was helping to give her peace of mind!* When she followed a simple program that permitted her to eat wholesome foods but eliminated sugar, she was better able to withstand the constant barrage of tumult surrounding her. Gone were her headaches. Gone were her screaming nerves. Now she felt able to cope with her noisy environment, thanks to the elimination of sugar.

The Secret Benefit of a
Sugar-Free Program

For sugar to be metabolized, the body leaches out the needed B-complex vitamins that would ordinarily help soothe and heal the nervous system. These vitamins help coat the nerve network with a myelin sheath that insulates the system against stresses and tensions of daily living. When there is an excessive or even a moderate intake of sugar, the body calls forth a supply of B-complex vitamins for metabolism of this sweetener. As a consequence, the nervous system becomes deficient in the B-complex vitamins. The myelin sheath becomes thinner and thinner. The coating wears out. The raw nerve becomes exposed. Any stress that the nerve might ordinarily be able to cope with, now becomes magnified. The nerve, in effect, lies open and gaping like a wound, because the myelin sheath is starved for the B-complex vitamins being used by sugar metabolism. This increases nerve sensitivity to tension and causes emotional as well as physical upheaval. A *simple* adjustment is to eliminate sugar from the eating program so that the B-complex vitamin store can be better used for nerve coating and protection against stress and tension.

Sugar Destroys Vitamins

Sugar is an artificial creation. The sugar molecule is a mixture of carbon, hydrogen and oxygen. It has no nutrients. As soon as it is consumed, it drains out the body's B-complex supplies in order for it to be metabolized. It enters into the bloodstream where it further disrupts normal vitamin content of the biological system. Excessive sugar intake may create a serious vitamin deficiency that can take its toll on the nervous system.

Risk of Vitamin Deficiency

A deficiency of the B-complex vitamin leaves the body vulnerable to the formation of *pyruvic acid,* a substance that accumulates in the cells and tissues and causes a grating or burning sensation. This reacts upon exposed nerves and increases tension-stress symptoms. To help protect yourself against a vitamin deficiency, eliminate sugar from your program.

HOW A SUGAR-FREE AND VITAMIN-HIGH PROGRAM HELPED RESTORE HEALTH

In a reported situation, marital discord was traced to faulty diet. When sugar was restricted and vitamins were increased, the persons were able to experience emotional health and freedom from nervous tension.

Depression Corrected with Vitamins

At age 34, Rose S. was always tired, showed poor concentration, suffered from chronic emotional depression. Her home life had deteriorated. She was separated from her husband. She was treated by a suggestion that she give up sugar from the shaker and in foods. Then Rose S. was to eat wholesome foods and whole-grain products as well as lots of fresh fruits and vegetables. Within several months, her improvement was noted. Her depression was corrected. She felt happy again. She soon rejoined her husband. It is believed that the elimination of vitamin-destroying white sugar had helped restore the health of her nervous system. The wholesome foods gave Rose S. needed nutrients to sustain her nerves and to help strengthen her natural resistance to daily tension. Vitamins became natural tranquilizers!

Irritation Ends with Sugar Elimination

At age 53, Theodore E. was a nervous business executive. He was irritated upon the slightest provocation. He suffered from pounding migraine headaches. His wife could not endure his chronic irritability and nervous unrest and there was talk of a divorce. Theodore E. went on a simple program: *elimination of white sugar.* He was also put on a program emphasizing whole grain breads and cereals, wholesome fruits and vegetables, lean meats, and fish. Now the vitamins could help insulate his nervous system and were not being threatened by "theft" by the sugar intake. Within eight weeks of this easy, natural program, Theodore's irritability ended. His headaches were gone. He became very easy and pleasant to live with. His marriage was saved. As a reward to his wife for her sympathies, he gave the both of them a six-month voyage around the world.

Sugar is a vitamin antagonist as it rushes rampaging throughout the digestive system, devouring the B-complex nerve vitamins, then into the bloodstream for more vitamin destruction. It upsets the blood sugar levels and also predisposes to nervous unrest by vitamin deficiency. The simple program of elimination of sugar from the shaker, from cooking, avoiding processed foods containing sugar (read the label), and emphasizing whole grain breads and cereals can do wonders in creating emotional health and a better nervous system.

WHY A SALT-FREE PROGRAM IS GOOD TO YOUR NERVOUS SYSTEM

Anna G. came from a family that indulged in very salted foods, heavily spiced stews and sharp meats and fish. She fell into this salt-eating habit as she matured. Now, she noted she was the victim of recurring nervous headaches. She would feel her nerves pounding in her temples. She could hardly endure even hushed noises. There were days when the ringing of the telephone in her house would give her a bad case of jangled nerves and the onset of a headache. She became terrible to live with.

Help Comes from a Neighbor

Because she could not tolerate the ringing telephone, she often kept it off the hook. A neighbor had tried to reach her and after getting a busy signal for hours, suspected something wrong, and came over to see Anna G.. She found her lying on the couch, with a cold towel on her aching head. She was so irritable, that she snapped at the neighbor. But the neighbor sympathised, offered to stay with Anna G. for a day or more and help her. The neighbor brought her food from her own house. It was salt-free since the neighbor was on a special diet to control high blood pressure. This simple salt-free diet so alerted Anna G. that within one day, her headache was gone and she no longer felt nervous. After three days, she felt happy, joyful. No longer did she mind the telephone. No longer did she scream when someone talked loud. Now she was good to live with again, thanks to the elimination of salt.

The Secret Benefit of a Salt-Free Program

Salt increases the irritability of sensitive nerve tissues and brings on tensions and stress. Salt has a corrosive or grating reaction upon the body's vitamins. On a salt-free program, vitamins are able to build and rebuild the body's tissues and nerves to alkalize the body's fluids and thereby quiet the nerves. Salt tends

to create an over-acid bloodstream that is destructive to many of
the valuable vitamins and minerals, too. In particular, salt appears
to drive potassium out of the body, changing the delicate acid-
alkaline balance of the tissue cells, leading to a tense and constricted nervous system. Vitamins that work with potassium are
now disturbed and the nerves react as they cry out in response
and protest against irritation. A simple program is to eliminate
salt so that the cells and tissues and the bloodstream can be adequately nourished by vitamins to help maintain a healthy nervous
system.

HOW TO USE THE MIRACLE B-COMPLEX
VITAMINS AS NERVE HEALERS

The B-complex vitamins are of invaluable aid to those sub-
jected to emotional and physical stress. Folks who are faced with
tension-producing situations in our modern times may feel emotional upheavals and chronic fatigue because of this tension-
drain. To help protect against tension, to help heal your nerves,
look to the miracle healing power of the B-complex vitamins.
They can act as natural stress-shields.

Tension-Melting Tonic: In a cup of fruit or vegetable
juice, mix one tablespoon of non-processed wheat germ, one
tablespoon of blackstrap molasses, one tablespoon of rice bran.
Stir vigorously. Drink this slowly. Plan to drink three glasses
throughout the day.

Benefits: This Tension-Melting Tonic is a powerhouse
of the B-complex vitamins pyridoxine, thiamine and also pantothenic acid. In this special combination, they help feed your
adrenal glands so that a sufficient amount of hormones can come
pouring forth to help you meet the challenges of tension. In effect, the Tonic helps melt tension by insulating your nervous
system against irritations and disturbances.

Mid-Day Nerve Healer: In a cup of vegetable bouillon
or even a cup of soup, stir in two heaping tablespoons of powdered Brewer's yeast. Stir until dissolved. Then drink slowly. Plan
to take this in the middle of the day to help protect your nerves
from tensions that precede and follow the Noon hour.

Benefits: The Brewer's yeast will provide you with niacin, a B-complex vitamin that helps "buffer" your nerves against constant onslaught. The Mid-Day Nerve Healer sends niacin together with other B-complex vitamins throughout your bloodstream, to soothe and relax the network of nerves that crisscross your body from head to toe. It is also reported that niacin (abundant in this Mid-Day Nerve Healer) is the vitamin used to treat schizophrenia, an emotional disorder. Many folks troubled with severe mental illness have become healed when taking Brewer's yeast in a tonic, just as described above. It's Nature's miracle of natural healing.

Natural Sleeping Potion: In a cup of warm milk, stir one tablespoon of raw wheat germ and rice germ. Sip slowly. Plan to take this Natural Sleeping Potion about 30 minutes before retiring. It will soothe your nerves and help you enjoy untroubled sleep.

Benefits: The raw wheat germ and rice germ offer you a treasure of thiamine, the B-complex vitamin that helps soothe your nerves. The benefit here is that *raw* germ is a prime source of thiamine which might otherwise be destroyed by processing. To further help feed your nerves needed thiamine, *avoid* the use of baking soda. This destroys thiamine.

WHY SEEDS ARE SOOTHING TO
THE NERVOUS SYSTEM

Jeff H. is an efficiency expert under such constant tension, that he has difficulty in keeping his emotions under control. Everyone has his own ideas about business acumen and interferes in Jeff's duties.

To help soothe his nervous system, Jeff H. eliminated sweets, pastries, cakes, cookies, pies and anything else containing vitamin-robbing sugar. Instead, he will munch seeds — sunflower seeds, sesame seeds, various nuts, throughout the day.

Benefits: Seeds and nuts are Nature-created sources of thiamine and most of the B-complex vitamins. In particular, the thiamine will take up the mineral magnesium in the seeds and nuts, and use this mineral to help soothe the nervous system, help improve nerve conduction impulses, gently promote a better transmission at the myo-neuro junction and balance healthful muscular contraction. When you munch chewy, crunchy seeds and nuts, this balance occurs so that your nervous system is soothingly relaxed. Jeff H. feels that by eliminating sugar, and using delicious seeds and nuts, he feels better so that he can cope with the tensions of daily living with more resistance. All this, thanks to the eating of seeds and nuts. They make tasty and nutritious substitutes for sugary confections.

THE MIRACLE STRESS-SHIELD POWER
OF PANTOTHENIC ACID

A deficiency of pantothenic can make all the difference in the world to the body's resistance to stress. This B-complex vitamin has a built-in stress-shield power that can help you resist the ravages of tension-filled daily living. Nature has supplied this vitamin, together with others, in many wholesome foods that are available almost anywhere. You may find it in liver, poultry, whole grain breads and cereals, vegetables, eggs, peanuts, soybean flour.

Stress-Shield Sampler: In a glass of skim milk, stir two heaping tablespoons of Brewer's yeast. Add one tablespoon raw wheat germ. Sip this slowly. You might drink this in place of the nerve-jangling "coffee break."

Unique Benefits: The tremendous source of pantothenic acid goes to work immediately to help regulate the secretion of nerve-needing adrenal gland hormones. The vitamin also helps regulate digestive enzymes and control stomach acid secretion to help guard against ulcer formation. This helps improve emotional health. The vitamin also prompts the adrenal glands to secrete vital steroids to regulate dozens of metabolic functions to help you cope with stress and tensions of daily living.

But a *benefit-plus* available with this easy Stress-Shield Sampler is that pantothenic acid will take the calcium out of the milk, then use the B-complex vitamins in the Brewer's yeast and wheat germ to help control the amount of lactate in the system. The B-complex vitamins use the calcium to bind with lactate, thereby neutralizing this substance, helping to dilute its nerve-grating threat. Once this happens, the nervous system is soothed and you are able to meet the challenges of daily living. This is the benefit-plus available with the simple, delicious and natural Stress-Shield Sampler. It takes a few minutes to prepare. It uses ordinary items available almost everywhere, as well as in health stores. Yet it offers you a dynamic source of built-in resistance to tension. It's the natural tranquilizer!

Note: Pantothenic acid, like others of the B-complex family, works better in its nerve-soothing function when it is given in combination with the other related B-complex vitamins. You will find such a balance in raw wheat germ, Brewer's yeast, desiccated liver, most whole grain unbleached foods. Soybean flour, soybeans, sunflower seeds, dark buckwheat, sesame seeds are other good sources of pantothenic acid with the rest of the B-complex family. It is this *balance* that is needed to help your metabolic processes function with total body biological harmony!

THE MIRACLE VITAMIN THAT HELPS
HEAL EMOTIONAL DISORDERS

In many reported situations, folks have been sent to mental hospitals and diagnosed as having brain damage because of a deficiency of one basic nutrient — *Vitamin B_{12}.* It is also reported that many of the complaints of emotional distress in mature years may be traced to a vitamin deficiency. This may cause severe psychotic symptoms which may vary in severity from mild disorders of mood, mental slowness and mental defect to severe psychotic symptoms. Frequently, these mental disturbances may be the first of Nature's warning signals that there is a Vitamin B_{12} deficiency. Corrected in time, it may help heal emotional disorders and obviate the need for confinement.

How Vitamin B_{12} Saved a Man
from a Mental Hospital

In a reported study, Edward D., at age 33 and a candidate for a college degree, suffered a "psychotic breakdown." He was diagnosed as being completely out of touch with reality. He felt a snapping sensation in his head. He envisioned space as being so reduced, that he felt like a dwarf. He was hospitalized, given sedation. His symptoms were controlled but *not* healed. Now he felt lethargic, lonely, insecure. Work on his Ph.D. thesis was impossible. He submitted to psychoanalysis but with little results. A laboratory test of his bloodstream showed that he was very deficient in Vitamin B_{12}. He was given supplements. Almost at the beginning, he felt better. His memory improved. Soon, he could go back to work on his Ph.D. thesis.

He was given more Vitamin B_{12} supplements until he was able to experience a recovery to the degree that he could leave the hospital. Thanks to the use of this "miracle vitamin," Edward D. was saved from a mental hospital!

Happy Mood Elixir: Into one glass of fresh fruit juice, stir one tablespoon of desiccated liver, a potent source of Vitamin B_{12}, along with other Nature-balanced B-complex vitamins. Drink this once a day.

Benefits: The *Happy Mood Elixir* gives you a supply of Vitamin B_{12} with niacin (and most other B-complex vitamins) that join with the Vitamin C to help nourish the glandular network, to feed your trillions of body cells, to insulate your nerves from outside erosion, and to help give you a feeling of contentment and happiness. The nutrients in this elixir promote a healthful utilization of fats and carbohydrates, helping to produce better energy (of the mind as well as of the body) and blood sugar levels. In particular, the *Happy Mood Elixir* is a treasure of the vitamins that manufacture fresh *nucleic acids* which direct the growth and maintenance of every single cell in your brain, as well as the rest of your body.

Suggestion: Feed yourself ample amounts of Vitamin B_{12} by eating lean liver at least twice a week. Lesser amounts are found in whole grain breads and cereals. Soybeans offer Vitamin B_{12}, too. Nature has put an assortment of the B-complex vitamins in these foods, ready to help you enjoy better health of your mind and your body.

FOODS TO HELP SOOTHE YOUR MOODS

To enjoy balanced emotional and physical health and soothed moods, take advantage of balanced eating as offered by Nature. You will help your body nourish itself and your mind and life will then be very beautiful. Plan to schedule these wholesome foods into your eating programs for better emotional health.

Whole Grains: A prime source of nearly all the B-complex vitamins that help nourish the nervous system. These include whole grain breads, cereals, natural brown rice, rye, oats, corn, wheat, soy. Use as breakfast for a good way to start off the day with vitamin-powered emotional vigor.

Fruits: A delicious source of needed Vitamin C to help make collagen, the substance that binds together nerve cells. Daily, eat fresh seasonal fruit salads. Drink fresh fruit juices, too.

Vegetables: A good source of many vitamins that work with minerals to help create better nerve health. They help round out the body's need for a *balanced* intake of vitamins and minerals, with enzymes which then prompt the metabolism of such nutrients. Daily, eat a raw vegetable salad. Drink lots of fresh raw vegetable juices, too.

Meats: A highly concentrated source of Vitamin B_{12} and protein which work together to nourish the bone marrow and nervous system. Especially nourishing meats are liver, kidney. Chicken and turkey are low in fat but very high in vitamins that work together with minerals and protein. Plan to eat a meat dish at least twice weekly.

Fish: Especially beneficial because fish is a prime source of ocean vitamins, the natural food that helps create a balanced body harmony. Fish is also a good source of phosphorus, a mineral that combines with vitamins to help nourish the trillions of body cells, particularly those of the brain. Fish should be eaten several times weekly.

Beans: These are excellent sources of most known B-complex vitamins. Feature them regularly. You may have a mixture of different cooked beans with a sprinkling of wheat germ and some plant oil as a dressing for a veritable golden treasure of emotion-soothing nutrients. Soybeans are as close to meat as possible with the valuable B_{12} potency. A plate of cooked soybeans together with a raw vegetable salad sprinkled with Brewer's yeast and vegetable oil is a powerhouse of "brain feeding" vitamins, minerals, essential fatty acids, enzymes, and protein.

Dairy: A valuable source of Vitamin A to help in the assimilation of other nutrients. Whole milk, buttermilk, yogurt, natural cheeses are all prime sources of vitamins and minerals with some protein. A wholesome combination that adds up to soothing emotional tranquility, thanks to Nature.

Seeds and Nuts: An excellent source of the vitamins that work together with minerals and proteins to nourish the nerve and brain cells. Seeds and nuts make excellent snacks, offer a better source of energy than sugar foods, help keep the metabolic process in balance. They also help prevent the formation of toxic substances that might otherwise upset the body harmony and predispose to emotional unrest. Use seeds and nuts for snacking, as "fillers" in meat loaves, stews, casseroles, in baking. For a soothing Mind Relaxant, just pulverize an assortment of seeds and nuts, then mix the powder with a fresh vegetable juice and drink slowly. The rich supply of Nature-created organic vitamins, minerals, proteins, enzymes, all converge to offer a soothing coating feeling upon your nerves, helping to give you a feeling of mind relaxation. It's all there, thanks to Nature, ready for you!

BALANCE PROMOTES SOOTHING RELAXATION

Your food program should be balanced so that your body receives the organic vitamins it needs to help promote soothing relaxation. Eat wholesome foods, emphasize the intake of organic vitamins as created in foods by Nature, and you will enjoy the peace and natural tranquility that you are entitled to have.

SUMMARY

1. In the form of foods, you can take natural tranquilizers that will help soothe your nervous system and enable you to cope with the stresses and strains of everyday living.

2. Edna D. was able to soothe her nervous system by the simple method of following a sugar-free program that helped preserve her supply of soothing B-complex vitamins.

3. Rose S. eliminated white sugar from her diet and switched to wholesome vitamin-containing foods. Her emotional depression eased. She had better energy and better emotional health.

4. Theodore E. switched from white sugar to whole grain foods and vitamin foods that insulated his nervous system so that he felt like a new man.

5. Anna G. went on a salt-free program and recovered from nervous illness.

6. To soothe your nerves with vitamins, enjoy such natural tranquilizers as a Tension-Melting Tonic, a Mid-Day Nerve Healer, a Natural Sleeping Potion. Just a few everyday ingredients that carry a powerhouse of nerve healing. All are made from natural foods found almost everywhere.

7. Jeff H. found that simple seeds and nuts offered him unique vitamins that helped soothe his nervous system and keep his emotions under control.

8. Use panthothenic acid, in a Stress-Shield Sampler (3 simple ingredients) to protect you against corrosive tensions of hectic living.

9. Vitamin B$_{12}$ is a miracle of Nature in its ability to heal emotional disorders. Edward D. used it to recover from a psychotic breakdown and he was "saved" from confinement in a mental hospital.

10. To help put yourself in a better frame of mind, use just 2 ingredients to make a Happy Mood Elixir. Drink it and feel your emotions becoming refreshed, airy, bright and alert. You'll be happy all over, thanks to the vitamins in this miracle all-natural beverage.

11. Soothe your moods and enjoy better emotional strength with an assortment of vitamin-high wholesome foods. You can actually feast your way to emotional health.

6

How Organic Vitamins Help Give You a "Forever Young" Mind

Wake up your mental youthfulness with Nature's organic vitamins. These miracle health builders act as energizers to the billions of cells that are involved with the functioning of your brain. A balanced nutritional program emphasizing certain foods will help nourish your system so that your brain can be "fed" essential vitamins that help keep it awake and alert. When your brain or mind is awake, your body will enjoy youthful alertness and speedy reflex action. Nature has put brain-nourishing vitamins in many foods that help give you a "forever young" mind. You need only eat these tasty foods to give your brain a feast of youthful nourishment.

THE VITAMIN THAT HELPS GIVE THE "BREATH OF LIFE" TO YOUR BRAIN

The brain that "breathes" is a brain that helps give you a young mind. Nature has created one outstanding vitamin that is head and shoulders above all others in helping to give the "breath of life" to your brain. It is Vitamin B $_6$ or *pyridoxine*.

This organic vitamin sparks the metabolism of carbohydrates and protein into brain-feeding amino acids. Pyridoxine helps maintain a balance of white and red blood cells and influences the content of oxygen in the bloodstream which then bathes and nourishes the millions of cells in the brain. Most essential is the way in which pyridoxine controls the blood levels of urea and uric acids. This helps keep these liquids from becoming too elevated (one of the first symptoms of mental decline). Pyridoxine also controls and regulates the amount of nitrogen and oxygen in the bloodstream so that the brain is given a steady supply of Nature-balanced ventilation. Pyridoxine also works with magnesium, a magic mineral, to help alert the activity of dozens of body enzymes to perform their brain-feeding functions. Pyridoxine helps maintain this body harmony so that your brain is kept young through healthful oxygenation.

How Marilyn F. Uses Vitamins to Restore Youth to Her Brain

As a department store buyer, Marilyn F. needs an alert mind when dealing with sales people from leading wholesalers. But she had problems with coming up with simple prices or discounts that younger buyers could rattle off instantly. Marilyn F. was always looking through her price charts or else calling her super visor for the simplest information. There were times when Marilyn F. had "blind spots" and her thoughts just could not come together. More serious was her increasing forgetfulness. There were important deals that were completely forgotten. Her younger co-workers had no difficulty in remembering negotiations, facts and figures. But if Marilyn F. forgot to write down every little detail, she forgot the entire business deal! Then she forgot that she had even written it down! Fearing that memory weakness could lead to job loss, she set about a simple yet effective nutritional program, as suggested by a 67-year wholesaler who had also endured "blind spots" until she discovered that a simple vitamin made all the difference between "senility" and a "forever young" mind.

Brain-Feeding Pyridoxine

Marilyn F. had to correct her food program to emphasize the intake of pyridoxine. She followed this easy five-step brain-feeding program:

1. *Youthful Yeast Tonic.*   Mix one teaspoon of Brewer's yeast flakes in a glass of fresh vegetable juice. Stir until dissolved. Drink one glass early Noon, another glass in Mid-Afternoon and a third glass in the Evening. *Benefit:* The pyridoxine in the Brewer's yeast works with the magnesium in the vegetable juice to send a shower of nourishment throughout the bloodstream and take up oxygen to be transported to the brain cells. Once the brain cells can "breathe," they can keep you thinking alertly with youthful vigor.

2. *Miracle Molasses Mix.*   Mix one teaspoon of black-strap molasses in a cup of piping hot water. Add a little skim milk. Stir vigorously. Drink as a "coffee break" beverage. *Benefit:* The B-complex vitamins in the molasses work harmoniously. Pyridoxine is a powerhouse of oxygen carrying vigor to the brain when it is boosted by the other B-complex vitamins together with minerals. You get a Nature-balance in this Miracle Molasses Mix.

3. *Brain-Feeding Breakfast.*   Two grain foods that are rich sources of pyridoxine as well as the other B-complex vitamins and minerals (along with many other nutrients) are wheat bran and wheat germ. Just mix several tablespoons of these two foods with granola or any *whole grain* cereal in a bowl of milk or fruit juice. For added power, sprinkle a bit of Brewer's yeast over the top. Eat this wholesome Brain-Feeding Breakfast when you expect a mind-boggling day ahead. *Benefit:* There is a treasure of pyridoxine and nearly all other known B-complex vitamins in these whole grain foods. They are needed in the morning because the night's sleep has siphoned off oxygen from the brain cells. To give your brain a youthful "get up and go" power in the morning, help whip it into shape with a stream of nutrient-carrying oxygen in this all-natural, inexpensive and deliciously effective breakfast.

4. *Liver Elixir.*   Mix one tablespoon of desiccated liver in a glass of fresh vegetable juice. Drink this healthful tonic at least once a day to give your body the raw materials out of which brain cells are made. *Benefit:* Desiccated liver is one of the richest sources of pyridoxine together with amino acids that work to build and rebuild brain (and body) cells and tissues. The B-complex in the liver join with its amino acids and help rebuild the fragile and damaged brain cells. Once the honeycomb of the brain

has been rebuilt, oxygenation from the pyridoxine in this Liver Elixir helps provide the "breath of youth" to your mind.

5. *Vitamin Meat Loaf.*   Mix together equal portions of chopped liver, heart and kidney. Shape into a loaf. Add wheat germ and wheat bran as "binders" to make the loaf more solid. Bake or broil until done. You can now eat a main dish that is chock full of the needed pyridoxine, together with nearly all other known vitamins, many minerals and also proteins, that work together to help oxygenate your entire system from head to toe. *Benefit:* It is this combination of nutrients that helps create the "forever young" brain that gives you alertness and speedy reflex action.

Marilyn F. Enjoys Second Youth with Simple Program

The simple five-step brain-feeding program supercharged this department store buyer's emotional health so that her well-nourished and well-oxygenated brain could respond with instant reflex action. She no longer had memory lapses. She could rattle off facts and figures with the alertness of younger co-workers. She became so clear in her thinking, she was soon given a promotion, winning out over another buyer who was twenty years younger! Now Marily F. was convinced that organic vitamins in the five-step program could do more than just restore and replenish the vitality of her brain. It could make her "forever young" in her mind, and her body, too!

WHY FRESH FRUIT SALADS CAN REVERSE THE AGING TIDE

Ralph O'D. had nothing wrong with his hearing. But when you said something to him, you received a blank stare. Often, folks had to keep repeating the same sentence to Ralph O'D. until he finally got the message. There were times when his memory was so fuzzy, that he stopped in the midst of whatever he was doing, wondering just why he was performing the task. Ralph O'D. also had a habit of staring blankly at a person. This indicated that he was aging as well as having faulty memory. He might have continued declining were it not for the suggestion of an in-law who had a surprising agile mind, even if he was a foxy grandpa. This in-law said that fresh fruit salads had performed a "miracle" in helping to keep him young in body, spirit and most important, young in mind. The in-law suggested that Ralph O'D. follow this one vital rule:

After Each Main Meal, Have a Large Raw Fruit Salad

This simple, yet amazing program was followed by Ralph O'D. for over two weeks. Gradually, his thoughts grew more coherent. His memory became young again. His thoughts were refreshingly alert. He not only regained knowledge of better thinking, he could now read complicated technical reports and statistical data with the clarity of a youngster.

The Secret "Mind Food" in Raw Fruits

A secret "mind food" in raw fruits can do much to help stem and reverse the aging tide. In particular, this "mind food" has an exhilarating and super-effective power when the fruits are eaten at the *end* of a main meal. This "mind food" is Vitamin C and it has a unique effect on helping correct problems of so-called senility and aging mind.

How Vitamin C Helps Correct the Aging Mind

Many folks are unable to thoroughly metabolize the fats in foods. With a slowing down of metabolism in the middle years, there is a problem of accumulation of fats in the system. This may lead to conditions of hardening of the arteries or atherosclerosis and this may also "choke" those channels leading to the brain. This brings about conditions of so-called senility.

Vitamin C is seen to help neutralize the elements in fats (especially the triglycerides) that are produced by digestion of fatty and sugary meals. In a sluggish metabolism, after a fatty or

sugary meal, the blood plasma becomes clogged with serum triglycerides which are end products of these foods. The body needs
to "wash" out these choked up products. The body can do this by
using Vitamin C (as found in raw fruit juices and raw fruits) in a
unique manner.

*Vitamin C alerts the body to create an enzyme known as
lipo-protein lipase (LPL). Vitamin C helps draw this LPL from the
walls of healthy capillaries to then help break down the triglycerides into free fatty acids, along with the cholesterol. Vitamin
C uses this LPL substance to help clear the blood vessels as if
they were washed with a magic juice. This helps control the de-
bilitating effects of atherosclerosis. Vitamin C is the spark that
ignites the LPL enzyme to perform in a self-scrubbing manner
within your system. Once the arteries are scrubbed clean, then
oxygen and nutrition can flow through open channels to nourish
the brain. This is Nature's way of protecting your brain and your
body against aging. All this is possible through the miracle of
organic Vitamin C as found in raw fresh fruits.*

When you finish your main meal with a raw citrus fruit salad,
you send forth a shower of this vascular-cleansing vitamin
throughout your system to help control problems of atherosclerosis and help to keep open the channels to your brain. It is Nature's way of protecting you against senility or malfunctioning
of the brain.

How Vitamin C Helps
Rejuvenate the Brain

The nerve tissue composing your brain needs a large and
constant supply of oxygen and nutrition, waking or sleeping,
thinking or idling. Your brain ceases after a few seconds if this
supply is cut off. Irreparable damage may be caused in a few
moments. Your brain needs at least 750 cubic centimeters of
blood per minute, pouring through the carotid (main artery of
the head) and vertebral arteries. Vitamin C is needed for a very
beneficial purpose: this organic vitamin prompts the body to
make *collagen* that helps bind up and heal and regenerate the
millions of cells and tissues of which your brain is composed.

Vitamin C sparks the manufacture of this substance by traveling through the arteries and veins of your body.

A deficiency of Vitamin C means that the number of brain cells decrease. There is shrinkage. Furthermore, with slowed up metabolism in the middle years, collagen fibers may shrink and "choke off" the surrounding tissue. In a sense, this surrounding brain tissue becomes *suffocated* and *wrinkled.* A deterioration of collagen is a symptom of the aging process.

Yet a plentiful supply of Vitamin C will help spark the making of more collagen which can then help form more tissue in the brain as well as throughout the body. So Vitamin C is Nature's organic way to help rejuvenate your brain through regeneration of new collagen for brain cells.

Suggestions: Eat lots of fresh citrus fruits daily. Drink lots of fruit juices daily. Finish each main meal with a large raw fruit salad. This is the healthful and natural way to give your body the magic vitamin that can then make collagen and give you millions and millions of healthy brain cells. It is the "key" to a young mind!

THE MIRACLE REJUVENATION VITAMIN

Nature has a secret plan to help keep you looking, feeling and thinking perpetually young. That plan calls for the use of a miracle rejuvenation vitamin that has a powerhouse of brain boosting benefits. This is the miracle Vitamin E. It is found in cold-processed seed, nut, fruit and grain oils. It is found in whole grain foods. It is found in raw and nonprocessed seeds and nuts. Nature put Vitamin E into these simple, everyday foods to help protect your brain and your body against aging. It's easy to use this vitamin. The rewards are many. A lifetime of youthful thinking is ready for those who use this vitamin.

How Vitamin E Gave Susan Y. a New Lease on Life

If Susan Y. had one problem it was that she loved the taste of fat. Years of eating fatty, marbled meats not only gave her symptoms of atherosclerosis, but she was becoming dull-witted. This housewife would forget simple everyday responsibilities. At the local shopping center, she would make errors in paying for purchases. She would often forget to make needed purchases. Susan Y. made various promises to friends about getting together with them, and speedily forgot those promises. She was slow-witted, had to fumble for the correct phrases to say. When the condition worsened, she went to the house of a friend who agreed to help her.

Simple Program.   The friend helped Susan enjoy her love of fats — but the "soft" or liquid types of polyunsaturated fats, instead of the animal or heavy meat fats. Susan's meals were prepared with free-flowing plant or seed *oils.* All meats were carefully trimmed. Butter was restricted. It took about two weeks before Susan could recover. She not only lost excess weight, but her thinking became sharp, clear, youthfully alert. Her memory was as excellent as that of a youngster. She no longer mumbled or fumbled, or had bouts of forgetfulness. Now her mind was young again, thanks to the use of plant oils. Her friend had actually used Vitamin E to help give Susan Y. a new lease on life.

The Secret of the Miracle Rejuvenation Vitamin

When you use polyunsaturated cold nonprocessed vegetable oils as a *substitute* for hard animal source fats, you send a gushing stream of Vitamin E right through your bloodstream. Once there, Vitamin E performs this secret miracle:

Vitamin E helps protect against cellular peroxidation and the production of free-floating roots and debris that would damage the body cells, inhibit the formation and transport of oxygen. By guarding against this peroxide rancidity, Vitamin E helps keep the bloodstream fresh and pure and thereby send valuable nutrients to all body cells and the tissues of the brain. Vitamin E sends oxygen (food) to the brain and this gives the brain the "forever young" alertness a well-nourished organ can provide.

Sources of Vitamin E.   Safflower seed oil, corn oil, peanut oil, soybean oil, rice bran oil, sesame oil, wheat germ oil, avocado oil, cod liver oil.

How Vitamin E Protects Against Senility

When you use these cold-pressed oils in any recipe that calls for a fat, you give your body a treasure of valuable source of Vitamin E that has a unique way of protecting your brain and body against symptoms of senility.

Here's how — polyunsaturated lipids and oxygen are needed to keep you alive and youthful. But when these two ingredients combine, they may form peroxides. This predisposes to the formation of free radicals (roots) of lipid peroxidation and is the forerunner of *aging* of the body and mind. This peroxide destroys cells, weakens enzymes, reduces energy production. It also reduces the ability of the body and brain to renew and to resist and recover from ravages of daily living.

But Vitamin E sends valuable substances shooting throughout the bloodstream to neutralize the aging effects of lipid peroxidation. Vitamin E helps construct the various membranes of the individual cells of the body and the brain. Vitamin E helps the membranes hold the brain cells together to allow the flow of nutrients into the cell, to prompt the flowing out of waste products such as carbon dioxide to be cast out of the body. It is this self-renewal process that is sparked by Vitamin E, the miracle of rejuvenation.

Hope for Eternal Youth with Plant Oils

Vitamin E in the plant oils helps prevent oxygen from combining with the essential fatty acids to form peroxides and free radicals. This helps protect against damage (aging) to the cellular membranes. This helps give your body a great supply of essential fatty acids that are protected against becoming rancid by Vitamin E. This reduces the amount of cellular destruction that causes the aging process.

Simple Program: For each raw fruit or vegetable salad, use cold-processed plant oils as a salad dressing. Sprinkle with a bit of lemon juice for Vitamin C intake and also add a bit of honey to give you needed vitamins and minerals. This is a healthy "forever young" dressing. *Replace* hard fats (animal sources) with soft fats (plant sources). It's the simple and natural way to fortify your body with needed Vitamin E — the rejuvenation vitamin!

HOW PITUITARY POWER HELPS PROMOTE BRAIN REJUVENATION

The pituitary is situated on the underside of the brain. It secretes hormones that influence the functioning of the hypothalamus, an extention of the nervous system. To enjoy youthful tranquility, youthful reflexes and youthful thinking, your pituitary must be adequately nourished by vitamins so that it can perform this hormone-making function. When your pituitary is given an assortment of vitamins and minerals, it can help maintain a balance between the other body glands to promote an even temperament and a better emotional outlook. The pituitary needs adequate nourishment.

The Pituitary Power Food
to Promote Emotional Well-Being

A cup of ordinary cottage cheese to which has been added wheat germ and Brewer's yeast, with several slices of fresh fruits, can become a "meal in a cup" that is a powerhouse for the pituitary gland.

Benefits: The vitamins in the grains and fruits tend to *amplify* the effective metabolism of the minerals such as calcium and iron of the cottage cheese. The vitamins send these minerals through the bloodstream to nourish various organs, especially the pituitary gland. Cottage cheese is a tremendous source of Vitamin A which acts as a propellant throughout the bloodstream and uses minerals to perform an energizing effect upon the pituitary. So the vitamins *amplify* the effective metabolism of the minerals in this simple food to help create "pituitary power" that results in better thinking capabilities.

Suggestion: Feed your pituitary a cup of cottage cheese with wheat germ and Brewer's yeast as main meal, whenever you expect to have to use your thinking cap. Finish with a plate of fresh raw fruit slices with a salad dressing of cold-pressed polyunsaturated oil and honey with a sprinkle of lemon juice. This is a simple, satisfying meal that offers a rich treasure of vitamins needed by your body and brain to give it "go power" no matter what your age!

Cheese and Fruit for Brain Nourishment

Combine natural cheese with fruit for a meal that gives your brain much needed nourishment. Vitamin C uses the calcium from the cheese to improve the health of your brain nerves, to help promote natural detoxification and offer you protection against fallout, food additives and other toxic substances that have accumulated in the system. Vitamin C and calcium will also help protect your brain against fluorides in your drinking water. Every stressful situation uses up Vitamin C which your body does not store *except* in your pituitary. Your brain is usually the first to react to a Vitamin C shortage so get a supply from fresh fruit that is eaten with cheese giving you calcium for further insulation against body pollution. It's the delicious way to nourish your brain, your body, your thinking and your mind! It's the natural way to help stay and keep your brain younger... longer.

ESSENTIAL POINTS

1. Use pyridoxine to give your brain "the breath of life." Marilyn F. used this simple vitamin in simple foods to help correct her mental "blind spots" and enjoy youthful thinking and better memory.
2. Try the five easy brain-feeding pyridoxine foods for better brain power.
3. Ralph O'D. discovered that fresh fruit salads can reverse the aging tide when the vitamins corrected fat metabolism and helped nourish his brain cells.
4. Susan Y. used plant oils to help nourish her brain. Vitamin E was a miracle rejuvenation vitamin that protected against senility.
5. Everyday foods such as cheese and fruit become powerhouses of stimulation for the brain-rejuvenating pituitary gland.

7

The Step-By-Step Vitamin Way to Freedom from Arthritis

A well-nourished body can build resistance to the spectre of arthritis. With proper care, a body that already has been invaded by arthritis can help gain remarkable improvement. The key to enjoying freedom from arthritis is in using nutrition, along with better living programs, to help correct the errors in metabolism that may have caused symptoms in the first place. Vitamins are natural medicines that can help restore body equilibrium and protect you from bone-joint ill health.

A STEP-BY-STEP DOCTOR PREPARED PROGRAM FOR ARTHRITIS RELIEF

"No person who is in good nutritional health develops rheumatoid or osteoarthritis," says Robert Bingham, M.D.[1] who has been able to heal arthritis by correcting the food program of his patients. The orthopedic physician explains, "Nutritionists know that nervous and mental and emotional stress interfere with appetite, digestion, absorption of food, the choices of food, nutritional habits and dietary patterns. Emotional stress exerts a con-

[1] "Arthritis and Diet," by Robert Bingham, M.D., *Journal of Applied Nutrition,* Winter, 1972.

trol on the glands of internal secretion, particularly the thyroid, adrenals and pituitary, and they play an important role in bone and joint metabolism. Naturally, any disturbance in the nervous and emotional function of a person produces biological changes which can affect the bones or joints."

To help correct this metabolic error, Dr. Bingham uses corrective nutrition for his arthritic patients. Each patient is treated as an individual and this may be the secret of success in healing. The doctor begins by making a list of each patient's likes and dislikes in foods as well as those which cause allergies. He also takes into consideration the patient's weight and whether gain or loss is needed. Each patient is then given a list of suggested foods that will help bone growth, development and repair and protect against the increase of arthritis. Emphasis is placed upon vitamins.

Simple Vitamin Program

Dr. Bingham notes that most of the arthritis patients are deficient in vitamins so he begins by suggesting 1000 units of Vitamin D from natural sources such a halibut liver oil to be taken daily with 25,000 units of Vitamin A. This is for the *treatment* stage. For prevention, he suggests one-half of this amount.

To help the vitamins perform their rebuilding, Dr. Bingham then suggests this step-by-step program:

1. Obtain bed rest at least 16 hours a day.
2. Boost the amount of water consumed up to 8 or more glasses a day.
3. Slowly decrease all drugs to the minimum the patient can take without too much pain. Reduce and slowly eliminate all corticosteroid medications. (This is a doctor-supervised program.)
4. The food intake should emphasize high protein.
5. Eat fresh raw and natural foods as much as possible to further increase the body's supply of depleted vitamins. If possible, use a blender or grinder to offer variety in preparation and taste.
6. Give up the use of alcohol, tobacco, refined carbohydrates and saturated (hard) fats.

7. Obtain a prescribed amount of vitamins, minerals and enzymes.

Simple Vitamin-Protein Booster

Dr. Bingham notes that most arthritics show a deficiency in Vitamin C and protein. Therefore, he recommends 2000 milligrams of natural Vitamin C each day, and 3 glasses of raw milk because it has *a natural vitamin-created anti-stiffness factor* which is destroyed by pasteurization. If raw milk is unavailable, then pasteurized milk is acceptable. It is believed that the Vitamin C amplifies the effect of both protein and calcium so that these nutrients are able to build and repair the ailing joints and promote relief.

Use Fresh, Natural Foods

Dr. Bingham explains that "It is important to keep the principles in mind that to preserve the natural food intact including proteins and amino acids which have not been damaged by heat, hormones and enzymes which have not been altered by cooking, drying, storage or preservation, and vitamins in the highest biological efficiency, that the foods must be as fresh and ripe as possible, grown by organic methods, free of residues of poisonous pesticides and fertilizers and delivered and prepared in as natural and palatable a form as possible."

HOW TO HELP VITAMINIZE YOUR BODY TO PROTECT AGAINST ARTHRITIS

To further vitaminize your body as a natural way to protect against arthritis, here are more suggestions:

Be Cautious About Aspirin

This is a drug and should be used solely with your doctor's approval and with extreme caution. Aspirin masks your pain but it destroys huge amounts of Vitamin C in your body. If you must take aspirin, protect against vitamin loss by increasing your intake of Vitamin C. *Suggestion:* Each day, drink several glasses of fresh citrus fruit juice. Increase your intake of fruits as salads for breakfast, lunch and dinnertime, too. It's the natural way to fortify yourself with Vitamin C and protect against aspirin destruction.

To Protect Against Vitamin Destruction by Drugs

Extensive use of cortisone may destroy many vitamins and protein, too. Often, the damage may strike your bloodstream, bones, nervous system, kidneys and liver. To protect against the threat of vitamin destruction by cortisone, boost your daily intake of fresh yellow and green leafy vegetables for Vitamins A and C; also increase your intake of nuts and seeds for essential fatty acids and protein and other vitamins. Use whole grain breads and cereals to give yourself needed Vitamin B-complex that may be destroyed by drugs. It is the natural way to protect your body against vitamin deficiency which may worsen the problem of arthritis.

Eliminate Refined Foods and Sweets

These are made with chemical preservatives and baking soda which drain out the body's already deficient amount of Vitamins A through E. Instead, switch to wholesome whole grain foods and fresh fruits for sweets that will help *add* rather than subtract your body's store of needed health-building vitamins.

Correct Living Methods

Dr. Bingham describes an average arthritic as being overweight, poorly nourished on a high carbohydrate diet, deficient in vitamins, enzymes and protein. Therefore, correct your living methods and gain a normal weight, reduce intake of starch-sugar foods to control carbohydrate destruction of vitamins, and eat lots of wholesome fresh foods to give yourself needed vitamins, enzymes and protein. They work to build health to help correct problems of arthritis and make you enjoy the good life which you deserve!

Melt Tensions

Dr. Bingham notes that nearly all arthritics have a history of emotional distress. It is recognized that stress and tension can drain out the body's supply of needed nutrients such as Vitamins B-complex and C. A deficiency of these nutrients weakens the body's self-defensive mechanisms and arthritic distress may occur because of this metabolic error. Ease up on situations that cause stress and tension. Fortify yourself with lots of whole grains and fresh fruits to give yourself the needed stress-shielding vitamins. You'll feel better all over.

Good nutrition with vitaminization are the keys to helping protect against the problems of arthritis. It's Nature's secret for offering freedom from arthritis.

THE NATURAL SWEET THAT WILL HELP SOOTHE ARTHRITIC PAINS

Ida C. reportedly was troubled with arthritis for many years. In particular, she had painful swelling in her knee. She had read about the healing benefits of honey as a natural sweet and she began her simple program, as follows:

Each day, she took five tablespoons of honey. She also increased her intake of wheat germ, Brewer's yeast, whole milk, a generous green salad with an occasional fruit salad. All were enjoyed with a lemon juice dressing with honey, too.

Benefits: Her arthritis pain disappeared. Within two weeks after beginning the honey program, the swelling in her knee was gone. Now she could sit on the floor with both of her knees lying flat.

Secret of Honey Healing

When Ida C. took honey, she was able to use its vitamins to help correct the ratio of calcium to phosphorus in the bloodstream. It is reported that inflammation as well as arthritic distress is often traced to a vitamin deficiency. The absence of sufficient vitamins means that the delicate calcium-phosphorus balance becomes upset and this predisposes to arthritic disorder. Honey is a prime source of natural vitamins that will use its power to help balance the levels of calcium and phosphorus in the body. This eased Ida C.'s symptoms and helped correct the metabolic disorder that causes arthritis to flare up. It was a simple, yet welcome vitamin way of soothing arthritis.

To help give your body the raw materials (vitamins) which can be used to maintain mineral balance and protection against arthritis, use honey daily. It's the natural and sweet way to enjoy good health.

THE VITAMIN THAT CAN CORRECT
ARTHRITIS DISORDERS

Janice L. had problems with extreme pain in her joints. She would wince if she had to bend her painful fingers to thread a needle. She could hardly bend her knees when getting in and out of an automobile. Walking produced such pains that she had to stop and rest every few yards. If she sat down, it was with difficulty. It was more distressful when she had to "unwind" her painful knee and hip joints to have to get up again. She almost always needed some support. She had to carry a cane which made her feel depressed. Yet there were times when her arthritic symptoms vanished. In particular, she noted that she experienced welcome relief after spending a weekend at her daughter's home where she dined on healthful liver as well as farm-fresh foods raised on her daughter's farm. This offered a clue to her arthritis. Namely, she was vitamin deficient since her own food program consisted largely of processed foods.

Simple Vitaminization Offers Blessed Relief

Janice L. boosted her intake of foods containing Vitamin A. She also eliminated artificial and bleached or processed foods in favor of wholesome, natural foods. This helped give her so much improved health, that her swollen joints subsided. She could bend with comfort. She could clench her fists with no outcry of pain.

She could sit down and get up with ease. Most delightful was being able to dispose of the cane. All this, thanks to the easy vitaminization program.

Why Vitamin A Is Helpful for Arthritic Relief

The body's liver needs an ample supply of Vitamin A in order to strengthen its cells and tissues. The liver uses Vitamin A to help protect against bacterial invaders. A deficiency means that the cells and tissues are weak and permit the invasion of corrosive elements that fetter themselves to body joints and predispose to a problem of arthritis. It has been noted that *many arthritics have liver disorder.* The liver is unable to transform carotene into Vitamin A and the body becomes deficient. The simple program calls for boosting liver health with Vitamin A so that it can offer protection against bacterial invasion which upsets the metabolism.

Official U.S. Government Recommendation for Vitamin A

The U.S. Department of Agriculture says[2] "Vitamin A is needed for normal growth. It also helps keep the skin and inner linings of the body healthy and resistant to infection. Vitamin A occurs only in foods of animal origin. However, many vegetables and fruits, particularly the green and yellow ones, contain a substance called carotene that the body can change into Vitamin A.

"Liver is outstanding for Vitamin A. Important amounts are also found in eggs, butter, margarine, whole milk and cheese made with whole milk. Carotene is found in largest amounts in dark-green and deep-yellow vegetables and in deep-yellow fruits."

Your Easy Liver Feeding Program

Twice weekly, eat lean broiled liver. This sends essential vitamins with proteins to your own liver to make it strong and

[2] *Family Fare: A Guide to Good Nutrition,* Home and Garden Bulletin No. 1, May, 1970. U.S. Department of Agriculture, Washington, D.C.

healthy. Then boost your vitamin intake with lots of dark-green and deep-yellow vegetables and deep-yellow fruits, as recommended by the U.S. Government. It's the natural way to boost the health of your liver which symbolizes a fortress against bodily infection and the risk of metabolic disorders that cause arthritis. *A liver that is nourished with Vitamin A can then help cleanse the body of toxic wastes that might otherwise create the erosion of destructive arthritis.*

A "BIOLOGIC VITAMIN PROGRAM" FOR ARTHRITIS RELIEF

To help relieve and banish arthritis, the vitamin program followed should be one that will help reverse the depleted efficiency of body chemistry and return it to a condition of normalcy. A "Biologic Vitamin Program" is one that will provide the body with the natural vitamins needed to help bring about corrective healing. Such a program can be followed by noting the suggestions of Robert Bingham, M.D.[3] who begins by saying, *"Applied nutrition in everyday life is the only way a human being may avoid arthritis and it is the first and best step for a patient to take to treat his arthritis."*

Restore Biological Health with Vitamins

"Diseases of the bones and joints which are due to deficiencies in a single nutritional factor are many. They include scurvy, a Vitamin C deficiency; rickets, Vitamin D deficiency; osteoporosis, from a lack of calcium and protein; neuropathy, from Vitamin B-complex deficiency; and degenerative joint diseases due to a combination of nutritional deficiencies." Dr. Bingham adds that these same nutritional deficiencies lower body resistance to become vulnerable to bacteria, viruses and parasites. To help correct biological imbalance, you should be adequately nourished with vitamins. They serve as the foundation for better health and protection against arthritis.

[3] Speech before 1967 annual seminar of the American Nutrition Society, in Pasadena, California.

Restore Body Health

"Secondary arthritis is often caused by diseases which interfere with the absorption, digestion and metabolism of certain vital nutritional factors." These include problems of the digestive system, food allergies, glandular ailments and changes in body biology. To help guard against overlapping problems, the entire body needs to be healed through vitaminization. This helps "insulate" the body against problems of arthritis.

Restore Adequate Nutrition

Build resistance and recovery with good nutrition. Dr. Bingham says, that by examination and analysis of folks suffering from forms of arthritis, he finds specific deficiencies involved. The "deficiencies are in Vitamin C, the B-complex vitamins, calcium, Vitamin D and iron. Iron deficiency anemias are found in 10 per cent to 15 per cent of both the younger and older groups. Poor iron absorption from deficiencies in the B-complex vitamins, gastric acidity and the trace minerals associated with iron are found." This suggests the boosted intake of the three aforementioned vitamins as well as calcium and iron. They work together to restore adequate nutrition and boost biological health.

Restore Vitamin D

Dr. Bingham says, "In spite of the fact that generations ago Vitamin D deficiency was so well recognized that all children were given cod liver oil, today the propaganda about 'good wholesome food' and dependence on intermittent administration of multiple vitamins has increased the number of cases we have seen with Vitamin D deficiencies and rickets. The reliance of some families on prepared milk and processed foods has so decreased their natural Vitamin C content that in some cases, Vitamin C is now added to evaporated milk." This suggests the increased intake of Vitamin D from foods and also from cod liver oil supplements. Vitamin C is also valuable in helping to restore good biological vitaminization of the body to help correct arthritic unrest.

Official U.S. Government Recommendation for Vitamin D

The U.S. Department of Agriculture says,[4] "Vitamin D is important in building strong bones and teeth because it enables the body to use the calcium and phosphorus supplied by food. Few foods contain much Vitamin D naturally. Milk with Vitamin D added is a practical source. Small amounts of Vitamin D are present in egg yolk, butter, liver; larger amounts occur in sardines, salmon and tuna." Fish liver oils are excellent sources of Vitamin D, too.

Official U.S. Government Recommendation for Vitamin C

The U.S. Department of Agriculture says,[4] "Vitamin C helps form and maintain cementing material that holds body cells together and strengthens the walls of blood vessels. It also assists in normal tooth and bone formation and aids in healing wounds.

"Citrus fruits — oranges, grapefruit, tangerines, lemons and their juices — and fresh strawberries are rich in Vitamin C. Other important sources include tomatoes and tomato juice; broccoli; brussels sprouts; cabbage; green peppers; some dark-green leafy vegetables such as collards, kale, mustard greens, spinach, turnip greens; potatoes and sweet potatoes, especially when cooked in the jacket."

Restore Body Activity

Dr. Bingham points out, "Our sedentary occupations, more riding in automobiles than walking, foods high in sugar, starches and fats have produced an overweight population, particularly in women and older people. The human digestive system, being naturally lazy, absorbs these simple types of foods more quickly

[4]*Family Fare: A Guide to Good Nutrition.* Home and Garden Bulletin No. 1, May, 1970. U.S. Department of Agriculture, Washington, D.C.

and completely than it does the proteins which may or may not be in normal supply. As a result, the average elder person is deficient in bone and muscle protein, bone calcium, good joint cartilage and is overweight with excessive fat deposited in the tissue, the body organs and the arteries." So for the sake of better digestion and assimilation, get yourself more activity. It helps send vitamins throughout your body and protects against sluggishness.

Restore Total Body Harmony

Dr. Bingham adds succinctly, "Osteoarthritis or degenerative arthritis of the joints is *basically a disease of poor circulation to the joints.* The increased weight and increased fat associated with arteriosclerosis provides a basis for gradual joint destruction before the patient is aware that much of this has occurred." This suggests maintaining healthful weight. Guard against obesity which impinges on circulation and may lead into arthritic distress. Furthermore, "Environmental dangers to nutrition, such as pesticides in foods impaired by smog and even radioactive fallout are becoming hazards which must be carefully watched and studied. *Complications of nutrition caused by toxic medications, the cortisone drugs, medications for ulcer remedies, for constipation, pain-relieving and tranquilizing medications and even the antibiotics can adversely affect the patient's digestion or absorption of necessary nutrients from foods."* It would be wise to seek natural methods to help correct digestive and other disorders and guard against the careless use of patent medicines which can disrupt body harmony and create ill health. For restoration of *total body harmony,* emphasize the use of healthful foods, adequate vitaminization, better body care.

When your body is nourished with a good "Biologic Vitamin Program," it can then resist and recover from arthritic distress.

Suggestion: Arthritics who are over-medicated often have serious nutritional deficiencies. Cortisone interferes with the availability of pyridoxine to the cells and tissues. A malnourished liver indicates poor vitamin and iron absorption. To help make up for this deficiency, try to eat organ meats (liver, heart, kidney) several times a week. Eat desiccated liver if you dislike the taste of complete liver. Also add beans, seeds, nuts, raw vegetables, raw fruits, whole grains to supply your body with a well-rounded source of nearly all known vitamins. They work together to help provide you with the total body harmony that gives you better health and insulation against arthritic distress.

WHY B-COMPLEX VITAMINS ARE NEEDED BY THE ARTHRITIC

Many arthritics have difficulties in metabolizing carbohydrates (sugars and starches). This suggests a B-complex deficiency. This vitamin is needed to accompany carbohydrates on their way to the digestive tract. An arthritic who is deficient in the B-complex vitamins will develop increasing nervousness and digestive disorders as well as problems of anemia. *Stress overlaps problems of arthritis.* To help protect yourself against stress, fortify yourself with B-complex vitamins. This helps offer a soothing relaxation and insulation of the nervous system which can help make arthritis less severe and often promote its healing. The B-complex vitamins are needed for metabolism of other nutrients needed to maintain good body balance and equilibrium.

To enjoy freedom from arthritis, enjoy good nutritional health! It's easy with wholesome foods available for a modest cost. The reward may well be a lifetime that is protected against arthritis.

MOST IMPORTANT POINTS

1. Vitamins can help correct the emotional stress that accompanies arthritis and help create better feeling.
2. A doctor's program calls for Vitamins A and D daily. He also uses a supervised and all-natural seven-step program that reportedly helps heal arthritis in his patients. Take Vitamin C daily.
3. Drink raw or pasteurized milk daily because the Vitamin C supplement amplifies the metabolism of the protein and calcium in body joints to promote arthritis healing.
4. Use fresh, natural foods as prime sources of body-healing vitamins.
5. Be cautious about careless use of aspirin and drugs. Replace body shortages with Vitamins A and C in healthful

foods. Eliminate refined foods and sweets which are destructive to vitamins. Use natural sweets such as fresh fruits. Improve basic living habits.

6. Ida C. was healed of joint swelling by using honey and wholesome foods.

7. Vitamin A in foods helped relieve Janice L. of arthritis symptoms. It is the one vitamin needed to have a healthy liver: the key to better metabolism. Follow official U.S. Government Recommendations for vitamins.

8. Restore total body harmony with the simple "Biologic Vitamin Program."

9. Emphasize intake of B-complex vitamin foods to help soothe stress and insulate the nervous system from arthritis flare-up.

How to Build
Natural Immunity with Vitamins—
Your Fortress Against Allergies

You can help build resistance to the ravages of asthmatic-bronchial distress, respiratory allergies and colds by utilizing the vitamins in simple, everyday foods to create natural immunity within your system. When you vitaminize your body and follow simple programs aimed at building up your natural antibodies, you can help protect yourself against common and uncommon allergic infectious attacks. Nature has put these miracle vitamins in ordinary, everyday foods to give you this shield against the onslaught of respiratory infections.

Give these foods to your body and let the vitamin build a natural fortress against allergies.

HOW TO USE VITAMIN A TO BUILD
NATURAL IMMUNITY AGAINST ALLERGIES

Vitamin A has a miracle power in being able to give you natural immunity against the germs of infectious diseases. Once Vitamin A is flowing freely in your bloodstream, it gives your body a "fortress" against virus germs that abound in the air and enter your body through breathing. With Vitamin A, your body is able to inhibit or reduce the health-destroying powers of such virus germs.

Miracle Immunity-Building Power of Vitamin A

This vitamin builds your immunity by weakening the effect of the disease germs; this vitamin also provides for the health of the mucous membranes. It preserves the healthful physiological functions and anatomical structure of the respiratory tract, aids in the regeneration and restoration of these membranes to protect against virus germ infestation.

Creates Natural Antibodies

Give your body Vitamin A from simple foods and you can help yourself create all-natural antibodies to resist allergic and respiratory infections. Antibodies are gamma-globulin substances formed in the spleen or lymph nodes to act as an important defense against infections. These antibodies are formed with the presence of Vitamin A. A deficiency means a reduction or weakening of your body supply of antibodies. You become more vulnerable to allergic infections. Vitamin A helps create more and stronger antibodies so that your body can enjoy healthful immunity to respiratory disturbances.

The Magic Cold-Fighting Power of Vitamin A

The key to cold-fighting and resistance to allergies is in the moisturizing substance known as *lysozyme*. This substance is secreted by the mucous membranes lining the nose, mouth and bronchial tubes. Coating this region is a substance known as *cilia*, resembling tiny hairs under the microscope. The cilia sweeps foreign matter such as germs, toward the pharynx (back wall of the nose, mouth and throat) where it can be swallowed or excreted. But in order for the cilia to function, it requires the moisturizing substance, *lysozyme*. This substance needs Vitamin A in order to function. Otherwise, the cilia cells die, the *lysozyme* supply is diminished and cut off. Now the antiseptic secretions of the nose and throat are no longer functioning. When a germ comes along, your body has little or no defense against it. So

Vitamin A feeds your cilia to create *lysozyme* which is a magic cold-fighter. It is the all-natural way to build immunity.

HOW TO USE FOODS TO CREATE NATURAL IMMUNITY

Ample amounts of Vitamin A are needed to provide for the health of the mucous membranes to resist germ infection and create natural immunity. Do *not* wait until you have a cold or an allergic attack before getting enough Vitamin A. By the time an attack occurs, the sensitive tissues of your nose and throat will be weakened and much more likely to succumb to a secondary or even chronic infection. Build immunity before any attack and you may avoid such attacks through natural immunity.

Animal Sources of Vitamin A: Fresh calf and beef liver are excellent animal sources. Fish liver oils are prime sources of Vitamin A. They contain many more times the amount of Vitamin A than just about any food.

U.S. Government Recommendation for Plant Sources of Vitamin A

The U.S. Department of Agriculture[1] recommends these plant sources: Dark-green and deep-yellow vegetables and a few fruits, namely: apricots, broccoli, cantaloupe, carrots, chard, collards, cress, kale, mango, persimmon, pumpkin, spinach, sweet potatoes, turnip greens and other dark-green leaves, winter squash.

Simple Guideline: In general, you can be guided by the yellow color of plant foods. This yellow comes from carotene which changes to Vitamin A after it is eaten. It is best to include at least one yellow vegetable in each day's menu, along with plenty of greens. This is the natural way to build natural immunity, using Nature's foods.

[1] *Family Fare: A Guide to Good Nutrition,* U.S. Department of Agriculture, Washington, D.C., House and Garden Bulletin No. 1, 1970.

HOW DOROTHY G. USED VITAMIN A TO BUILD IMMUNITY AGAINST ALLERGIES

Dorothy G. was always sniffling. A slight weather change brought a hacking cough to her throat and tears to her eyes. A little house dust would choke her throat; she would erupt in what she called an "asthmatic fit" of coughing that left her shaken and worn out.

Dorothy G. could hardly use a whisk broom because a few specks of dust would tickle her nostrils, provoke her breathing apparatus. Often, she would start to sputter and cough, and have to run into another room or stick her head out of the window to catch her breath. Dorothy G. endured these allergies for more years than she cared to remember. She was at a loss to know what to do.

Simple Food Starts Natural Immunity

Remembering that when she was a child, her mother gave her fish liver oil in early winter to protect her against colds (it always worked), she decided to try it even though she was an adult. Each day, Dorothy G. took two tablespoons of cod liver oil in a glass of fruit juice. She also increased her daily intake of seasonal fresh *yellow plant foods*. Once a week, she ate broiled liver. She also ate lots of fresh fruits and drank fruit and vegetable juices throughout the day. It took just nine days of this program before she could enjoy natural immunity.

Resists Allergic Attacks

Dorothy G. could sweep up a cloud and have negligible respiratory symptoms. She could breathe freely and deeply. Gone were the hacking coughing fits. Her eyes no longer watered. Even in cold weather, she enjoyed freedom from colds which she had previously caught regularly. Dorothy G. discovered that vitamins in foods, especially Vitamin A, offered her natural immunity against allergies. Now she would take two tablespoons of fish liver oil every single day throughout the year, and eat broiled liver, and also enjoy plant foods. This gave her the protection she sought . . . the natural way! Life was worth living!

Wide Variety of Foods Containing
Vitamin A

To help build your fortress against allergies with Vitamin A, you should enjoy some of these foods: liver and giblets from animals and poultry, too. Natural Swiss and cheddar cheeses are good supplies. Try eggs made in the form of a cheese omelet or a chicken liver omelet for a triple-A supply. Sun-dried fruits such as apricots, available in wintertime at most specialty food stores, many supermarkets, health stores, are prime sources of Vitamin A. Try a baked squash as among the highest in carotene value that is when transformed into Vitamin A. It's the tasty and delicious way to insulate yourself with the vitamin that creates natural antibodies and a form of immunity against respiratory and allergic disorders.

THE FRUIT VITAMIN THAT GIVES YOU
NATURAL "COLD INSURANCE"

Nature has put a vitamin in fruits that can actually help give you natural "cold insurance." Just eat the fruit or drink the fruit juice (or do both) and you will be feeding your billions of cells and tissues with this miracle vitamin. You will then help build amazing resistance to the infectious onslaught of winter germs and enjoy what may be called "cold insurance" the natural way.

This miracle is *Vitamin C.*

Your body cannot manufacture Vitamin C and it must come from outside sources. Your body cannot store Vitamin C and you must have an adequate amount every single day. A slight deficiency or shortage may reduce your body's resistance to respiratory ailments, particularly colds, and you may become victim to chronic and increasing winter ailments. This risk could be reduced if your body has ample Vitamin C to build a form of "cold insurance."

How Vitamin C Gives You This
"Cold Insurance"

When you eat a citrus fruit or drink its juice, you send a supply of Vitamin C to your system. Speedily, Vitamin C brings

about a metabolic conversion of body substances to create a substance known as *collagen*. This is a "cement-like" ingredient
that makes up a large percentage of your total body protein and is
distributed throughout the intercellular spaces of your body. It
occurs typically as long, intertwined protein fibers. This collagen
is used to build, rebuild and heal broken cells and tissues so that
they can resist the ravages of infectious bacteria. Without Vitamin C from citrus fruits, collagen production declines and the
body becomes vulnerable to colds and other infections.

Promotes Health and Well-Being

This magic vitamin uses collagen to help give you energy,
protect against fatigue, protect against listlessness, put a better
color into your skin, soothe your muscles, guard your joints and
bones. Vitamin C-nourished collagen also helps ease problems
of a fever, fast pulse and shortness of breath. When your body is
adequately nourished with Vitamin C, it can better resist colds
and other ailments.

Nourishes Tissues

As an effective means of creating "cold insurance," this
plant vitamin maintains the integrity of connective tissues and
cells and this helps guard against the susceptibility to winter
infection. *Unique Benefit:* A cold attack uses up a lot of Vitamin
C just at a time when your body needs this nutrient in larger
amounts to nullify the infections of germs. So when you eat lots
of fresh fruits and drink fresh juices immediately upon the onset
of a cold, you will be able to give your body the working materials
needed to dilute and conquer the invading germs. This is a unique
benefit of Vitamin C, available in citrus fruits and juices, as
created by Nature for your better health.

Protects Against Viruses

Many viruses and some non-viral filter-passing substances
can cause the onset of a cold, as well as many other respiratory
attacks. But Vitamin C offers a special type of protection against
such viruses. This plant vitamin is involved in the release of cer-

tain hormones that become converted to norepinephrine, a vital neurohormone. This is a powerful amine that protects the body against the invasion of viruses. In particular, it shields the central and autonomic nervous systems with this amine to guard against lethargy and weakness and metabolic reactions from virus attacks. Yet your body needs Vitamin C to create this process. It is the natural way to help protect yourself against viruses in any climate.

A MEDICAL DOCTOR'S PROGRAM FOR PROTECTION AGAINST COLDS

Edme Regnier, M.D.[2], says that based upon years of study, he has been able to control, cure and prevent the common cold by the use of Vitamin C. He speaks from personal experience. This physician suffered 20 years of recurring bouts of inflammation of the middle ear (known as otitis media) and also noted that virus cold infections brought about such attacks. He also had a lifelong history of chronic cold catching. He decided to try to protect himself from such problems with Vitamin C. He discovered that when he fortified his body with this simple plant vitamin, his colds were less frequent, less severe. Soon, they did not occur. He enjoyed freedom from ear trouble, too. He tells of a program to be followed that helped himself and many of his patients: (Program to be followed for 10 to 11 days).

Step One: At the first sign of a cold, take 750 milligrams of Vitamin C; thereafter, take 625 milligrams at three-hour intervals until bedtime; take 750 milligrams every three hours through the day. Follow this program three to four days.

Step Two: Maintain the same timetable of natural medication, but reduce daytime doses of Vitamin C to 400 milligrams; reduce bedtime and getting-up doses to 500 milligrams. Follow this program three days.

Step Three: Maintain the same timetable of natural medication, but reduce daytime doses to 200-250 milligrams of Vitamin C; reduce bedtime and getting-up doses to 300 milligrams. Follow this program three days.

[2] Edme Regnier, M.D., *There Is a Cure for the Common Cold,* Parker Publishing Co., West Nyack, New York 10994.

Step Four: For one day, take 250 milligrams of Vitamin C every four hours during waking hours. On the last day, take 250 milligrams of Vitamin C every six hours during waking hours.

Take Adequate Vitamin C

Dr. Regnier emphasizes the importance of taking the specified amounts of Vitamin C daily and adhering to his program. He says that if you wish to enjoy natural immunity and protection against colds, then you should not reduce the amount of Vitamin C taken daily. "Smaller doses of Vitamin C," says the doctor, "or longer intervals between doses may prolong the overall duration of symptoms of the cold itself. In other words, if the required amount of the vitamin is not going to be taken, it is much better not to take any ascorbic acid (Vitamin C) at all."

Edme Regnier, M.D. tells of treating and healing countless patients by prescribing Vitamin C for colds. He says that there was not one person who failed to obtain successful results as regards his symptomatic response if his intake of Vitamin C was sufficient and also well timed. This suggests that at the very first sign of a cold, immediately start boosting your Vitamin C intake. It may heal and cure the common cold, according to the doctor.

Note that in cases of fever or hard physical exertion, the body uses up more Vitamin C at a much faster rate than usual. So it is wise to replace that which is lost with Vitamin C as a natural "cold insurance" program of Nature.

SIX COLD-FIGHTING AND BODY-HEALING BENEFITS OF VITAMIN C

Here is what happens when you feed your body Vitamin C, as explained by a pioneering researcher, Fred R. Klenner, M.D.[3] who says, "We have been able to assemble sufficient clinical evidence to prove unequivocally that Vitamin C is the antibiotic of choice in the handling of all types of virus diseases. Furthermore, it is a major adjuvant (help) in the treatment of all other infectious diseases." Dr. Klenner lists these six basic cold-fighting miracle powers of Vitamin C:

[3] Fred R. Klenner, M.D., "Use of Vitamin C As an Antibiotic," *Journal of Applied Nutrition,* Winter, 1953.

1. Vitamin C combines with toxins and/or virus invaders to form a compound which is then destroyed by oxidation, thereby cleansing the system.
2. Vitamin C is directly related to the formation of proteins in the blood (antibodies) that produce immunity against certain infections and toxins.
3. Vitamin C prevents and lessens tissue damage.
4. Vitamin C causes body cells to be more permeable, thus allowing the entrance of immune factors.
5. Vitamin C has a natural anti-histamine-like action.
6. Vitamin C functions as a dehydrator and diuretic.

In combination, these functions provide healing of colds and respiratory-allergic reactions and also perform the desired natural "cold insurance" if you take Vitamin C regularly.

Helps Heal Pneumonia

A patient was under treatment for virus pneumonia when he suddenly developed cyanosis (a condition in which the skin turns blue because of lack of oxygen in the blood). The man refused to be hospitalized for supportive oxygen therapy. To relieve the condition, Dr. Klenner administered 2000 milligrams of Vitamin C. *Benefits:* The vitamin reportedly would act as a gas transport and aid in cellular respiration. *Results:* Within 30 minutes, the man responded favorably. His breathing stabilized. His color returned to normal. Some six hours later, this pneumonia patient could sit up and eat dinner. His fever which had been very high, dropped three degrees less. The patient received another 1000 milligrams of Vitamin C that night and then again at six hour intervals for the next three days. Within 36 hours of the first vitamin therapy, he was pronounced "clinically well."

Fred R. Klenner, M.D. believes Vitamin C is a natural cold-fighter. He writes, "Could it be that, by maintaining a high blood level of this vitamin, all body tissue is allowed to return to normal in spite of the existing fever and the presence of the specific virus organism, and that, acting as a respiratory catalyst, it (Vitamin C) enables the body to build up adequate resistance to the invader?"

Dr. Klenner emphasizes, *"We argue that Vitamin C, besides being an essential vitamin, is a super-antibiotic!"*

The doctor also suggests the use of Vitamin C for problems of polio, pulmonary virus infection, virus encephalitis, virus pneumonia and measles. (Nearly all of these ailments are triggered by a virus attack. The reasoning is to use the miracle of Vitamin C as a natural way to build immunity.)

Recovers from a Virus

A patient was suffering from virus encephalitis (brain inflammation). Dr. Klenner reports him as having a "skin cold to touch, color cadaver-like, eyes closed, nasal discharge, throat red. The temperature was 103.8°. Breath and heart sounds practically inaudible. Areas of the back presented an appearance similar to that seen in rigor mortis." Dr. Klenner says the patient also suffered convulsive seizures of the right arm and leg which began some 12 hours before hospital admission. The treatment consisted of 1000 milligrams of Vitamin C at the start, and then repeated every four to six hours. The doctor also prescribed mustard plasters for the chest, dextrose in saline and a special croup tent carrying vapor of compound tincture benzoin.

Results: Just two hours after the first administration of 1000 milligrams of Vitamin C, the patient could drink orange juice. This is notable since it was the first food of any type he could ingest in 24 hours. Twelve hours and some 3000 milligrams of Vitamin C later, the patient could move his right leg. One hour and more Vitamin C and now he could hold a bottle of orange juice with both hands. From that point on, says Dr. Klenner, "the recovery was eventful." In effect, Vitamin C had helped neutralize the harsh effects of the virus infection, had helped the body form its own antibodies and created a form of natural immunity and eventual healing.

Dr. Klenner sums it up by saying, "Hippocrates declared the highest duty of medicine to be to get the patient well. He further declared that of several remedies, physicians should choose the least sensational. Vitamin C would seem to meet both requirements."

Other Benefits: Dr. Klenner has used Vitamin C to help treat tetanus and other conditions requiring the quick neutralizing of poisonous toxins. He says that large amounts of Vitamin C have helped heal folks with arthritis. Vitamin C was also effective in the treatment of folks with severe burns. Of course, this Vitamin C therapy was under strict medical supervision. But Vitamin C is a miracle nutrient of Nature and it is necessary for basic body health and should be used in healthful foods for good resistance and natural immunity.

WHERE TO GET MIRACLE VITAMIN C

U. S. Government Recommendation: The U.S. Department of Agriculture[4] recommends these sources of Vitamin C:

Good: Grapefruit or grapefruit juice; orange or orange juice; cantaloupe; guava; mango; papaya; raw strawberries; broccoli; brussels sprouts; green peppers; sweet red pepper.

Fair: Honeydew melon; lemon, tangerine or tangerine juice; watermelon; asparagus tip; raw cabbage; collards; garden cress; kale; kohlrabi; mustard greens; potatoes and sweet potatoes cooked in the jacket; spinach; tomatoes or tomato juice; turnip greens.

MAINTAIN BODY BALANCE
FOR NATURAL IMMUNITY

Harry R. Litchfield, M.D. says,[5] "It is quite evident that the daily required amount of Vitamin C should be increased in the presence of infection to stimulate the activity of its 'fighting' blood cells. To do this, there must be a high blood level of ascorbic acid. However, it is not just a question of how much Vitamin C is required for body metabolism, but the relationship of Vitamin C to other vitamins, enzymes, food intake and the presence or absence in the diet of substances stimulatory to ascorbic acid." So maintain healthful body balance with all of the needed nutrients. It helps put power into Vitamin C.

[4]*Family Fare: A Guide to Good Nutrition,* U.S. Department of Agriculture, Washington, D.C., House And Garden Bulletin No. 1, 1970.

[5]*Live and Be Well,* by Harry R. Litchfield, M.D., Libra Publishers, Inc. New York, N.Y. 1972.

Be Cautious About Aspirin

The careless taking of aspirins during a cold spell may deplete Vitamin C and worsen the situation. Dr. Litchfield notes that aspirin-taking can have adverse effects upon the body. "It is therefore evident that Vitamin C is *rapidly depleted* resulting in disturbance of its function in the formation of intercellular substances of cartilage, dentine and bone and the substance called collagen which holds the fibrous tissue together. So take citrus fruits or Vitamin C daily." Aspirin would appear to deplete Vitamin C so if you wish to build natural immunity that would hopefully eliminate the need for chemical drugs, be sure to get lots of fresh fruits, vegetables and juices daily. It's the healthful and natural way to build antibodies to resist cold and virus infections.

Simple Program

Bernard Bellew, M.D., says[6] that "the body functions best when it is saturated with Vitamin C." He recommends the use of a supplement. His simple program is as follows: *"In general, Vitamin C is anti-flammatory and should be taken in doses as high as 2000 milligrams every hour or two in the presence of acute inflammation in the body, until there is some resolution or relief. An example of inflammation would be the common cold or acute gastritis."*

THE MAGIC HEALING POWER OF BIOFLAVONOIDS

Bioflavonoids (often called Vitamin P) are healing substances found in the white pulp of citrus fruits. They are biologically active in that they help strengthen your blood vessels and capillaries to resist the ravages of infections. Folks troubled with allergic symptoms may be in need of bioflavonoids.

Healing Benefits: A virus attack or an allergic reaction may be traced to unhealthy capillaries in need of bioflavonoid nourishment. These nutrients help keep the capillaries neither too week or too strong. These nutrients maintain the *permeability* of

[6]*Diet Dynamics* by Bernard Bellew, M.D., Sherbourne Press, Los Angeles, California, 1972.

your capillaries and provide an osmotic pressure that protects you against fragile breakdown. Nourishing fluids must pass through the capillaries. Bioflavonoids produce this miracle balance so that the capillaries are healthful and reasonably strong. They help *neutralize* or *screen out* and otherwise nullify the volatile effects of virus infections. How is this balance maintained? By the availability and nourishment of bioflavonoids.

Sources of Bioflavonoids: Fresh fruits and vegetables. Try the citrus fruits but whenever you eat an orange, grapefruit or cut up a lemon for seasoning or juice or dessert, *do not throw away the pulp. Look at the small white core that runs down the middle. There is your treasure trove of organic bioflavonoids. Take out the white core and chew it and swallow it. You'll be giving yourself Vitamin C together with the precious capillary feeding bioflavonoids.* If you do this regularly, you should be able to insulate yourself with natural virus-fighting vitamins and help enjoy freedom from allergy and respiratory infections.

In addition, rose hips or acerola cherries (sold at most health stores) as well as bell pepper are more sources of the bioflavonoids. Try buckwheat for more of this virus-fighting vitamin. Make a salad using green pepper strips (include the white pulpy portion where bioflavonoids are concentrated) with buckwheat honey and a sprinkle of lemon juice. If you wish, add citrus fruit wedges but be sure to include the white strings which will give you bioflavonoids-plus! It's the delicious way to feed yourself miracle vitamins for natural immunity.

HELPING TO BUILD NATURAL IMMUNITY

Vitamin A: Needed to work with other vitamins. You will find a lot in yellow or deep green vegetables such as carrots, cantaloupe, parsley, kale, squash, green peppers, fish liver oil, whole eggs.

Good Ventilation: Avoid stuffy rooms. Crowded rooms with many people breathing may cause colds or allergic attacks. Maintain good ventilation or try to leave such a room.

Good Moisture: Your nose and mouth tissues contain vitamins that need moisture in order to stay healthy. So avoid dry rooms. In your house, if it's dry, place flat pans of water beneath your radiators. Or boil a kettle of water in the kitchen now and then. Keep well-watered potted plants around the house. This helps create healthy humidity. Although Vitamin A is useful in maintaining the normal suppleness of your mucous membranes, it will lose efficiency in very dry air.

Take Walks: Keep yourself active but walk only in good weather. Avoid very cold weather. When cold air hits the lungs, it constricts the tiny blood vessels which must extract oxygen from the air you breathe. The result is you get reduced oxygen which can set off a heart condition. So walk on a nice day. Keep your back to the wind. Avoid cold wind or rain blowing directly in your face.

Keep Calm: Ever notice how an allergy or respiratory attack strikes after a frenzied round of activity? It is believed that excess tensions drain your strength. They force your body into a stress syndrome; this means your body's metabolism pumps vitamins to your tired tissues to keep you going. The risk here is that your body is depleted of vitamins and a virus or germ can then seize you and you do not have sufficient natural antibodies to fight back. So keep calm. Avoid excessive tensions of your mind and body. Fortify yourself with food vitamins to build resistance to viral attacks. Let wholesome foods with natural vitamins help make your body a fortress against allergies.

IN REVIEW

1. Vitamin A has a miracle immunity-building power to shield you against the symptoms of respiratory ailments. It makes *lysozyme,* the body's own cold-fighting substance. This acts as a natural antiseptic.
2. Enjoy some of the Vitamin A foods as recommended by the U. S. Government.
3. Dorothy G. used yellow plant foods and cod liver oil as well as broiled liver to help build immunity to her allergies.
4. For "cold insurance," consider Vitamin C in the foods recommended by the U. S. Government. It helps protect against viruses.

5. A medical doctor offers a Vitamin C program to reportedly prevent and cure colds.

6. Vitamin C has six cold-fighting and body-healing benefits. A doctor used this miracle vitamin to help heal pneumonia and virus encephalitis in his patients.

7. Be cautious about aspirin. Use bioflavonoids in salads. Maintain better home ventilation and better body care. You can easily build a natural fortress right within your body, using simple foods, and free yourself from allergy-respiratory distress.

9

How to Rebuild Your Internal Organs with Vitalic Vitamins

You can reap the rewards of shining good health when you use Nature-created vitalic vitamins for the rebuilding of your internal organs. Ordinary, everyday foods can become sources of healing for your gallbladder, kidneys, liver and pancreas. When these organs are healthfully nourished, your entire body bounces back with youthful vitality. Treat your internal organs with vitalic vitamins as found in foods, and they will serve you healthfully so that you can enjoy the best that life has to offer. Let us see how you can help rebuild *four* important internal organs by using vitalic vitamins in ordinary foods that give an extraordinary power of healing.

HOW VITAMINS CAN BE GOOD TO YOUR GALLBLADDER

Location and function of gallbladder: This organ is a small bag attached to the underside of the liver in which bile is stored and concentrated. When food passes from the stomach to the intestine, the gallbladder contracts and ejects bile into the duo-denum (first part of the intestine near the stomach). Problems include inflammation and gallstones which are insoluble deposits precipitated from the bile. This may lead to intolerance of fatty foods because fat needs bile for its digestion and stimulates the gallbladder. You need a healthy gallbladder because it uses bile for the emulsification and digestion of fat in the intestine. A poorly functioning gallbladder means a deficiency of bile and poor fat digestion. This may cause the growth of toxic wastes which putrefy. This causes gas and indigestion. It may also be involved with the formation of gallstones. With healthful foods, your gallbladder can be nourished with vitamins to keep it in good functioning order.

The Food That Vitaminizes Your Gallbladder

The B-complex vitamins are used by your gallbladder for stimulation and emptying. Vitamins A, D and E are also needed by the gallbladder for nourishing of its cells and tissues and to carry across the intestinal wall into the bloodstream. Your gallbladder uses these vitamins to promote the emulsification of fat. Vitamin A is especially needed for bile processing and folks troubled with faulty gallbladder functioning often show a deficiency of this vitamin. One such food that is a prime source of these and complementary essential fatty acids and minerals is *lecithin.*

The vitamins in lecithin help emulsify fats, keep them broken up in very tiny and separate particles. These vitamins help keep circulating fats emulsified while also helping to control the buildup of cholesterol to protect the gallbladder from formation of stones. Lecithin is the natural way to vitaminize your gallbladder.

Where to Get Lecithin

To help improve your gallbladder, lecithin is a wholesome vitamin food. It is found in soybean oil and most other polyunsaturated unhydrogenated vegetable oils. Lecithin is a substance found in *soybeans.* If you will eat soybeans as a healthful meal several times a week, you will be good to your gallbladder. Health stores sell lecithin granules which may be sprinkled over salads, used in soups, stews, casseroles. You may also mix one table-spoon of lecithin granules in a glass of vegetable juice and drink as a healthy tonic that is brimming with vitalic vitamins for the health of your gallbladder. Just one such drink a day can do very much for your internal organs.

How Elizabeth T. Flatters Her Gallbladder with a Simple Program

When she felt slight spasms in her stomach, Elizabeth T. decided to flatter her gallbladder at the very start. This preven-tive method is wise. She has a simple program. *Before each meal, she takes one tablespoon of any polyunsaturated unhydrogenated oil.* The benefit here is that the oils are more readily absorbed than solid fats and increase the production of bile acids and leci-thin while decreasing the cholesterol content of bile. The oils send a supply of soothing vitamins to help "coat" her internal organs and shield them from distress. Of course, Elizabeth T. eats wholesome foods, too, for added benefits. But she would not begin any meal unless she first has this one tablespoon of oil for vitaminization and flattering of her gallbladder. Now she feels no spasms, enjoys her food and has a contented gallbladder, thanks to the vitamins in the oils.

For healthful nourishment of your organs, increase your intake of Brewer's yeast, soybean flour, wheat germ, fresh and powdered skim milk, nuts, various non-hydrogenated nut butters and liver lightly broiled in oil. *Avoid* hydrogenated or "hard" fats. With good care, your gallbladder can be good to you, too!

HOW VITAMINS CAN BE KIND TO YOUR KIDNEYS

Location and function of your kidneys: These are bean-like organs, about four and one-half inches in length, located at your backbone between the thick muscles of your back and stomach. The major function of your kidneys is to filter blood which is carried to it by your arteries, then distributed via a capillary system to the filtration site and then returned to the veins. Your kidneys serve a function as your body's filter plant through which some 150 quarts of liquid pass daily. Each kidney consists of a million tiny filters which strain waste products (those left from protein digestion) out of the blood, dissolve them in water and excrete them in the form of urine. The blood enters one end of each tiny tube in the kidney and then leaves through the other and smaller end. When the kidneys are under-nourished, problems result. These include edema or dropsy in which there is an accumulation of water in the body. There may also be development of several types of stones which present painful health hazards. Malfunctioning of the filtering system means that the waste substances in the blood cannot be discarded and toxic infection or uremic poisoning results. Your program for better health calls for being kind to your kidneys . . . with the miracle of Nature's own vitamins in simple foods.

The Foods That Help Nourish Your Kidneys

Foods containing Vitamin A are needed to nourish your kidneys. This vitamin helps feed the tiny kidney tubules which are lined with mucous membranes. A deficiency may cause the tubules to become plugged with dead cells; less urine can be formed, excessive water retained in the body prompts a blood pressure increase and urea back up into the blood. You need foods with Vitamin A to help nourish and cleanse your kidneys and keep you well.

Foods containing the B-complex vitamins are needed to help regulate the acid-alkalinity of the body fluids. These vitamins do this in unison with the lungs, helping them retain or release a greater or lesser amount of carbon dioxide, depending upon the body's need for maintaining the optimum level of acidity. These vitamins are needed to regulate the balance because the body fluids bathe the cells of all the tissues and are in continuous communication with the internal biological functions of the cells.

Foods containing Vitamin E are also needed to nourish the walls of the kidneys and keep the cells and tissues in healthy condition. Vitamin E works with other vitamins to keep kidney tubules clean so that the dead cells are washed away and speedily repaired. This protects your kidneys against nephritis (inflammation) controls the volume of urine, balances the water in the bloodstream. These vitamins are needed by your kidneys for helping to keep you healthy and fit.

Where to Get These Kidney-Feeding Vitamins

If you will prepare one large bowl of shredded carrots, sprinkle with desiccated liver, then some wheat germ, and use a salad dressing made of polyunsaturated oil with a sprinkle of lemon juice, you will be giving your kidneys (and body) a tremendous source of these essential health-building vitamins. You will have a treasure of Vitamin A, B-complex, as well as Vitamin E. In this combination, they go to work to help nourish your kidneys and make you feel good all over.

How Peter I. Is Kind to His Kidneys with an Easy Program

Problems of water retention as well as chronic fatigue, poor digestion and a "bitter taste" in his mouth alerted Peter I. to the need for being kind to his kidneys for better health. Quite often, the accumulation of toxic wastes and urea in the bloodstream is traced to a malfunctioning kidney and this creates the "bitter taste" in the mouth due to excess acid. Peter I. followed a very simple but highly effective "be kind to the kidneys" program. Here it is:

Eliminate all harsh spices and condiments. Eliminate coffee and commercial tea. Foods should be as wholesome and natural as possible.

Boost the intake of needed Vitamins A, B-complex and E by preparing a simple main dish consisting of soybeans with a raw yellow and green vegetable salad that featured a dressing of wheat germ oil with a bit of honey and a sprinkle of lemon juice. He would also eat *organ* meats such as kidney, liver, heart because these are prime sources of vitamins that nourish the body organs. For beverages he would enjoy fruit or vegetable juices, herb teas and coffee substitutes such as Postum.

Benefits: These everyday foods are prime sources of more than just the needed kidney-nourishing vitamins. They also contain minerals, enzymes, proteins and essential fatty acids that are used by the vitamins to *amplify* their activities. In brief, vitamins take up these other nutrients and use them for the building and rebuilding of the kidneys, and body.

Peter I. soon was relieved of his water imbalance, he felt more energetic, his digestion improved. When the "bitter taste" in his mouth went away, Peter I. felt very happy. So did his kidneys because he treated them with kindness!

HOW TO USE VITAMINS THAT LOVE YOUR LIVER

Location and function of your liver: This organ is the largest gland of your body and completely fills the part of your abdomen that is covered by the right side of your diaphragm and rib-cage, a little below your waistline. It is part of your digestive tract. The liver manufactures, changes or breaks down many substances into other substances. Digestive products arrive at the liver for changing. Carbohydrates are changed into glycogen which is stored by the liver and released to the body as needed. The liver breaks down fats so they may be oxidized (burned) in the cells. The liver passes off bile (residue left from the breakdown of red blood cells) into the excretory system. It also stores iron and fibrogen which are two valuable blood components. When healing is needed, the liver releases these substances into the body. The liver stores a blood-forming factor and guards against anemia. The liver also absorbs toxic wastes from the digestive tract and then releases them or else nullifies their poisonous effects. A malnourished liver may lead to virus attack such as hepatitis, poor circulation, biliousness, jaundice and the vague symptoms of just feeling unwell, indigestion and unnatural weight loss. Cirrhosis of the liver can be a serious consequence of ill health and poor nourishment.

The Foods That Help Nourish Your Liver

Because of its function as an organ of metabolism, your liver needs such food vitamins as A, the B-complex, D and E, as well as minerals, enzymes, proteins. These food vitamins alert the liver to produce enzymes which then perform the actions of metabolism and also activate body hormones for good health. These food vitamins protect against serious liver degeneration and offer protection against toxic drugs and chemicals. This includes pollution which is breathed in daily and absorbed through the skin. A well-nourished vitaminized liver can do much to protect against body damage from such chemical infiltration of your body. Healthful foods are fresh fruits and vegetables, lean meats, Brewer's yeast, seed oils and fish as well as fish liver oils. Broiled liver is, perhaps, the best food for your liver.

How Arlene Q. Loves Her Liver with a Deliciously Healthy Program

Problems of poor digestion, a sallow complexion, increasing stomach pains, and an embarrassing "gas" feeling of biliousness, alerted Arlene Q. to the need for showing a little love to her liver. The unique benefit of this deliciously healthy program that she followed is that in addition to helping to treat her liver with loving kindness, it boosted her basic health and made her realize that life can be very beautiful. All this, thanks to the vitaminization of her liver and her body. Here is the simple and tasty program followed by Arlene Q.

1. *Emphasize Natural Foods.*   She had to cut down on saturated or "hard" fats so she eliminated refined, processed foods. Bakery products, commercial mixes, deep fried foods, hydrogenated products all contained "hidden" hard fats. She would eat wholesome, natural foods. Fruits and vegetables were freshly prepared. Lean meats, lean liver, poultry, fish, and any bread products had to be as natural as possible. This gives her liver and body a tremendous treasure of vitamins.

2. *Desaturated Butter.*   Arlene Q. liked butter. But as a hard fat, it was too much for her liver to metabolize. So she found a tasty way to "desaturate" the butter. Here is what she did. Put one pound of butter in a blender. Add 1/4 cup sesame seed oil, 1/4 cup of lecithin granules. Whiz a few moments. Then refrigerate until use. This gave Arlene Q. a desaturated butter that had

all the taste of hard butter, but with far less cholesterol and hard fats. A special benefit is that the sesame seed oil was a prime source of Vitamin E and other nutrients that was nourishing to her liver. The lecithin gave her liver a tremendous supply of most known vitamins, including the necessary B-complex family. She could have her butter, and eat it, too!

3. *Increase Vitamin A and E Intake.*   These two vitamins are especially valuable for nourishing the cells, tissues and walls of the liver. Since the liver has to absorb or metabolize carotene to be formed into Vitamin A, it is essential to feed these vitamins to this organ. Arlene Q. was able to give her liver the love it needed by daily taking a simple food. It was halibut liver oil. (Any fish liver oil will do.) She took two tablespoons daily. This gave her liver the needed Vitamin A for cell nourishment; it gave her liver the needed Vitamin D to promote better metabolism; it gave her liver the needed Vitamin E to prompt better metabolic and oxidative processes. This also helped to protect the liver's supply of Vitamin A and the important fatty acids. *Vitamin E protected Vitamin A and the essential fatty acids from destruction by oxygen.* All this available to Arlene Q. by the simple act of taking two tablespoons daily of halibut liver oil. A natural powerhouse of liver nourishment.

4. *Eat Seeds Daily.*   Your liver needs a variety of vitamins. You can get them from any types of seeds such as sunflower, sesame, pumpkin. Arlene Q. would munch on them daily, either as snack foods (to replace junk foods) or else she would sprinkle seeds over a raw vegetable salad. Sometimes, when baking a liver loaf, she would add a handful of seeds. This gave her a tremendous supply of needed vitamins and the most important fatty acids. The liver absorbed these nutrients and gave Arlene Q. a feeling of soothing contentment.

5. *After Dinner Liver Tonic.*   Arlene Q. would take this easy After Dinner Liver Tonic daily. Just one tablespoon of sesame seed oil with one tablespoon of lecithin granules.

Secret Liver Benefit: The nutrients help "prime" the liver and lower the fat level of the bloodstream. The rich fatty acid supply helps keep skin moist, also helps utilize cholesterol and protect it from forming fats. This two-ingredient After Dinner Liver Tonic also is a powerful emulsifying agent, aids in the body's transportation of fats, helps the liver cells remove fats and cholesterol from the blood. A nourished liver with these two ingredients can help the cholesterol metabolism much more effectively. It made Arlene Q. feel good after eating her dinner.

6. *Keep Skin Pores Open.*   Your internal organs have to breathe! Your liver has to cast off wastes through your skin pores so keep them open. Arlene Q. did it by simply adding a cup of apple cider vinegar to her final bath water rinse. The benefit is that it helped restore the natural acidity of the skin. Healthy skin is acid. Most soaps are alkaline forming and clog the pores. So Arlene Q. opens her pores so her liver can send wastes out of her body by this simple bath program.

Results: Arlene Q. found that this simple six-step "liver loving" program so improved her health, she felt as if reborn. Her digestion and metabolism became youthfully restored. Her complexion was bright. Her stomach was contented and free of pains. The embarrassing "gas" biliousness was gone. She loved her liver with healthful vitamins ... and her liver loved her, in return, with the rewards of feeling good from top to bottom, from the inside to the outside.

HOW VITAMINS HELP PAMPER YOUR PANCREAS

Location and function of your pancreas: Located near your stomach, this is a broad strip of soft glandular tissue. It is situated across the back of the abdomen, mostly under cover of the stomach. It is broadest on the right where it nestles in the curve of the duodenum, wrapped around the portal vein and closely applied to the arteries of the liver and the bile duct. The function of the pancreas is for better digestion but its basic concern is that of secreting pancreatic juice, released into the intestines, to help the other digestive juices break down food for assimilation. The pancreas needs vitamins to be able to produce a hormone called insulin. This vitamin-sparked hormone ignites the flame for burning sugars and starches transforming them into energy and heat. A vitamin-starved pancreas may lead to deficient insulin. In this case, the sugar cannot be burned; instead, it flows into the urine, after the blood has become saturated with it. This creates problems of diabetes. A malfunctioning pancreas cannot metabolize properly and a problem of hypoglycemia or low blood sugar ensues. So the key to better body health is to pamper your pancreas.

The Foods That Help Nourish Your Pancreas

One miracle vitamin is Vitamin B_6 or pyridoxine that is food for your pancreas. This vitamin transforms protein into tryptophane, an essential amino acid which it then uses to nourish the pancreas. In particular, it uses this amino acid to help maintain even blood sugar through healthful metabolism. Vitamin B_6 also helps magnesium, a mineral, control blood sugar and the pampering of the pancreas. All the B-complex vitamins are especially valuable to help maintain good pancreas health. A deficiency usually predisposes the feeling of thirst that is common among diabetics and this suggests an ailing or vitamin-starved pancreas. Vitamins A and C also work to help use sugar for the burning of fat for heat and energy. These vitamins influence the complete utilization of fat, and protect the body from the problem of acetone acidosis. Even mild vitamin deficiency and a weak pancreas can cause symptoms of acidosis in which the person feels weak, nervous, headaches and has bouts of nausea. To pamper your pancreas, feed it Vitamins A, B-complex especially pyridoxine, C and the others through wholesome yellow and green vegetables, liver, whole grain foods, fresh citrus fruits. These vitamins are needed by your pancreas so it can function adequately to protect you against disruption of the delicate insulin flow so that your sugar metabolism is healthful. Nature has put vitamins in foods to help pamper your pancreas.

Where to Get These Pancreas-Pampering Vitamins

Use whole-grain breads and cereals; avoid hydrogenated or "hard" fats and reduce intake of animal fats. Nuts and seeds are healthful. Fish is a desirable food because it contains a natural fat that is highly unsaturated and is used by Vitamin A for pancreas nourishment. Fresh fruits and vegetables are important, too. This is a list of simple yet very healthful foods that add up to loving pampering for your pancreas.

How Julie U. Enjoys Her Foods While Pampering Her Pancreas

Julie U. was aching all over. She had bouts of frequent perspiration over her body; she was nervous, had embarrassing compulsive drinking (of water) urges and feelings of excessive energy and then a complete let down. This would suggest that her pancreas was in need of better care. She had been told she had symptoms of hypoglycemia as well as poor metabolism. She set about a simple corrective eating program.

The "secret" of the healing success of this program is in its vitamin power. It helped nourish her *entire body* and this had a beneficial healing upon her vitamin-starved pancreas. Here is how Julie U. enjoyed her foods while pampering her pancres.

Eggs — two per week.

Milk — 1 quart of skim milk daily.

Meat — lean broiled liver at least twice per week.

Dairy — cottage cheese with wheat germ; the cheese was to be from skim milk.

Poultry — lean white chicken or turkey at least twice weekly.

Fish — lean fish for the treasure of ocean vitamins.

Soups — fortified with powdered milk for more vitaminization. Homemade soups were a "must" and they had to be clear and without creaming.

Plants — fresh fruits and vegetables. A rule was to eat them *raw* for maximum vitaminization. Those vegetables needing cooking would be steamed lightly in *oil* to preserve vitamin content.

PEP-UP PANCREAS PUNCH: In a bowl (or blender) mix 1 tablespoon lecithin, 1 tablespoon seed oil, 1 cup yogurt, 1 cup skim milk, 1 tablespoon Brewer's yeast, 2 tablespoons wheat germ, 1 tablespoon soy flour or powder. Mix together with an egg beater or else run through the blender for a few moments.

Julie U. would drink this early in the morning. *Benefits:* The secret here is that pancreas tissues can be rebuilt at maximum speed only when all basic nutrients are supplied at one time. The *Pep-Up Pancreas Punch* is a natural treasure of Vitamins A, B-complex (especially pyridoxine) Vitamin C, Vitamin D, Vitamin E and also has many minerals and proteins, together with needed unsaturated fatty acids. In *combination,* the nutrients soothe and pamper the pancreas, nourishing the cells and tissues and helping it function smoothly.

Results: This simple daily food guide, together with the *Pep-Up Pancreas Punch* sent a shower of healthy vitamins to Julie's pancreas, as well as to the other internal organs. They so nourished her pancreas that she soon was freed from nervous perspiration; she had no abnormal thirst urges, and her energy was youthful and more stable. Gone were her ups and her downs. She pampered her pancreas and she entered a new phase of contented living.

Special Tip: Brewer's yeast and soy flour offer boosting vitamins but *no* sugar or starch. This is beneficial for folks anxious to control their insulin requirements and want better health. As for milk, this does contain sugar and may often be restricted. *But* you can have your milk — in the form of *yogurt!* The benefit here is that in the process of making yogurt, the milk sugar is broken down to lactic acid which can be enjoyed by the pancreas-pampering person.

For good health, use vitalic vitamins to help nourish your internal organs. Let foods be your healing medicines in the form of vitamins as created by Nature. A healthy insides mean a healthy outsides. It is a miracle of health awaiting you with organic vitamins in simple foods.

HIGHLIGHTS

1. Elizabeth T. is good to her gall bladder with a simple vitaminization program. Easy to follow. Healthful, too.
2. Peter I. is kind to his kidneys by following simple common sense eating programs. He enjoys better health through well-nourished kidneys.
3. Arlene Q. loves her liver with a simple and tasty six-step program. She is able to enjoy good food and nourishes her liver and her body, too.
4. Julie U. pampers her pancreas with some slight dietary adjustments. She finds the Pep-Up Pancreas Punch to be a super-duper vitamin booster. It has made life very beautiful, indeed.

10

Cholesterol-Controlling Vitamins for Better Heart Health

Nutritional science has recognized the importance of a set of ingredients in plant foods that can effectively help control the amount of cholesterol buildup in the bloodstream. With these vitamin-like ingredients available in the body, the blood vessels, arteries and heart can be "washed" and kept youthfully clean so that the entire body can enjoy better health and longer life. These ingredients are known as *essential fatty acids* and have come to be called *Vitamin F*. They offer hope for cholesterol washing for better heart health. Nature has placed these essential fatty acids, or Vitamin F, in grain foods so that when eaten in the form of grains or oils, they can help protect the body against cholesterol accumulation. It is the natural way to use this Vitamin F to help improve your health.

THE MIRACLE HEART-HEALING POWER OF VITAMIN F

To understand how Vitamin F can be so effectively heart-healing, let's see what cholesterol is and how you can control its buildup.

Cholesterol.   A fat-like substance found in most animal

foods; in your body, it is a normal and essential constituent of the blood and nerve tissues, as well as other organs. Your liver manufactures cholesterol from fats, proteins and carbohydrates. It is a necessary substance for body health. But it is the *excess* of cholesterol that can be a risk to the health of your arteries and heart. By using Vitamin F (described later), you can help control buildup of cholesterol and promote a natural "washing" away of this fat-like substance.

Arteriosclerosis.   Also known as "hardening of the arteries," this is precipitated by a buildup of patches of cholesterol-like fatty material and other substances in the smooth inner wall of the artery. In addition, the artery becomes less elastic. This causes a form of "hardening" that reduces body health.

Blood Clot.   This is caused when continual deposits of cholesterol in the artery wall tend to squeeze the opening through which the blood flows. There is a choking of the normal cells of the wall. When cholesterol buildup is unchecked or "unwashed" by Vitamin F, then it may squeeze the artery until it blocks off the flow of blood. A clot may break loose and travel to smaller arteries, causing various blood clots.

Heart Trouble.   If the coronary arteries (those arteries supplying the heart) are involved, the result can be catastrophic. The heart muscle, like tissues throughout the body, is dependent on a constant supply of oxygen from the blood supply. Body cells can live and function briefly without this supply. If a major artery to such a vital organ as the heart is blocked, a large part of the heart muscle soon becomes incapacitated. This precipitates a "coronary" or heart attack. If arteries in the brain are involved, a "stroke" results. If the arteries are given sufficient Vitamin F through essential fatty acids in plant foods, they can be kept "clean" and the bloodstream can flow youthfully to help nourish body cells and the heart. In effect, Vitamin F is Nature's own *detergent* for the arteries and heart. When Vitamin F is given to your body, it washes and cleanses your internal network and creates a sparklingly clean, natural, antiseptic benefit. It adds up to a miracle of good health for your heart, your body and your life!

Vitamin F Has Three Components

The essential fatty acids or Vitamin F consist of three healthy components:

1. *Arachidonic Acid.* This sub-vitamin is useful in helping to control cholesterol and to help melt down accumulated deposits from arterial walls throughout the body.

2. *Linoleic Acid.* This sub-vitamin has the beneficial effect of helping to lower cholesterol. It is also necessary for growth and reproduction and helps protect you against excessive loss of water, and water-soluble vitamins B-complex and C. It also appears to shield the body against radiation. It helps build a better skin. It enters into many other metabolic functions that help promote better heart and body health.

3. *Linolenic Acid.* This sub-vitamin helps stimulate the manufacture of intestinal bacteria needed to produce B-complex vitamins that help promote better skin health. (Soybean oil has some 7 per cent linolenic acid.) It also cooperates with the two preceding sub-vitamins to help promote body harmony and health and also control of cholesterol.

All three of these ingredients that make up Vitamin F enter into the metabolic process to maintain health of the intestines, blood and lymph systems, the liver and muscular energy and the heart. Your body fat contains about 10 per cent linoleic acid, for instance, and it is believed that if you have more of this Vitamin F component, you will help control cholesterol accumulation and keep your arteries and heart in better health.

Official U.S. Government Recommendation for Essential Fatty Acids

The U.S. Department of Agriculture says[1] that linoleic acid (one of the sub-components of Vitamin F) is most essential for better health and must come from foods "because it cannot be formed by the human body." The official report tells us;

"Sources of linoleic acid include many grain oils and seed

[1] *Food, Yearbook of Agriculture,* "Fats and Fatty Acids," U.S. Department of Agriculture, Washington, D.C.

oils which contain 50 per cent or more. Fats from nuts, peanuts carry 20 to 30 per cent. Outstanding exceptions are walnuts, which has more than 60 per cent of linoleic acid and fat from coconuts, which have about 2 per cent.

"Fats from such fruits as avocado and olive contain about 10 per cent of linoleic acid. Those from leafy vegetables and legumes run higher, 30 per cent or more, but the total amount of fats in greens is low."

Government Recommendation. "The diet should provide some linoleic acid every day. Linoleic acid is necessary for growth and reproduction and helps protect against excessive loss of water and damage from radiation. It is essential for normal skin conditions."

Cholesterol Control. "When it is fed as 25 per cent or more of the fat, linoleic acid lowers blood cholesterol in adults under certain dietary conditions. *Corn oil contains more than 6 times as much linoleic acid as olive oil.* High cholesterol in the plasma is lowered by relatively high intakes of linoleic and perhaps other polyunsaturated fatty acids, by high intakes of niacin (Vitamin B_3) . . . by strict vegetarian-type diets, as well as by stepped-up energy metabolism such as from regular exercise, thyroid hormone and other agents that stimulate metabolism."

Vitamins Ease Arteriosclerosis. "Damage to arterial walls in the presence of high plasma cholesterol," continues the U.S. Government report, "has been lessened or averted in experimental animals by higher dietary intakes of magnesium, pyridoxine and Vitamin E."

Vitamin F, which contains all three of these sub-vitamins, arachidonic acid, linoleic acid and linolenic acid, may well hold the key to better health of the arteries, the heart and life, itself.

VITAMIN F SOURCES:
GOVERNMENT RECOMMENDATIONS

The U.S. Department of Agriculture says[2] that these types of essential fatty acids are needed for the transportation of the

[2] *Family Fare,* Home and Garden Bulletin No. 1, U.S. Department of Agriculture, Washington, D.C.

fat-soluble vitamins A, D, E and K. They recognize linoleic acid, the sub-segment of Vitamin F as being important. They recommend these sources:

"Linoleic acid is found in valuable amounts in many oils that come from plants — particularly corn, cottonseed, safflower, sesame, soybean and wheat germ. They are referred to as 'polyunsaturated' fats or oils. Margarines, salad dressings, mayonnaise and cooking oils are usually made from one or more of these oils. Nuts contain less linoleic acid than most vegetable oils; among the nuts, walnuts rate quite high. *Poultry and fish oils have more linoleic acid than other animal fats, which rank fairly low as sources.*"

U.S. Government Suggestion on Cholesterol Watching

The U.S. Department of Agriculture notes further that "cholesterol content of the diet is but one of many factors that influence the cholesterol level in blood." How can you be a cholesterol watcher? The official source tells us which foods do and do not have this fatty substance:

"Cholesterol is found only in foods of animal origin. It is not present in fruits, vegetables, cereal grains, legumes, nuts or in vegetable oils or other foods coming from plants. Organ meats, such as brains, liver and kidney and egg yolk contain the largest amounts of any foods. Shellfish supply appreciable quantities. Other foods of animal origin contain smaller quantities."

Suggestion: To control and protect against the possibility of excessive cholesterol buildup, substitute plant food for animal foods wherever possible. Trim away all fats from animal foods. Eat smaller portions of animal foods and increase your intake of the cholesterol-free foods recommended by the government. Increase your intake of the Vitamin F or linoleic acid foods such as oils and grains as recommended by the government. You'll have all the delicious taste of fat with plant oils but with none of the cholesterol. You'll also be giving your body Vitamin F to help wash and cleanse your arteries and keep your heart properly nourished and oxygenated.

THE SIMPLE VITAMIN F PROGRAM THAT PROMOTES BETTER HEART HEALTH

Marie E. experienced stiffening of her fingers. Her breath came in short gasps; at times, she thought she felt a wrenching tightness in her chest. Often, when she would carry a shopping bag or load of wet laundry, she would experience such breath difficulties, that it was tortuous for her to make her way into her home where she would collapse on the bed, breathing for air. She noted her pulse was weak. She saw that her skin color was pale. Often, she would break out in a hot and cold sweat. It also was difficult for her to get out of bed because of her short breath. Marie E. was concerned about improving her heart. Yet she liked the satisfying taste of fat and was reluctant to give up her heavy intake of animal foods. Then she was told that fat is not a taboo. The secret is in the "right" kind of fat that can *help* her health. It calls for substitution with this "right" fat and reduction of the "wrong" kind of fat. It would give her the joy of tasty fat but with virtually no cholesterol. She feared she had a cholesterol buildup that was involved with her health decline. So she followed this easy program:

1. Reduction and even elimination of hard fats such as butter and margarine (except when made with polyunsaturated liquid oil, rich in Vitamin F, and without any animal fats.)

2. Dairy products could be enjoyed but they had to be low or fat free. These include skim milk, buttermilk, cottage and other low-fat cheeses.

3. Egg yolks were limited to twice weekly. Instead, enjoy egg whites as a prime source of vitamins and protein but with *no* cholesterol.

4. All meats had to be very lean and trimmed. Portions were moderate and prepared with Vitamin F-rich plant oils.

5. Lean poultry (especially turkey) could be enjoyed for its low fat content.

6. A high intake of raw fruits and vegetables as well as a wide assortment of seeds and nuts. This gave a boosting supply of needed essential acids and cholesterol-washing Vitamin F. A tasty way to scrub-clean the arteries throughout the body.

7. Baked goods had to be made with skim milk or oils for good Vitamin F supply. Commercially prepared bakery products were reduced or eliminated, except if they had been made with fat-free ingredients and were *free* of animal products such as butter or animal fat.

8. To enjoy delicious and healthy fat, and supercharge the body with Vitamin F, an assortment of nut butters could be enjoyed on whole grain bread (made without animal fats). Any type of plant oil could be enjoyed as a delicious source of Vitamin F.

Results: This four week program gave Marie E. an assortment of foods for taste variety and "safe" fats in the form of plant oils and plant foods. Her fingers became more flexible. She could breathe easily now. Gone was the tight feeling in her chest. Her skin color improved. Her pulse was good. Her hot and cold sweats ended. She could get out of bed with youthful agility. The results were prompted by cutting down on cholesterol foods and replacing with "washing" essential fatty acids. Vitamin F in these plant and seed and nut oils helped wash her arteries and helped protect against unnatural cholesterol buildup. Marie E. has heartfelt thanks for Vitamin F. She follows the simple eight-step program as part of her daily life . . . which has years and years of health ahead of her.

YOUR VITAMIN F SALAD DRESSING — CHOLESTEROL FREE

Because salad dressings are usually made with egg yolks and saturated fats, they are high in cholesterol. Here is a special salad dressing that is a powerhouse of Vitamin F or essential fatty acids, but is *completely cholesterol free*.

1 cup safflower seed oil
Juice of 1 lemon
1 teaspoon paprika
1 tablespoon tomato juice

1/2 cup apple cider vinegar
1 teaspoon sea salt or kelp
1 tablespoon honey

Place all ingredients into a jar with a tight fitting lid. Shake until well blended. Shake again when ready to pour over salad.

YOUR VITAMIN F MAYONNAISE
— CHOLESTEROL FREE

Commercial mayonnaise is "loaded" with cholesterol. Folks who love mayonnaise can indulge in this unique recipe that has NO cholesterol, and has the added benefit of being a prime source of cholesterol-washing essential fatty acids.

2 cups water	1/4 cup cornstarch or
1/4 cup honey	arrowroot powder
1 teaspoon sea salt	1 teaspoon dry mustard (optional)
1/2 cup apple cider vinegar	1 cup wheat germ oil

Combine water and cornstarch. Cook over low heat, stirring constantly until thickened and clear. Combine remaining ingredients in a bowl. Gradually beat in hot liquid until smooth and blended. Chill. Then use as you would mayonnaise.

THE SIMPLE FOOD THAT IS A
MIRACLE HEART SAVER

Lecithin is a simple food that is a potent source of Vitamin F and other nutrients that can become a miracle heart saver.

Lecithin is a bland, water-soluble, granular powder made from de-fatted soybeans. Biochemists call it a *phosphatide*. This means that it is an essential component of all living tissues and cells. As such, lecithin plays a valuable role in building body health. Lecithin is available in granules at health stores. You can also feed yourself a supercharging power of Vitamin F by eating soybeans and getting the lecithin as Nature created it in a natural form. The Vitamin F in soybeans (out of which lecithin is made) is the highest of all known foods, pound for pound. Eating soybeans regularly will give your body a supply of Vitamin F-containing lecithin. It's the delicious way to be good to your heart.

TEN HEART-SAVING BENEFITS
FROM VITAMIN F IN SOYBEANS

Vitamin F is found in soybeans in its lecithin content. If you eat soybeans regularly, this miracle vitamin can do the following for you. . . and your heart:

1. *Lowers Surface Tension.*   Vitamin F in lecithin is ef-

fective in lowering the surface tension of aqueous solutions. The reason is that one side of the molecule prefers fat, while the other is attracted by water. This unique action makes Vitamin F in the lecithin an effective emulsifying agent, capable of dissolving cholesterol deposits.

2. *Improves Absorption.* Vitamin F in lecithin increases the digestibility and absorption of fats because of its emulsifying abilities. It also enhances both the absorption and utilization of Vitamin A and carotene (the precursor of Vitamin A as obtained from a meatless source). It increases the blood level and storage of Vitamin A.

3. *Fat Metabolism.* Vitamin F in lecithin boosts the metabolism of fat. The enzyme, lecithinase, which is produced in the body, sets free choline (a B-complex vitamin) which helps control the accumulation of fat in the liver. Choline is able to alter fat into another form, or otherwise remove its accumulation in a body part. Vitamin F in lecithin has the power to energize choline.

4. *Contains Lipotropic Agents.* Vitamin F in lecithin is a prime source of lipotropic agents which are needed to metabolize fats. It contains both choline and inositol (members of the B-complex family) which help perform the fat metabolization process.

5. *Improves Skin Health.* Vitamin F in lecithin is helpful in healing such skin problems as psoriasis, dry skin, eczema, scleroderma, senile atrophy of the skin, seborrhea, acne and keloid formation because this miracle vitamin causes fat absorption, lipid transport and helpful cholesterol metabolism of the skin, itself.

6. *Diabetic Help.* Vitamin F in lecithin reportedly may be able to decrease the needs of insulin requirements by better absorption and metabolism of sugars and starches via the pancreas.

7. *Better Absorption.* Vitamin F in lecithin improves the absorption of fat and lowers the susceptibility for problems of sprue (improper digestive absorption of fats and carbohydrates) and diarrhea.

8. *Improves Liver.* Vitamin F in lecithin helps correct deranged fat metabolism and this helps improve the health of the liver.

9. *Improves Kidneys.*   Vitamin F in lecithin helps correct a problem of choline deficiency or other lipotropic agents which protect against kidney necrosis or cellular deterioration.

10. *Internal Cleansing.*   Vitamin F in lecithin helps clear up vitreous opacities (the forerunner of cholesterol deposits — a colorless thickening).

Vitamin F or the essential fatty acids in soybean lecithin helps control cholesterol and helps protect the body against cholesterol buildup. It is a miracle of Nature, available to you in a simple bean!

How to Use Soybeans: Wash soybeans under fresh running water. Then fill a jar with equal amounts of soybeans and new water. Let soak overnight. The next day, pour the soybeans and water into a kettle and cook until the beans are tender. Eat the soybeans and sip the water as an excellent source of needed vitamins and minerals. You will be feeding your body a treasurehouse of lecithin and Vitamin F — the miracle protector of your heart!

How to Use Lecithin: Lecithin granules are available as a food supplement at most health stores. You may take two tablespoons in a glass of fresh vegetable juice for a healthful "cholesterol washing" beverage. Or else, sprinkle over breakfast cereal, bake with casseroles, loaves, stews, use in soups. This simple program gives you a rich source of the essential fatty acids (Vitamin F), which is the newest all-natural way to use miracle vitamins for the health of your heart, your body, your life!

SUMMARY

1. Essential fatty acids, known as Vitamin F, help protect against problems of cholesterol, arteriosclerosis, blood clot and heart trouble. Vitamin F consists of three components, considered sub-vitamins, which help promote this cholesterol-washing effect.

2. The U.S. Government has issued official recommendations for the intake of essential fatty acids and how to use this Vitamin F for better health.

3. Marie F. corrected stiff fingers, chest pains and shortness

of breath by a low animal fat program and cholesterol washing in eight easy steps. She uses Vitamin F in plant, seed and nut oils daily.

4. Enjoy a Vitamin F Salad Dressing — it's cholesterol free. All the taste of fat but with *no* cholesterol. Instead, a treasure of cholesterol-washing Vitamin F.

5. Use the Vitamin F Mayonnaise for delicious salad topping with *no* cholesterol but lots of healthful Vitamin F.

6. Lecithin in soybeans is a prime source of essential fatty acids that reportedly can promote ten heart-saving all-natural reactions in the body. A simple food with a powerhouse of cholesterol-washing Vitamin F.

7. Easily prepare and use both soybeans and lecithin for adequate Vitamin F nourishment of your heart, arteries and your life, too!

11

Twenty-Five Youth-Building
Secrets of Vitamin "E"

Vitamin E was discovered in 1922 by two American scientists, Drs. Herbert M. Evans and Katharine S. Bishop, as they tried to discover whether fertility was dependent on some nutritive substance different from those which produced growth and adulthood. The two doctors noted that test subjects were able to conceive but could not carry to full term. But when these subjects were given lettuce, the fertility problem was corrected. The doctors observed that when the subjects were given a simple food, *unbleached wheat,* they became fertile and could conceive.

Dr. Evans noted that single daily drops of golden yellow wheat germ proved remedial. Test subjects who could not otherwise become pregnant were now able to bear young when they took this natural food in the form of wheat germ as a grain or its fresh cold-pressed oil. Because this miracle substance enabled subjects to bear offspring, it was given a special name. The doctors took *tocos,* the Greek word for "childbirth," and *phero,* the Greek verb meaning "to bring forth" and the suffix *ol,* for "alcohol" (basic molecular structure) and called this miracle substance *tocopherol.* It was the birth of Vitamin E.

What Is Vitamin E?

This nutrient is a fat and oil-soluble vitamin that is highly concentrated in the adrenal glands found above the kidney. The adrenals use Vitamin E to help regulate sodium and potassium in the blood, produce certain sex hormones and help the body respond to stress. It is also highly concentrated in the fatty tissues of your body and such internal organs as the liver and heart.

Biologically, Vitamin E is a combination of seven oil-soluble substances known as *tocopherols — alpha, beta, gamma, delta, epsilon, eta* and *zeta.* Of these, the one called *alpha tocopherol* is regarded as the most valuable and potent in building and rebuilding youthful health. A food highest in alpha tocopherol is a food highest in *usable* Vitamin E.

Oils, Grains, Seeds, Nuts, Plant Foods

Nature has placed Vitamin E in such natural sources as oils from most grains, seeds and nuts. Good sources include corn oil, wheat germ oil, soybean oil, sunflower seed oil, peanut oil, avocado oil, whole grain unbleached products, nuts of all varieties, fresh fruits and leafy vegetables. Other good Vitamin E sources include whole grain and cereal products, fresh fruit and vegetable juices. By using these wholesome tasty foods in your regular diet, you will be nourishing your body with Vitamin E, together with a wide assortment of nearly all other vitamins as well as important minerals, enzymes and proteins. They also help promote better assimilation of Vitamin E in your system.

Official U. S. Government Recognition of Vitamin E

The U. S. Department of Agriculture, through the official National Research Council has recognized the need for Vitamin E for better health. The Council has a Recommended Daily Dietary Allowance of 25 to 30 units as important for health. You can easily get this *minimum* amount in 3 tablespoons of corn oil or 1 tablespoon of soybean oil, or 2 tablespoons of wheat germ oil. If you will use this oil on a raw vegetable salad, you will be nourishing your body with this miracle Vitamin E. You can also use Vitamin E to help build and rebuild your youthful health in a variety of ways. Here are 25 such youth building secrets made possible through the miracle of this organic vitamin.

YOUTH SECRET #1 —
STIMULATES HAIR GROWTH

An adequately Vitamin E nourished body does help stimulate hair growth. The biological activity of the hair bulb depends on the high level of energy production in the cells which need a supply of natural glucose and oxygen. Vitamin E protects the body's stores of oxygen and it is believed that the further protection with more Vitamin E in the body will help energize the hair bulb to produce better growth.

YOUTH SECRET #2 —
HEALS WOUNDS

In a reported situation, George B. caught his foot on an aluminum threshold and tore some skin loose from his heel. It started to bleed profusely. It was late at night and George B. could not get to a first aid station. He had a Vitamin E capsule so he bit one open, spilled the oil into the wound, then put on a band-aid. He repeated this simple treatment every morning during a week of travel. He did lots of walking. George B. notes that the skin grew back. There was no infection. There was no visible scar. Vitamin E helped promote this healing.

YOUTH SECRET #3 —
REVITALIZES BLOODSTREAM

Vitamin E from foods is a natural anti-thrombin (dissolves blood clots) in the bloodstream. When the bloodstream has enough Vitamin E in circulation, it appears to protect against clots occurring inside the vessels. It is natural and does not interfere with the *normal* clotting of the blood. It appears to help accelerate the healing of burns and wounds.

YOUTH SECRET #4 —
MAINTAINS HEALTHFUL INTERNAL OXYGEN

Vitamin E is a natural anti-oxidant in the body; that is, it helps perform the youth-giving function of oxygen conservation.

It reportedly helps decrease the oxygen requirement of muscles by as much as 43 per cent and makes the narrow stream of blood which gets through the narrowed coronary artery in many heart patients adequate to prevent the occurrence of anoxia (lack of oxygen) which is the trigger that sets off angina or heart pain. Better oxygen, thanks to Vitamin E, helps protect the heart.

YOUTH SECRET #5 — MELTS UNWANTED INTERNAL SCAR TISSUE

Vitamin E has the miracle youth function of helping to prevent production of excessive scar tissues; it also is able to help melt away unwanted internal and external scars.

YOUTH SECRET #6 — HELPS DILATE BLOOD VESSELS

Vitamin E is a dilator of blood vessels. By opening up the body's vascular network, it enables blood to flow more freely, so that the entire organism can be nourished and kept youthfully healthy with this free-flowing lifestream. This helps open up new pathways in the circulatory system to guard against clots and problems of hardening of the arteries.

YOUTH SECRET #7 — PROTECTS AGAINST AGING

Vitamin E promotes an antioxidation process in the system which helps protect against aging. It is noted that the aging process is initiated by the interaction between certain substances which create free radicals or root endings circulating in the system. This type of peroxidation is the forerunner of cellular deterioration that predisposes to aging. Vitamin E plays a youthful role in preventing oxygen from combining with essential fatty acids to form the age-causing peroxides or radicals. It may be the key to "preventive aging" as offered by this miracle vitamin found in foods.

YOUTH SECRET #8 —
SOOTHES THE EYES

In a reported situation, Jeannette McC. was troubled with dimming eyesight. She had excessive watering from the eyes which was embarrassing. She was told that at her age (86), she would have to expect sight deterioration. Jeannette McC. decided to use natural Vitamin E. She applied a coating of this vitamin to her eyelids and let it become absorbed throughout the night. After three days, she reported that her eyesight improved and went "back to normal" and that the watering ended. Her eyes felt better and at her so-called advanced age, she could see better than youngsters, thanks to the external use of Vitamin E.

YOUTH SECRET #9 —
HELPS HEAL BURNS

The "quick healing power" of young people is restored to grownups, thanks to Vitamin E. In a reported situation, Helen A. turned on the hot water which came out with a spurt and hit her on the ankle. It caused a red and partly blistered spot larger than a dollar. Helen A. applied liquid Vitamin E to the burned area and it was "painless' as if nothing had touched her ankle. The burn healed rapidly, as it would to a youngster.

YOUTH SECRET #10 —
REJUVENATES SKIN

At age 80, Frances F. was troubled with eczema that suggested forms of psoriasis. Considering her age, it was believed that nothing could help her recover or experience any form of rejuvenation. Frances F. was told that Vitamin E could well stimulate the processes within her system that would promote skin rejuvenation. She went on a simple program by which she increased her intake of Vitamin E in cold-processed oils and lots of fresh fruits and vegetables, as well as eating seeds and nuts. Frances F. followed this easy and *all-natural* program for several months. Soon, she was completely free of any signs of eczema or so-called psoriasis. Her scalp, which had been entirely covered, and her body which had large blotches, became healed. She knows that Vitamin E promoted this rejuvenation since she took nothing else. It was a natural miracle of a natural vitamin in everyday foods.

YOUTH SECRET #11 —
HELPS STRENGTHEN THE HEART

Vitamin E in foods appears to resemble the action of digitalis, a drug administered to strengthen weakening or ailing hearts. It is possible that when foods with Vitamin E are made part of the daily program, it can be the natural way to strengthen the heart and keep it youthfully healthy.

YOUTH SECRET #12 —
IMPROVES TISSUE OXYGENATION

Vitamin E helps guard against the aging problem of oxygen deficiency. It nourishes the tissues with "youth giving" oxygen. It is unique in that it is one of the active components of the terminal respirating chain in the mammalian skeletal and heart muscle tissue.

YOUTH SECRET #13 —
PROTECTS AGAINST THROMBOSIS

Vitamin E helps, safely and naturally, to promote a youthful and thrombus (clot) free bloodstream. It is able to act on the atravascular clots already formed and help bring about dissolution. It is safe because it is natural. Many chemicalized anticoagulants may cause side effects and clash with other processes in the body. But Vitamin E is the natural way to protect against thrombosis.

YOUTH SECRET #14 —
BOOSTS YOUTHFUL MUSCULAR RESPONSE

The action of Vitamin E on the muscles is believed to be due to increased utilization of oxygen by the muscle. This is helpful to more than just body muscles but to the heart, too, because it is a muscle. Well-nourished muscles can give youthful health to the body, thanks to Vitamin E.

YOUTH SECRET #15 —
IMPROVES CAPILLARY WALLS

Aging brings with it problems of inflammatory and degenerative processes of the body's capillary-cellular walls. Vitamin E is able to help nourish these walls, thoroughly oxygenate them, and to help delay or even reverse the aging process by rejuvenating the circulatory mechanism.

YOUTH SECRET #16 —
CONTROLS CHOLESTEROL

The aging problem of cholesterol on the arteries can be controlled with Vitamin E which helps "wash" away the thick porridge that accumulates in and on the arterial walls of the body. When Vitamin E promotes better "cholesterol washing," the body's arteries become clean and youthfully resilient. Life then becomes beautiful!

YOUTH SECRET #17 —
REJUVENATES LEGS

Vitamin E is known for being able to increase collateral circulation around the deep, obstructed veins of the legs. Often, problems of varicose veins can be relieved or even prevented if the body is adequately nourished with Vitamin E. This natural vitamin decreases ankle congestion, soothes leg ache, halts varicose progression, reduces skin irritation, promotes better flexibility of the legs, helps bulging veins to regress. Limbered up youthful legs may be the reward of sufficient Vitamin E.

YOUTH SECRET #18 —
BETTER SUGAR METABOLISM

Vitamin E may help duplicate the action of insulin in controlling glucose levels and protecting against sugar imbalances that lead to problems, such as diabetes. Vitamin E appears to help the pancreas metabolize sugar and spares the use of insulin. It is a natural regulator.

YOUTH SECRET #19 —
SOOTHES CHEST PAINS

Also known as angina pectoris, problems of chest pains can be relieved by making available more oxygen. In particular, the oxygen need is very great after undue excitement, exertion or after eating a heavy meal. Vitamin E offers a double benefit: it helps increase heart blood flow and then reduces oxygen need. This helps soothe chest pains.

YOUTH SECRET #20 —
CREATES YOUTHFUL REJUVENATION

Vitamin E sets off a biological process so that the body is better able to assimilate and utilize protein. The youth vitamin also helps improve the nitrogen balance of the system, which is a key to self-regeneration. Vitamin E helps reduce the level of serum cholesterol deposits, boost calcium absorption and *protect* against the metabolic changes usually associated with age. This helps ease the formation of so-called aging ailments such as arthritis, hypertension, osteoporosis and arteriosclerosis. Vitamin E maintains better metabolism and thereby helps guard against the aging process.

YOUTH SECRET #21 —
IMPROVES VASCULAR HEALTH

A unique secret of Vitamin E is its ability to promote "collateral circulation" which means simply that when an artery or a smaller blood vessel is blocked, this vitamin helps the body create a new artery around the aging portion. This improves the health of the body's blood vessels and promotes better health and youthful vitality.

YOUTH SECRET #22 —
ERASES LEG CRAMPS

In problems of *intermittent claudication,* in which there are leg cramps making it difficult or uncomfortable to walk (a symptom of hardening of the arteries), Vitamin E is helpful in opening up blockages and thereby helping to send a fresh stream of blood through the arteries. This helps erase problems of leg cramps.

YOUTH SECRET #23 —
MUSCULAR STRENGTH

Vitamin E is able to help bring about the synthesis of a substance called *acetylcholine* from choline and acetate (B-complex vitamins). The body then takes up this extracted substance to help correct and ease the muscular weakness and wasting that is often symptomatic of advancing age. It helps strengthen the body's muscles and promote a feeling of youthful vigor.

YOUTH SECRET #24 —
NATURAL DIURETIC

In situations of internal toxemia or congestion, a self-cleansing is healthful to rid the body of accumulated wastes. Vitamin E appears to initiate this biological process so that a natural diuretic and self-cleansing process is created. This helps free the body of accumulated wastes. A clean body is a youthful body, thanks to Vitamin E.

YOUTH SECRET #25 —
CELLULAR REJUVENATION

Vitamin E helps provide a breath of cellular life and youth throughout the body. It is a natural lipid anti-oxidant which helps wash the body's cells and tissues, helps give them needed oxygen, helps protect against the age-causing debris and guard against cellular destruction. Vitamin E is the guardian of the body's cells and the undisputed key to better health and vigor.

HOW TO FEED YOURSELF
THE YOUTH VITAMIN

Plant Sources: Nature has put Vitamin E in many plant foods. The largest naturally occurring potency of Vitamin E is in *wheat germ oil.* You can feed yourself a treasure of this golden youth vitamin by using cold-pressed non-processed wheat germ oil in salad dressings, in cooking, or anywhere that a recipe calls for the use of fat. Take one tablespoon of wheat germ oil in a glass of fresh vegetable juice for a powerhouse of the youth Vitamin E. Other plant sources include barley, navy beans, celery, corn, endive, wheat, kale, olives, parsley, peanuts, peas, rye products, sunflower seed products, safflower seed products.

Animal Sources: Vitamin E will also be found in beef, beef liver, veal, lamb, haddock, salmon, chicken, turkey, and most fish, although in smaller amounts. You would do your body a health favor by obtaining a *balance* of both plant and animal foods for the needed Vitamin E, among other nutrients, as well.

Select Natural, Nonprocessed Foods: Because modern milling and refining methods tend to bleach out and destroy much Vitamin E in foods, you will do well to select natural and non-processed foods. These are your prime sources of this healthful youth vitamin. Just select whole grain breads and cereals, wholesome fruits and vegetables. Replace much of your hard fat intake with the "soft fat" or the liquid oils of plants. These plant oils should be nonprocessed and cold-pressed polyunsaturates sold just about everywhere, in all health stores, as well as in most food markets. These are your prime sources of youth-building Vitamin E.

Good Sources: Salmon steak is a good source of Vitamin E. Whole grain oatmeal and most whole grain cereals, whole wheat flour products, unpolished natural brown rice, and most plant oils are your good sources of this healthful vitamin.

Ever since its discovery in 1922, this vitamin has been heralded as offering hope for youthful health and better living. Nature has created this vitamin and placed it in delicious, tasty foods. Now, it is up to you to reap the rewards of this healthful vitamin by eating the foods that are prime sources of youth and health.

MOST IMPORTANT

1. Vitamin E was isolated and identified in 1922 as having the power to promote youthful health.
2. This youth vitamin is found in most oils, grains, seeds, nuts,

plant foods. It has been officially recognized by the U.S. Government which recommends about 30 units daily as an absolute minimum.

3. Vitamin E in foods can offer you at least 25 youth secrets ranging from healing of skin wounds to sparing the body's use of oxygen and opening up constricted arteries.

4. To feed yourself the youth vitamin, obtain a balance of plant and animal and fish foods. Emphasize intake of natural and non-processed foods because refining methods tend to bleach out and destroy much Vitamin E.

5. The use of cold-pressed oils such as sunflower seed, safflower seed, wheat germ oil will give you ample fortification and protection against unnecessary aging through the internal healing of Vitamin E.

12

The Megavitamin Way to Emotional Health

Vitamins can be used as *natural tranquilizers*. An added benefit is that vitamins can do much, much more than soothe the nervous system. They can help correct the *cause* of the emotional upset and thereby bring about a natural healing so that the symptoms just melt away. Vitamins help correct the internal misbehavior of the body's delicate biochemical balance so that impulses and stimuli become more stable, more even, and the entire body responds with better emotional health. All this is possible when your body nourishes your mind with the miracle of Nature's organic vitamins as found in everyday foods.

THE VITAMIN THAT REPLACED "SHOCK TREATMENT"

The pioneering physicians who discovered the use of vitamins as therapy, Abram Hoffer, M.D. and Humphrey Osmond, M.D., tell of a typical situation[1] in which a simple, everyday vitamin replaced shock treatment and promoted healing.

Roger X. had become acutely ill (mentally), so that he had to be hospitalized. After several months of conventional treat-

[1] *How to Live with Schizophrenia,* University Books, New Hyde Park, New York, 1966.

ment which included shock treatment, Roger X. failed to respond. The doctors then substituted shock treatment with a natural method. They gave Roger X. huge doses of Vitamin B₃ (niacin), or several hundred times the normal daily requirement. Roger X. showed speedy improvement. Under this vitamin therapy, he recovered and then he could be discharged. Vitamin B₃ had actually replaced shock treatment and promoted the healing that other methods could not produce. This led the doctors to explore the avenues of healing by using nutritional methods under close supervision.

How Megavitamin-Orthomolecular Treatment Is Helpful

The secret of the success of vitamin treatment lies in the name given to this method. *Mega* means "large" or "more" so *megavitamin* means "more vitamins." *Ortho* means "straight" or "corrective" so *orthomolecular* means "corrective molecules" or "corrective organization" within the body. The benefit of the megavitamin therapy is to help balance faulty body biochemistry that may cause emotional unrest as a symptom of error. Drs. Hoffer and Osmond believe that when supervised supplementary programs are administered, the body's biological balance can be corrected and better health is then possible. This also includes better emotional and mental health. It is the natural way to help boost healing of nervous disorders with vitamins.

This means that vitamins help to adjust body nutrition so that the right molecules reach the right places, permitting the complex biochemical reactions within the brain to proceed more healthfully. Once vitamins have put body molecules in their proper niches, the system is able to function smoothly and there is healing of disorders and more soothing emotional tranquility.

Two Vitamins That Control Emotional Health

While emotional and body health require a balance of all nutrients, it appears that two vitamins have more decisive influence upon emotional health. These are the B-complex family and Vitamin C. The megavitamin program frequently calls for increased intake of these vitamins under supervision, together with a general nutritional improvement plan. When the body is fortified with the B-complex vitamins and Vitamin C, then the mind responds with better health and strength. In effect, these two vitamins may be called "Nature's tranquilizers."

THE VITAMIN THAT PROMOTED MENTAL HEALTH

In a reported situation, Irene Z. was so emotionally troubled that she required hospitalization. She took medication but reported that it did not keep her nerves under control. Furthermore, it kept her in a state of complete fatigue. She then started a very simple program. She increased intake of Vitamin B_3 or niacin. She reports that just taking this vitamin gave her a vitality in her body that nothing else could create. Vitamin B_3 helped her to concentrate and think more clearly. She started to get her self-confidence back and her attitudes toward other people became more friendly. She was able to share experiences, relate to people and start living again. Irene Z. feels that it was Vitamin B_3 that helped act as a natural tranquilizer. But more important, the vitamin corrected the *cause* of her emotional unrest and brought about corrective healing.

Food Sources

A powerhouse of Vitamin B_3 or niacin is found in a simple food known as Brewer's yeast. Sprinkle it over your whole grain breakfast cereals. Use it as a coating for lean meats or liver for double-barreled niacin fortification. Also use soybeans, wheat germ, whole grain breads. But a highly concentrated amount of Vitamin B_3 or niacin is found in Brewer's yeast, the simple but very effective natural tranquilizer.

THE VITAMIN PROGRAM THAT HEALED "CHRONIC" ILLNESS

Margaret D., reportedly suffered from a chronic emotional illness for 16 years. After tests by Drs. Hoffer and Osmond, it was believed that a defect in her body chemistry had created a poison in her system due to a malfunction of the adrenal glands or the liver. Margaret D. was put on a supervised megavitamin program with the goal to mop up the poison which could cause distortion of the senses, thoughts and moods.

Vitamin Healers

She was told to take 3000 milligrams daily of niacin and 3000 milligrams daily of Vitamin C. She also took Vitamins B_1, B_2, B_6, B_{12} and Vitamin E together with minerals. It took a considerable length of time before her emotional upheaval was soothed. Soon, the vitamins had corrected her faulty biological imbalance and her "chronic" illness could be considered cleared up.

Margaret D. says that this megavitamin program appeared to "mop up" the toxins out of her system. The vitamins promoted this mopping up or cleansing and once the toxins were reduced, her imbalance could be straightened out. Vitamins acted as natural healers and promoted needed reactions that made Margaret D. a well person.

THE MIRACLE "MIND HEALING" EFFECTIVENESS OF VITAMIN B_{12}

A psychiatrist, H.L. Newbold, M.D., tells of treating a 33 year old Ph.D. candidate who had suffered a psychotic breakdown two years before appearing for treatment. Dr. Newbold reports[2] that the student was completely out of touch with reality. He complained of a snapping sensation in his head. His conception of space was that it was very brief and he felt very tiny. Hospitalized and given tranquilizers, his symptoms eased but he still felt lethargic, lonely and insecure. He could not work on his thesis. Psychoanalysis did not produce desired benefits.

Corrective Nutrition Promotes Miracle Healing

Tests showed the student was very deficient in Vitamin B_{12}. He was given administered supplements. Within a short time, the young man said that he felt a "remarkable improvement." Gradually, with more Vitamin B_{12} supplementation, his emotional distress became healed. His memory improved. His learning ability was restored. Soon, he could participate in his class activities, and returned to work on his Ph.D. thesis. When Vitamin B_{12} was less frequently administered, he became tired and depressed. This could be corrected with more Vitamin B_{12}. In effect, this corrective nutrition did give the desired healing effects. It was the natural way to help heal the mind and make life worth living again.

HOW VITAMINS HELPED HEAL SENILITY

In a reported case,[3] Douglas Vann, M.D., tells of Mary H., an 84-year-old woman with symptoms of senility who was in a geriatric ward. She was diagnosed as being "grossly psychotic and demented." Then Mary H. was put on a nutritional program. Daily, she was given both folic acid and Vitamin B_{12}.

Vitamins Banish Senility: This vitamin-therapy produced "an unexpectedly rapid return to intellectual and behavioral normality, but with almost complete amnesia for the period of psychosis and dementia . . . She (now) lives in her daughter's home amongst half a dozen grandchildren, whose behavior toward her and in their own lives is entirely natural, and which she and they thoroughly enjoy." It is apparent that the vitamins helped restore her emotional health and eventually corrected problems of senility.

Food Sources of Senile-Healing Vitamins: Folic acid is found in Brewer's yeast and most leafy green vegetables. Vitamin B_{12} is found in liver, kidney, milk, salt-water fish, lean meats, soybeans. To fortify your body (and your mind) with these vitamins, it is healthful to eat them throughout the week.

Mind Healing Tonic: In a green vegetable juice, mix one tablespoon of Brewer's yeast and one tablespoon of desiccated liver. Stir vigorously. Add a bit of honey for extra taste. This Mind Healing Tonic is a powerhouse of nearly all-known B-complex vitamins but it is one of the richest sources of folic acid and B_{12}. In combination, these vitamins help correct biological error

[3] "Vitamins and Senility," *Medical Journal of Australia*, Nov. 11, 1972, Australia.

and "straighten" out the chemical processes in your body to help soothe and heal your mind.

Whole Liver: This is considered so rich in all known B-complex vitamins that it is the most natural "supplement" you can take. It would be body and mind soothing to eat broiled liver at least twice weekly. Folks who dislike the taste of liver can enter a world of taste thrill by preparing it in this simple manner:

Rub both sides of the liver with a juicy lemon slice. You can further "cut" the disliked livery taste by pouring lemon juice over the liver. Then coat it with a mixture of Brewer's yeast, unbleached flour, kelp (sea salt), paprika, some sunflower seeds.

In a pan, add three tablespoons of wheat germ oil. Heat. Now sear the liver slices for about five minutes on each side. You will see that the outside looks deliciously crusty. The inside will be juicy tender and flavorful.

When eating, include a tossed raw green vegetable salad and whole grain bread slices.

Benefits: You will be feeding yourself a treasure of the needed B-complex vitamins as well as Vitamin C and necessary minerals and proteins. This adds up to a supply of important nutrients that help correct any imbalance in your system and regulate emotional health.

VITAMINS THAT ACT AS BRAIN FOODS

Your brain is composed largely of nerve cells. There are nerve centers in the brain that control regulatory or automatic functions such as breathing, heartbeat, thinking, circulation, and so forth. Every move and every thought is governed by these brain-nerve cells. These cells need nourishment, just like other body cells. Your body supplies your brain with the fuel it needs from foods taken in and through metabolism. The B-complex vitamins such as thiamine, niacin, B_{12}, pantothenic acid, enter into the nourishment of your brain-nerve cells.

"Brain vitamins" are found in whole grain, non-processed wheat products, beans and peas, nuts and seeds, whole grain cereals, meat, eggs. Cold-pressed polyunsaturated oils will also give you appreciable amounts of such vitamins.

Mind-Feeding Vitamins

Niacin helps invigorate the health of the brain-nerve system and helps your cells metabolize other nutrients that enter into mind-feeding. Good niacin sources include organic peanut or any nut butters, whole grain bread and cereal products, wheat germ and all products such as oils made from wheat germ, Brewer's yeast. These are everyday foods but they have the unique ability of nourishing your mind to give you everyday vitality and a youthful emotional outlook.

The Vitamin That Heals Neuritis

Because so many emotional upsets start with "simple neuritis," it is essential to seek vitamin help for the problem as soon as warning symptoms are noticeable.

Usually, neuritis can be corrected as soon as Vitamin B_1 or thiamine is added to the food program. You can very easily do this by increasing your use of wheat germ and also Brewer's yeast. Thiamine goes to work to help soothe emotional upset, to help heal problems of recurring numbness and those vague, fleeting pains that may be felt in your hands, feet or shoulders. Thiamine is the vitamin that can help correct the biological imbalance that causes such symptomatic reactions of neuritis.

The emphasis here is on *unbleached* grains since these are your prime sources of thiamine and other B-complex vitamins. (Milling and refining will remove them.) Just eat a whole grain breakfast cereal sprinkled with Brewer's yeast and wheat germ, and fresh fruit, and you've got a good supply of thiamine and other needed vitamins to help soothe and protect your nervous system.

HOW TO BRIGHTEN UP THOSE BLUE MOODS WITH NATURE'S VITAMINS

If you have "blue moods" on Mondays (or any other time), it is Nature's suggestion that you need a boosting of simple vitamins. To brighten up those feelings of lethargy, poor energy or depression, here are some suggestions:

Perk Up with Pantothenic Acid

This B-complex vitamin is essential for the metabolism of carbohydrates and fats so that the nervous system is properly nourished. It influences the adrenal glands to secrete needed hormones for better disposition. Pantothenic acid is the vitamin that gives an antihistaminic effect to help resist allergies (often a symptom of a nervous disorder). Pantothenic acid also sparks intestinal bacteria to synthesize other B-complex vitamins in a complex chain that helps make a better emotional outlook. So a pantothenic acid deficiency may mean a B-complex deficiency which spells blue moods.

To perk up with this B-complex vitamin, just add Brewer's yeast or unbleached wheat germ to a bowl of soup or in a meat loaf, or in a glass of vegetable juice. Other good pantothenic acid foods are egg yolk, rice bran, salmon, peanuts, broccoli, soybeans.

How Niacin Helps Put a
Smile on Your Face

Body metabolism uses this vitamin to convert food into energy-yielding reactions to influence the nervous system and the connected brain cells. This makes you feel much better and you'll feel inclined to have a smile on your face. In particular, niacin will help spark the body defense mechanisms to guard you against such distressing problems as insomnia, irritability, poor appetite, neurasthena, anxiety, vertigo, chronic fatigue, a feeling of numbness in some body parts, headaches, depressive melancholy. Niacin can help transform a tired, apprehensive and gloomy person into one who looks upon everything with more optimistic cheer and pleasantness. A problem is that niacin, like the other B-complex vitamins, is easily perishable. Refining processes of grains will strip away this needed "smile vitamin." A simple trick is to eat non-refined and non-processed grains.

To help put a smile on your face, eat niacin in such delicious and everyday foods as wheat bran, Brewer's yeast, turkey, fresh liver, peanut butter, roasted peanuts, beef kidney, veal chops, among other foods. You will help give your body the needed nourishment to help make life cheerful and a smile will appear on your face.

Thiamine Brightens Up Your Moods

This everyday vitamin is known for being a natural "gloom chaser." Thiamine or Vitamin B_1, also known as the "morale vitamin" helps protect your nerves against fraying. It acts as a helper or coenzyme in many important energy-yielding reactions in the body. It "coats" your nervous system to guard against fraying and when your nerves are resilient and strong, you'll be able to wipe away gloom and feel brightened up at almost any age. Thiamine helps protect you against feeling cross or irritable, protects you against fatigue or energy loss.

Because thiamine is water-soluble, you lose much in cooking at high temperatures. *Avoid* products made with baking soda or bicarbonate soda as these chemicals destroy thiamine in your system. Thiamine, like the other B-complex vitamins, as well as Vitamin C, is *not* stored in your body. So you need some every single day. It's necessary for body health and for mind health since the two are so closely interrelated.

To help brighten up your moods, eat thiamine in non-processed grains, natural brown rice, Brewer's yeast, soybeans, whole grain bread products. Just be sure that the product is unbleached for good thiamine mood-brightening benefits. It's Nature's tasty way to help improve your disposition and make you feel bright, cheerful and happy. Remember that *thiamine* is found in the *germ* of cereal grains and also in the *outer coatings*. So your grain products should be unbleached since refining will strip away these two treasured sources of thiamine. If you plan on making natural brown rice, then use wheat germ and Brewer's yeast as "fillers" and you'll be rewarding your body with a tremendous supply of the needed vitamins that help you perk up, enjoy a smile on your face and brighten up your moods.

IN REVIEW

1. Vitamins can be used as natural tranquilizers. Roger X. was saved from further shock treatment by being treated with a vitamin. The megavitamin-orthomolecular treatment helps nourish the body and improve emotional health.
2. Irene Z. recovered from hospitalized emotional illness by receiving an increased intake of a simple B-complex vitamin.

3. Margaret D. recovered from "chronic" mental illness on a simple and all-natural vitamin program.

4. A 33-year old student recovered from hospitalized psychotic breakdown by a vitaminization program that healed his mind.

5. Mary H. was rescued from hopeless senility at age 84 on a nutritional program of just two basic vitamins.

6. Do yourself a favor and enjoy the Mind Healing Tonic. Whole liver, prepared as directed, can give you nutritional-flavor plus that it is good for your stomach and your mind, too.

7. Vitamins can act as brain foods. Heal neuritis, brighten up your blue moods, perk up your disposition with the described vitamin-rich foods that make life very beautiful.

8. Orthomolecular psychiatry or the use of megavitamins is helpful by supplementing and *not* replacing therapeutic treatments. Megavitamins are helpful when they are auxiliary to the other therapeutic and prophylactic measures used by psychiatrists.

13

How Raw Food Vitamins Help Rebuild Your Digestive System

Living vitamins found in *living foods* can help put *living health* into your digestive system. Raw foods are sources of dynamic vitamins that are used by enzymes for the rebuilding of your digestive system. This Nature-created combination of vitamin-enzyme action causes what is known as a *Double AA Value*. The vitamins in raw foods will *activate* and *amplify* the action of enzymes so that they can promote better digestive health. This Double AA Value of better vitamin-enzyme activation and amplification can then trigger off a set of biological chain reactions so that ingested food is acted upon. This Double AA Value acts upon food, extracting their vitamins, minerals, proteins, essential fatty acids, carbohydrates, liquids and other trace elements, to be used in building and rebuilding your digestive (and body) health. Without living vitamins in living foods, this process would be sharply reduced. Health would be reduced, too. Nature has put these living vitamins in an assortment of raw foods for your digestive and body health. The Double AA Value is the key to youthful health.

THE SECRET "VITA-ZYME" THAT HOLDS THE KEY TO YOUTHFUL HEALTH

Raw foods contain a secret or mysterious substance that reportedly holds the key to youthful health. It is a combination of vitamins and enzymes. Known as an *auxone,* this vita-zyme has the unique power of speeding up almost all known biological processes within your system. Without this vita-zyme, or *auxone,* found exclusively in *raw foods,* your digestive-assimilative processes would either slow up or halt completely. But Nature has put the vita-zyme into raw foods for your eating pleasure and health benefits. When you eat a luscious raw fruit or vegetable, or when you drink a fresh raw fruit, you send a powerhouse of digestive boosting vita-zymes shooting through your system. They go to work speedily to metabolize and assimilate other nutrients to nourish and rebuild your body from head to toe. The secret or little-known vita-zyme holds the power of furnishing energy for your breathing, giving vigor to your heart so it can pump blood, transmit nerve impulses and influence better digestive action. Vita-zymes are found almost exclusively in raw foods.

The Miracle of Organic Vita-zymes

Raw food vitamin created enzymes or "vita-zymes" are catalysts because they have the ability to create a digestive-biological reacton without themselves being transformed or destroyed in the process. Vita-zymes are spark plugs that energize the biological healing mechanisms of your body. When you eat raw foods or drink raw plant juices, the vita-zymes go to work to transform substances into nerves, bones, glands, muscles. The vita-zymes help store substances in your organs or glands for future use. The vita-zymes also metabolize minerals into bone and nerve; they help repair iron in your blood cells; they help promote healing; they serve to decompose toxic hydrogen peroxide and liberate digestive-rejuvenating oxygen; they create an oxidation process by joining oxygen with other elements to facilitate better respiration as well as digestive mobility; they help change toxic substances in the tissues and blood into a form of urea so that they can be eliminated from the blood and waste channels of the body and create better health. These vita-zymes are tremendous powerhouses of youth-building health.

SEVEN LITTLE-KNOWN FOOD SOURCES OF YOUTH-BUILDING VITA-ZYMES

These *auxones* or "acceleration substances" known as vita-zymes hold the key to digestive rejuvenation. They are found in these seven all-natural, everyday foods:

1. *Raw Fruits.*   Fresh raw fruits are prime sources of these vita-zymes that help rebuild your digestive system and promote better elimination.

2. *Raw Vegetables.*   Fresh raw vegetables contain vita-zymes that are used to maintain better blood health, offer needed roughage for better regulation and help nourish cells and tissues from head to toe.

3. *Raw Grains.*   Fresh raw grains in cereals or uncooked grain meals are prime sources of vita-zymes that use essential fatty acids for building better health of the internal organs.

4. *Raw Nuts.*   Fresh raw nuts are treasures of vita-zymes that prompt plant proteins to nourish the digestive system and to build and rebuild damaged cell networks through amino acid regeneration.

5. *Raw Seeds.*   Fresh raw seeds are almost complete sources of nutrition with nearly all known vita-zymes that help wash away accumulated wastes and control cholesterol deposits.

6. *Raw Oils.*   Fresh raw or non-processed and unrefined plant oils contain vital vita-zymes that protect against fat buildup and guard against cholesterol choking of the arteries and veins.

7. *Raw Juices.*   Fresh raw plant juices are prime sources of vita-zymes that are needed to spark the body's biological actions to assimilate all known vitamins, minerals, proteins and other elements so that life and health can continue.

Yes, raw foods contain the unique combination of vitamins and enzymes that offer you self-renewal through self-regeneration. If you want to experience the miracle of organic health, your food program should include *raw foods daily.* You will be giving your digestive system the vita-zymes it needs for survival and sustenance . . . and your better health, too.

HOW VITA-ZYMES HELP CLEANSE YOUR COLON

Raw food vita-zymes hold the key to cleansing of the colon, and better digestive health. This lower bowel of the large intestine needs natural cleansing in order to protect against the buildup of infectious bacteria. Nature offers a natural cleanser in the form of raw food vita-zymes.

How Alfred J. Used Raw Foods for Natural Colon-Cleansing

Alfred J. had problems of colitis. He felt embarrassed because of the unpredictable behavior of his bowels. Alfred J. knew that much of his distress could be traced to irregular eating habits, gulping down his foods, careless selection of foods, too. But he lived a super-active life as a salesman of roofing products and was always on the go. He also loved cooked foods. Only when his colitis became so unbearable, did he decide to use natural methods, advised by some friends, to promote healing.

Simple Colon-Cleansing Program

Alfred J. would begin each of his three daily meals with a *raw food*. For breakfast, he would begin with a raw fruit salad. For lunch, he would have a raw fruit or raw vegetable salad. For dinner, he would begin with a raw vegetable salad.

Alfred J. would partake of cooked foods but only *after* having had his raw food. It took just six days of this easy program for this salesman to enjoy superhealth by having had his colon cleansed. His colitis subsided and soon was healed. Alfred J. was able to enjoy better digestive health, thanks to *beginning* each meal with either a raw fruit or vegetable salad. Simple, yes. Effective, definitely!

HOW A RAW FOOD AT A MEAL'S BEGINNING IS A MIRACLE OF HEALING

Raw foods contain vita-zymes that help restore healing conditions that are essential to digestive health. When you *begin* a meal with raw foods, the vita-zymes can go to work to *prepare* your digestive system for the work ahead, without interference of food that has yet to be introduced. The vita-zymes then help regenerate the regulative systems so that foods to follow can be better metabolized, and nutrients from the foods (whether cooked or raw) can be better assimilated.

Establish Healing Environment

Raw food vita-zymes establish an anaerobic environment right in your digestive-intestinal tract. This environment helps beneficial coli bacteria grow and multiply and thus chase away the pathogenic or destructive ones. This environment is of enormous value in helping to maintain a cleansed digestive system that can give you *better assimilation,* which is the *key* to better health.

Vita-zymes in raw foods help protect you against digestive leucocytosis, which is a mobilization of white blood corpuscles and their concentration in the intestinal walls. When you *begin* a meal with raw foods, the vita-zymes speedily work to help control digestive leucocytosis so that white blood corpuscles are freed and can then perform other biological tasks; the vita-zymes help save the body the effort of a defensive action and thereby improves digestive-assimilation power.

If you eat raw foods *after* a meal, the vita-zymes are ineffective because the leucocytosis has already begun and impeded digestion. To the amazingly simple secret of better digestive health is this one: *Begin each meal with a raw food. You may eat cooked food after you have finished your raw food.*

HOW RAW FOOD VITA-ZYMES REJUVENATE YOUR SYSTEM

Raw food vita-zymes hold the key to rejuvenation by protecting against digestive leucocytosis. When you eat a raw food at the *start* of a meal, the vita-zymes then create an increase in the micro-electric vibrations of the cell tissues throughout the body and bring about repair and regeneration. Only raw food vita-zymes can create this process of cellular rejuvenation.

Once vita-zymes create the micro-electric vibrations, then cell respiration improves, cell metabolism is stimulated. The ability of resistance to aging is improved. Vita-zymes boost functions of the body's metabolism so that the billions of cells and tissues can be nourished and made healthy and youthful. Nature has put vita-zymes in raw foods to help create this youthful function.

MAGIC GREEN DRINK — VITA-ZYME REVITALIZER

Betty N. was troubled with embarrassing constipation. Other times, her stomach reacted to much of what she ate. There were recurring stomach pains that kept her awake much of the night. Often, whatever she ate, settled in her stomach "like a lump" and created bloating discomfort. Betty N. ate cooked foods regularly. On occasion, she would drink raw fruit juices. She also liked raw plant juices. These helped ease her symptoms. They also helped correct her constipation and contented her stomach so that she felt better. But when she mixed *raw vegetable juices* in a natural elixir, she discovered that her symptoms vanished. More important, when she *began* a meal with this Magic Green Drink, Betty N. could digest her food much better. Foodtime became funtime when she *began* with a simple Magic Green Drink. Now she enjoys life with a happy stomach.

How to Make a Magic Green Drink

In a juice extractor or a blender, put *washed* green vegetables of any variety. You may enjoy lettuce, scallions, watercress, sweet peppers, celery, cabbage, chard, kale, cucumber, parsley, green peas, collards, or any other *washed green vegetables*. Juice or blend the vegetables until you have a liquid. Then drink one or two glasses of this *Magic Green Drink* before a meal. Or just drink it as a natural stomach-soothing tonic. It is the natural way to help rebuild your digestive system.

Why Magic Green Drink Is
a Miracle of Health

The vita-zymes in raw green plants are prime sources of healing properties. Raw green plant vita-zymes help promote the formation of blood cells, stimulate respiration-nitrogenous metabolism of the cellular network. This helps boost the metabolism of protein into amino acids. The vita-zymes in the *Magic Green Drink* help stabilize blood pressure and improve the circulatory process. In particular, the vita-zymes will help create a soothing acid-alkaline ratio after food combustion. A unique benefit is that the vita-zymes do this very rapidly so that the digestive system is speedily soothed and then made receptive to the barrage of food to follow. The *Magic Green Drink* is a treasure of these vita-zymes that are needed to help rebuild and regenerate the components of the digestive system, which is often considered the "core" of good health. Green vegetables are prime sources of these special vita-zymes, unlike any other nutrients. That is why the *Magic Green Drink* is Nature's supreme health tonic and secret rejuvenator. It is the key to better health.

RAW GRAINS, NUTS, SEEDS —
DIGESTIVE REJUVENATION

Raw grains such as whole groats, flaxseed, rye, wheat germ, yeast flakes and raw nuts and seeds are prime sources of valuable vitamins and minerals, together with enzymes and proteins that add up to a feast of digestive rejuvenation.

Vita-zyme Potency. These raw foods are prime sources of Vitamins A through E as well as many minerals, plant proteins, together with natural enzymes. They offer a potency of vita-zymes that help preserve the youthful ratio of intestinal bacterial flora. They are flavorful, while imparting a shower of vita-zymes in the digestive system. They are potent sources of Nature's miracle vitamins, among other nutrients, needed to keep your digestive system youthful.

Vita-Zyme Healing Properties. When you eat a raw grain, nut or seed, you eat *live* food with Nature-created vita-zymes. These are botanical fruits of Nature, with the means of self-sustenance. These grains, nuts or seeds contain within their shells nearly all the elements needed for their own survival and nourishment. Archeologists have often unearthed such foods from thousands of years ago and discovered them to be fertile, alive and youthful. Nature has given the secret of *eternal life* to these grains, nuts and seeds. Now, Nature gives them to you to help feed your digestive system with the valuable vita-zymes. Generally speaking, these plant foods are wholesome, healthful, free of those tissue wastes and animal fats which abound in animal foods. The nutritive value of such foods may often be higher, biologically speaking, than most other edibles. Nature offers you a wide assortment of these grains, nuts or seeds for your health.

Program: Daily, eat whole grain cereals, eat raw nuts or raw seeds. You will find them in almost any health store, and just about every large food market. Plan to eat them daily. Chew them *thoroughly* because they are concentrated sources of vita-zymes. You have to release this treasure of nutrients which is possible by chewing. You will thus be feeding your digestive system the needed vita-zymes that are found in these raw foods as created by Nature.

Avoid roasted grains, nuts or seeds as this refining process has depleted much vita-zyme potency. Emphasize *raw* clean foods for good health.

THE EASY WAY TO FEED VITA-ZYMES TO YOUR DIGESTIVE SYSTEM

To put "life" into your digestive system, use "life" foods such as raw plants. Here is an easy program to follow. It helps supercharge your body from head to toe with youth-regenerating vita-zymes:

1. *Raw Foods Are First.*   Eat raw what can be eaten raw. Cook *only* those foods that must be cooked. *Begin* each meal with a raw fruit or vegetable salad or a raw plant juice.

2. *Use Cold-Pressed Plant Oils.*   The juice of seeds and nuts are known as oils. Safflower, corn, soy, wheat germ, sunflower, olive, and many others are prime sources of vita-zymes. Select the polyunsaturated cold-pressed oils that have *not* been heated or chemically treated (these processes destroy vita-zymes) that are available at almost any health store or large food market.

Use them freely as a substitute for hard fats in most recipes. If you must cook, do so briefly with the oils and discard after use.

3. *Keep Cooking to a Minimum.*   Cooking is destructive to many vitamins and some minerals. Enzymes are destroyed by temperatures over 120°F. For top-notch vita-zyme power, keep cooking to a minimum. If you eat a cooked meal, fortify yourself with "vita-zyme insurance" by starting with a raw salad or juice. Most animal products require cooking; but most plant foods do *not* so you keep cooking to a minimum and enjoy better vita-zyme rejuvenation.

4. *Salads Are Luscious.*   Raw fruit and vegetable salads are luscious sources of vita-zymes. Emphasize greens as these are richer in vita-zymes. Sprinkle with fresh fruit juice and a dab of honey for flavor-boost and nutrition-boost.

5. *How to Preserve Vita-Zyme Potency.*   Plan to buy fresh, raw vegetables. At home, wash the greens beneath free flowing cold water, drain, and plan to serve promptly. If you must store, put in a covered container in your refrigerator. If the plants have stems, then store them with the *stem ends down* so you'll get more vita-zyme potency out of them.

6. *Root Vegetables Are Vita-Zyme Powerhouses.*   Root vegetables appear to have greater vita-zyme potency than the others; of course, you should eat a variety for good health. Emphasize such root vegetables as beets, turnips, kohlrabi, carrots, celery root, salsify.

7. *Enjoy Vita-Zyme Root Fruits.*   Root fruits are higher in vita-zymes than others. Again, enjoy a balance. Enjoy root fruits such as tomatoes, cantaloupe, watermelon, honeydew. Also enjoy their freshly made raw juices for more vita-zyme fortification.

8. *Wash But Do Not Soak Plant Foods.*   To preserve vita-zyme potency, wash your plant foods but NEVER soak them since this drains out valuable nutrients. Instead, wash speedily in cold water, drain in a salad basket (or whirl in an old but clean pillow case) and then serve promptly. If you must store, cover with a towel or plastic bag and place in your refrigerator.

9. *Salad Dressings Can Be Healthful.*   Boost flavor and vita-zyme potency with a nutritious salad dressing. Just mix apple cider vinegar with honey and a sprinkle of lemon juice. You may prepare your salad dressing ahead, but do *not* add the dressing

until just before serving your salad. A tip is that a few moments before you are ready to toss your salad and dressing, put the salad bowl in your freezer. Then remove. You'll have deliciously crisp salad with a dressing just applied before serving.

10. *Soaked Grains Are Great.*   Yes, the taste and vita-zyme potency in soaked grains are great. Just soak any desired grains (wheat, barley, oats, rye, or natural brown rice *uncooked*) in milk or fruit juice in your refrigerator *overnight*. Next morning, add a bit of wheat germ, or some grated apples, and you'll have a delicious breakfast that is brimming with vita-zymes.

11. *Vita-Zyme Breakfast.*   Give your body more "go power" with vita-zymes in the morning by making this raw breakfast. The night before, grind wheat and barley, place in a bowl, add water or milk, let soak overnight in your refrigerator. Next morning, add sliced fruits into the bowl. Sprinkle with Brewer's yeast and sun-dried raisins. Eat as a delicious vita-zyme breakfast that will help you "get up and go" and . . . keep going.

12. *Snack Your Way to Youthful Vigor.*   Enjoy a snack while you vita-zyme your digestive system. Instead of the processed and chemicalized sugary-salted plastic "foods," select raw seeds, raw nuts, raw sun-dried fruits. Munch on fresh raw fruit slices. To replenish yourself, just peel a banana and eat your way to better health!

13. *The "Soft Drink" That Is the Safe Drink.*   Most carbonated fizz or soft drinks are high in chemicals, caffeine and artificial flavors. They are either high in sugar or else contain chemicalized artificial sweeteners. They are hardly regarded as "safe" if you want to build your health. A "safe" soft drink is one made of any fresh fruit juices. Stir vigorously. To give a "tart" or "piquant" taste to most fruit juices, just add a bit of lemon juice. You'll have all the "kick" of a fizz drink, but this will be a "safe" and vita-zyme health-building drink.

14. *Go on a Raw Food Fast.*   To give "full speed ahead" working power to vita-zymes, go on a raw food fast. For one day, eat and drink a wide variety of raw foods. This simple fasting program will do much to completely replenish your digestive system with needed vita-zymes. They can work in rebuilding cells and tissues without the interference of hot foods. You'll emerge feeling glad all over.

15. *End Meals with Raw Foods.*   Frequently, end your meal with a raw plant food (just as you would begin a meal with a raw food). When you do both, begin and end with raw plant foods, you give your body the vita-zymes needed to metabolize food molecules so they become parts of your living structure. This process liberates energy that is needed to nourish your life. It is the "secret" of rebuilding your digestive system and giving yourself the hope and promise of forever youthful health.

For *living* health, rebuild your digestive system with *living* foods that are prime sources of Double AA Value (activate-amplify) vita-zymes.

IN A NUTSHELL

1. Raw foods contain an *auxone* or "vita-zyme" which is a unique youth-building vitamin-enzyme substance that can supercharge your body with vibrant health.
2. You can enjoy these organic vita-zymes in seven different everyday foods.
3. Alfred J. used raw foods as a natural colon-cleansing program and helped correct digestive unrest and embarrassing colitis.
4. For a miracle of healing, begin every meal with a raw plant food.
5. Raw food vita-zymes protect against digestive leucocytosis and thereby boost your digestive rejuvenation functions.
6. Betty N. used a simple Magic Green Drink and so improved her digestive powers she corrected her constipation and bloating problems, and has a happy stomach.
7. Raw grains, nuts and seeds offer vita-zymes for digestive regeneration. Eat them regularly. Good taste. Good health.
8. You have a variety of 15 different ways to feed vita-zymes to your digestive system. Enjoy good taste with good nutrition and a youthful contentment.

14

Health Secrets from the American Indians

The early American Indians who inhabited this continent long before the arrival of explorers knew how to use herbs, seeds, nuts, plants for healing and prolongation of youth. The Indians were unaware that these plants contained vitamins, as such, but they did know that these healing plants from the woods and oceans produced youthful restoration of vitality. They did not know why Nature's plant vitamins healed, but they knew they worked and used them as remedies. Many of the American Indians worshipped these plants for their miracles of healing. This gave rise to a mystical appreciation of these plants. With the arrival of settlers, this knowledge was shared.

Before long, both Indians and newcomers were sharing their health secrets of using plants for healing. As science developed, it was noted that nearly all of the Indian plant healers were rich in vitamins. This was the secret of their success. But to the Indian who worshipped these mystical plants of Nature, he was concerned solely with their effectiveness. If an Indian could heal himself with a plant of Nature, if he could heal others with a plant of Nature, then it was accepted in his way of life.

Today, there is an increasingly revived interest in these traditional healing secrets from the American Indian. They are considered secret because they were freely practiced by the

Indians but were shared with only a select few of the newly-arrived settlers. Many guarded their secrets with great jealousy. There were some who were amazed at the healing effectiveness of these plants and decided that since Nature had created these healers, they belonged freely to everyone. So began fragmented writings which explained how such plants could be used for healing. This rich heritage from the American Indians has come down to our present society. Today, we recognize that Nature's plants from the fields, woods, forests and oceans are prime sources of vitamins with healing qualities that have miracle-like powers of effectiveness. The American Indian was wise in realizing that if a plant could heal, it was accepted. This same approach will help many folks enjoy better healing and better health, thanks to the wisdom of the American Indian.

WHERE TO OBTAIN THE HEALING VITAMIN PLANTS OF THE AMERICAN INDIAN

Many of the following vitamin-containing plants are available at many food outlets. If the health secret calls for the use of a herb, seek out your local herbal pharmacist. Look in the classified telephone directory of the nearest large city under "Herbs" or "Spices" or "Botanicals" and contact the outlet for the particular vitamin plant listed.

How to Make a Herb Vitamin Potion

Here are two basic methods: (1) To make an infusion or tea, steep one teaspoon of the leaves or flowers in one cup of boiling water for five to ten minutes. Strain and drink. (2) To make a decoction, boil the roots and/or seeds in one cup of boiling water for 15 to 20 minutes. Then strain and drink.

How Much to Take: The American Indians took just one or two doses during the course of an illness. The American Indians prescribed about one pint of the particular vitamin-plant healing juice. They recognized that a *small* amount of the plant healing juice could cure, but a *large* amount could cause side effects. So they suggested using small amounts.

Their mystical or spiritual leaders who dispensed medicinal secrets also suggested a form of fasting during and after the use of such remedies. It was felt that the plants could provoke more healing benefits if the system was free of the competitive influence of other foods. An ailing Indian would then abstain from food for a day or two during this plant remedy program. He reportedly recovered at a much better rate.

These plant vitamins could promote better healing if they could function *without* interference of other foods. In our modern times, we recognize the healing effect of vitamins when they saturate body tissues and organs without conflict from other nutrients. The Indians recognized this secret, too, even though they did not identify the force as natural vitaminization.

Mystical Healing

The American Indian gathered many secrets about the edible and healing plants of Nature that flourished abundantly in his environment. The American Indian worshipped Nature as the source of life and health. He lived in mystical harmony with his natural environment. He paid homage to the plant vitamins because he knew they offered him miracles of healing. Indian mystics prophesied that with the destruction of Nature would come the destruction of man's health.

Today, we see that this prophesy is reaching partial fulfillment. With chemicalization of the environment, there is a destruction of vitamins and a loss of health. Just as modern man begins to depend upon chemicals for his survival, so did the American Indian depend upon plant vitamins of Nature for his survival. In the hopes that our environment can be saved and that Nature can be given a rightful role in building youthful health, here are some of the legendary vitamin-healing secrets of the American Indian.

These plants are available at most herbal pharmacies; the other foods listed on commonplace items available at almost any marketplace. With these vitaminized plants of healing, there is much hope for youthful survival in our chemical age.

VITAMIN PLANT HEALING SECRETS

Wounds and Cuts.   Central American Indians pulverized the root of the buttercup, soaked it in tepid water, then applied to wounds and cuts. The buttercup leaves were rubbed upon blemished skin. It is believed that the plant vitamins A and C promoted healing.

Bruises.   Boil the leaves of the balsam from sweet gum bark, and apply this to the injured area. The vitamin A content is healing to skin tissues. The Mississippi Choctaws worshipped this concoction for its miracle of healing.

Natural Antiseptic.   To disinfect wounds or cuts that might otherwise cause an infection, the Mohegan Indians used the wild indigo root. They would boil the root in water, and then use the liquid as a natural antiseptic wash. Vitamins A and B-complex help sterilize infections and reportedly protect against further deterioration.

Natural Dusting Powder.   For problems of itching or scaling skin (comparable to the modern problem of Athlete's Foot), the southwestern Indians such as the Navajos or Zunis would use the pinon nut. (Currently available as Indian nuts, pine nuts and also called pignolias. Sold in many nut shops or health food shoppes.) Pulverize the pinon nuts and then use the substance as a natural dusting powder. It reportedly has a high amount of skin-healing Vitamin A and the needed essential fatty acids or Vitamin F that help promote an antiseptic action and better healing. Just shake into your socks and shoes to heal your foot sores.

Skin Blemishes.   The Shoshoni Indians would boil plantain leaves and apply as a moist dressing upon skin blemishes. Many believed it would help heal the symptoms of insect bites. Some Indian medicine men would suggest binding plantain leaves around the feet when a long trek through the woods or forests was necessary. It is believed (currently) that Vitamins A and C help nourish the skin of the feet and also ease muscular symptoms of fatigue.

Scratches or Skin Wounds.   Early Indians of the Rocky Mountain region would use boiled valerian roots (a volatile but effective herb) upon their scratches or skin wounds. This is a rich source of skin-feeding Vitamin A that regenerates tissues and cells.

Mystic Love Potion.   Wisconsin Indians (members of the Meskwakis tribe) would use many love potions. One was the Joe-Pye Weed. It was regarded a "love medicine" to be chewed to stimulate a "mood." It is also known as purple boneset and is available at almost all herbalists. The red and blue lobelia plants were chewed and eaten and said to cause intense emotion between two lovers. The early California and Nevada Navajos would make a tea of the dayflower herb which was said to increase desire even amongst the aged. These plants are prime sources of Vitamin E and Vitamin F which serve to activate the glands and enrich the hormone flow to rejuvenate the desires of healthful lovemaking.

Asthma.   Members of the Dakota and Winnebago tribes reportedly could relieve problems of asthma by eating skunk cabbage. This same vegetable is available at many large markets. Ordinary cabbage (try it raw or as a juice) is a prime source of Vitamins A and C which are needed to nourish and rebuild the health of the bronchial tubes and respiratory tract. This helps relieve, protect and heal asthmatic congestion.

Better Respiratory Health.   Indians generally relieved breathing or chest congestion by drinking a tea made from the boiled root of the mullein weed. This contains Vitamins A, B-complex and E that work harmoniously to promote healing of the arteries and connecting cellular networks of the respiratory tract.

Back Pains.   Apache Indians would use a tea made from the roots of the arnica plant. (History mentions this same secret remedy in use in Europe for hundreds of years.) Vitamins in the arnica plant activate a tart crystalline substance known as *arnicin* which appears to ease muscular spasms. Vitamins A and C are able to flow through congested areas and ease problems of backache.

Low Back Pain or Strain.   To help ease a wrenching low back pain, the Catawba Indians would boil gentian roots in hot water. This lotion would be applied to the aching region. It is believed that the heat opened up pores of the skin so that the mystical substances (identified as Vitamins A and C) could penetrate and soothe the twisted muscle.

Fever, Chills, Inflammation. To help correct these disorders, the Catawba tribespeople would rely upon the horsemint plant. (It is also known as thymol at many herbalists.) The Indians would crush the leaves and soak them in cold water. They would drink the liquid and would reportedly recover from problems of feverish chills or inflammation. This plant is a powerhouse of natural Vitamin C that is needed to soothe the respiratory tract and replace what has been lost through perspiration.

Chest Pains. Many Indians used the fragrant spikenard plant to relieve chest aches or pains. The Potawatomi Indians would make a chest pack of the pulverized root and apply to the chest. The Shawnee Indians would just apply natural grown spikenard to the aching region. The Cherokees would make a tea of spikenard roots and drink it to relieve congestion of the chest. The Indians of the Ojibwa tribe would mix pulverized spikenard roots with wild ginger, add a bit of water, and use as a moist poultice upon the aching chest. The spikenard contains vitamins A and C and a form of Vitamin E that helps nourish the muscles, balance oxygenation and promote better equilibrium and healing.

Blisters. The Indians who lived in the region around Lake Superior would pound sunflower roots and mix with powdered sunflower seeds and use this as a wet dressing upon blisters. It is said that the Vitamin E content in this mash helps promote healing as well as a natural anti-oxidation process of better antiseptic cleansing.

Bronchitis. Members of Indian tribes around the Illinois region would boil dried bergamot and use the tea as a means of relieving bronchitis. (Modern chemists have already discovered that the flowering tops and leaves contain a Vitamin C-like substance known as *thymol* which has a remarkable healing benefit.) The Indian tea made from dried bergamot is a prime source of Vitamin C which reportedly helps remove toxic wastes from the respiratory tract and helps promote healing of bronchial disorders.

Colds. Yes, Indians caught cold when exposed to harsh climatic elements. The Pillager Indians would make a salve of the leaf buds of the balsam poplar tree. They would then inhale this salve and experience relief of nasal congestion. The Vitamin C helped nourish the cells and tissues of the breathing apparatus and guard against infections. It was the natural way to help ease nasal cold distress and improve breathing.

Sore Throat.   Many Eastern Indians would praise the healing qualities of the pleurisy root herb. They would make a tea of the boiled plant and drink it to relieve sore throat. Often, just chewing the fresh root of the pleurisy herb, a source of Vitamin C and enzymes that are used to clear away phlegm and restore natural resistance to germs, would give prompt relief to throat congestion and chest tightness.

Burns.   The Zuni Indians of New Mexico would grind the yarrow plant, soak it in cold water, then apply the liquid to the burned region. It is believed that Vitamin A in yarrow joined with Vitamin E to utilize a pungent oil known as *cineol* which promoted healing of the burned skin.

Winter Ailments.   Whether a sniffle, a cold, a hacking cough or more serious winter distress, the Indians looked to plants for healing. Boneset tea with its concentrated Vitamin C was helpful to almost all Indians throughout the land. Other Indians would boil balm of gilead buds and then inhale the fragrance to help cleanse the cells of the respiratory tract. Vitamins in the balm of gilead buds take up *salicin,* an ingredient that is then transformed into salicylic acid in the body. Aspirin is largely composed of salicylic acid; so we see that balm of gilead buds with the vitamin-energized *salicin* may well be considered *natural aspirin.*

Body Aches and Pains.   Indians in the northeastern region of our country, closer to Canada, would use wintergreen for relief of body aches and pains. This is a highly concentrated Vitamin C plant that grows in these areas. The Indians would boil the leaves and drink as a Vitamin C tea. Or, they would soak a cloth in this Vitamin C tea and then apply as a natural poultice to the aching region. (Modern chemists recognize that oil of wintergreen has methyl salicylate which is a form of aspirin.) Wintergreen also has Vitamin B-complex which is helpful as a natural sedative.

Coughs.   Central Indians would use the bark of the wild cherry as a tea to help relieve problems of coughs as well as colds. This has a high amount of enzymes and Vitamin C that work together to help ease internal congestion. This unique combination promotes self-cleansing. Many modern medicines contain a concoction of wild cherry for cough relief.

Winter Discomforts. The Mohegan and Ojibwag Indians relied upon the dried inner bark of white pine for relief of winter ailments such as coughs, colds, sniffles, respiratory ailments. A very rich source of Vitamins A and C and enzymes, this plant is a miracle of healing. Many chemicalized cough syrups contain white pine. Indians would boil the inner bark and use the Vitamin C syrup as a natural cough syrup.

Better Health. Northern Pacific Indians would use sarsaparilla as a "miracle plant" for better health. This plant contains Vitamins A, B-complex and C and smaller amounts of Vitamin E and Vitamin F, making it a natural vitamin supplement. Nearly all of these tribes would chew sarsaparilla or eat the roots regularly to give them better health and strength.

Mohegan Indian Cough Syrup. Soak mullein leaves in blackstrap molasses and eat with a spoon. This gives you a potent source of the B-complex and C vitamins needed to help restore health of sore throat. It was said that the Mohegan Indians would use this "cough syrup" with amazing benefits. Coughs reportedly were eased and even healed overnight.

Dandruff. The Chickasaw Indians of northern Mississippi would rub corn oil into the scalp to help heal dandruff-like conditions and also to promote better health of their shimmering and enviably thick dark hair. Corn oil contains precious Vitamins E and F or the essential fatty acids, to nourish the scalp and hair follicles and to create natural moisture.

Diarrhea. For this embarrassing distress, many Indians would make a tea of Vitamin C rich blackberries and sip slowly. It is said that this healed their problems. Neighboring settlers who scoffed at this idea, succumbed to dysentery.

Digestive Tonic. Menominee Indians would boil the butternut (also known as a white walnut) meat and drink it as a tea to help correct an upset stomach. Many would eat these walnut meats regularly as food and also as a means of nourishing the stomach to protect it against ailments. Walnut meats contain Vitamins E and F which coat the stomach and make it feel contented and smooth.

Fever. The Indians of Texas (near the Gulf) would boil

the bayberry plant and drink the tea to relieve problems of fever or inflammation. It is a prime source of gland soothing Vitamins A and C.

Hair. You never saw a hairless Indian. Rarely did you see one with gray hair. It is believed that their vitamin plant remedies gave them abundantly dark hair. Some Indians soaked the leaves of plume and used the liquid as a rinse to keep the hair looking youthfully thick and dark. It is a source of Vitamins A and E. Blackfoot Indians would mix pounded roots of soap root with water as a wash. This plant contains high concentrations of Vitamin A for the scalp. Oregon Indians would soak wood fern in water and use this Vitamin A and C wash for the scalp and hair. Other Indians would boil flaxseed in water and use the cooled liquid, a prime source of Vitamin F, as a hair wash. It helped send the essential fatty acids to the follicles and nourish the hair roots, too.

Headache. Many Indians would boil Vitamin C rich skunk cabbage and eat it, drink the liquid, to help relieve headaches. It contains small amounts of B-complex which join with Vitamin C to help open up the tight arterioles that cause congestion and headaches. Modern cabbage contains nearly identical properties as skunk cabbage.

Hemorrhoids. Many Indians would apply Vitamin E oils to the affected region to soothe the painful bulges.

Stings from Insects. Winnebago Indians would apply crushed garlic or crushed onions or a mixture of both to the swollen region, and thereby relieve the pain from a sting. Enzymes took up Vitamins A and C to promote relief. Other Indians would apply Vitamin F containing sunflower meal to the sting to soothe and detoxify the burning.

Natural Laxatives. Early Spanish settlers in California were told of the "sacred bark" of the cascara tree for having natural cleansing actions. Indians of this region would boil a small portion of the bark in water, then sip the brew. The B-complex vitamins reportedly prompted relief. Modern scientists recognize that Vitamins A, B-complex and C take the cascara sagrada to induce peristalsis of the bowels to create a natural action. Vitamins in this bark appear to strengthen tone of the bowels. Many modern laxatives contain cascara as an ingredient. Modern

Cherokee Indians would boil Vitamin E high senna leaves and drink the potion as a natural laxative. Vitamin E helps lubricate the intestinal channel. Senna, too, is found in many commercial laxatives.

Oral Health.   For problems of mouth sores, Indians of the Northeastern section would pound Vitamin C rich barberry roots into a powder and use as a mouthwash with water. Other tribespeople would drink a tea of boiled barberry roots as a means of healing mouth sores or wounds. The Vitamin C reportedly helps strengthen the gums and soothes the lining of the tongue and lips.

Natural Mouthwash.   Peppermint leaves are prime sources of Vitamins A and C. When chewed after a meal, according to Menominee legend, will help make the mouth sweet and fresh. This natural herb, high in enzymes that are used by Vitamins A and C for oral cleansing, is available at most pharmacies. Just chew it and let the vitamins cleanse your mouth, naturally.

Bronchitis.   Yerba santa, a Vitamin A and C herb, was revered by many California Indians. They would boil the leaves and sip the tea as a means of easing problems of bronchitis. Early explorers said that many Indians worshipped the all-healing mystical powers of the yerba santa herb because when it was applied as a leaf poultice, it could cure chest congestions. The Vitamins A and C helped send enzymes to cleanse the blood, to help relieve arthritic-like symptoms or what was considered as stiffness of the limbs and chest tightness. Indians have always held the yerba santa in the highest of repute for its healing properties. It's Vitamin A and C content, with some Vitamin E to help maintain a better oxygenation of the bronchial system as well as better health, helps protect against bronchitis.

Natural Sedative.   Black cherry was a Vitamin A, B-complex and C herb that Indians used to help induce sleep or to calm down the system. A tea should be made with lukewarm or simmered water, instead of boiled water since the high heat may weaken some of the vitamins. These fruit vitamins take up a substance known as hydrocyanic acid, and use it in the body to induce natural relaxation and peaceful slumber.

Pimples.   Mid-western Indians would boil bergamot

leaves and apply them directly onto the pimples. The high Vitamin A and D content in this plant helps restore the health of skin tissues and guards against eczema and blemishes.

Hoarse Throat. The Ojibwag would chew the root liquids of the bloodroot herb (a good source of Vitamins E and F for replenishment of dehydrated tissues) for easing a hoarse throat. Other Indians would make a tea from the Vitamin C rich inner bark of slippery elm. Or else, chew vitamin rich goldenblossoms thoroughly and swallow the juice. Many Northern Indians, especially those in the cold climate of Canada, would relieve a sore throat by boiling the Vitamin A rich green needles of the white pine and then drinking the tea. Some Indians, chewed soaked Vitamin E containing senna leaves and then swallowed them for speedy relief of raspy throat. The Catawba Indians placed great faith in the persimmon fruit for throat soothing. This is a prime source of Vitamin C and enzymes that are used by vitamins to create natural astringent qualities and comfort of a sore throat.

MEDICINAL VITAMIN FOODS USED BY THE INDIANS

The Indians regarded food as a natural medicine with healing qualities. Today, we know that foods contain organic vitamins that are medicinal healers created by Nature. The Indians used such medicinal vitamin foods as:

Nuts. Indians would eat a wide variety of nuts such as peanuts, chestnuts, walnuts, acorns, beechnuts. These are prime sources of nearly all known vitamins and act as all-purpose or multiple vitamins as created by Nature. Try natural peanut butters, cashew nut butters, too. Grind nuts into a powder and sprinkle over any food for a natural and delicious all-purpose vitamin supplement.

Peas, Beans. Indians would eat such foods in the absence of meat foods and survive with hardy strength. These are plant vitamins which absorb nutrition from the soil. You get these vitamins *first hand,* as created by Nature. This may make them more beneficial than meat vitamins which have first been utilized by the animal's body and reach you depleted or second-hand. Peas and beans may be eaten as a side dish or a meal in themselves. Use in soups, casseroles or as fillers for many baked dishes.

Seeds. The unusual good eyesight and hearing of the Indians may well be traced to the eating of high Vitamin A through E seeds. Nearly all known eye and ear nourishing vitamins are found in sunflower, sesame or any other kinds of seeds. You might use pumpkin and squash seeds for a tremendous source of vitamins that are healthful and healing. Cook and bake with vitamin seeds, too.

Corn. To the Indian, corn was his "mother food." He recognized corn as the "giver of life." Indeed, corn is a life-giving food since it contains Vitamins A and C and, more important, the needed Vitamin E and the essential fatty acids or Vitamin F. This gives the blood-washing and cholesterol cleansing action needed for youthful health. The Indians worshipped corn, too. The Iroquois would boil corn kernels in water with meat and beans and eat this highly vitaminized meal. They would also toast ripe corn kernels until they popped. This gave a natural Vitamin A supply. It was a natural but healthful "pop corn" rich in Vitamin E. The Zuni Indians had a unique *Corn Drink*. They would grind popped corn until it was a soft powder. They would add some cold water and drink this Corn Drink during sacred ceremonies. It was said that this helped purify the body and give it the strength of a young brave. This is a prime source of Vitamin E, the "youth" nutrient. The Iroquois also worshipped corn and held elaborate ceremonies when drinking *Corn Coffee*. This sacred beverage (a rich treasure of Vitamins A and E) was made by boiling corn kernels for about 15 minutes (according to our modern time calculations) and then Vitamin C high maple syrup was added for a sweetener. The Iroquois would drink this *Corn Coffee* during sacred rites because they revered it as a source of supreme strength and youthful vigor.

Wild Rice. Not a rice, but a member of the grain family, it grows in ponds and swamps along the marshy borders of streams in the midwest. Indians from Minnesota (known as Menominees; their name was taken from the Indian word for wild rice which is Menomin) would boil this wild rice (a major source of Vitamin E and F) and eat it to give them strength. Large cults grew up in homage to the wild rice. Special festivals were held for wild rice as a source of strength and youthful vigor. Its high source of Vitamin E and F helped give it this honor.

Wheat. Nearly all Indians would use wheat for almost all foods. Here is a leading source of youthbuilding B-complex and E vitamins.

Asparagus. The Iroquois particularly worshipped asparagus (a high Vitamin A and C food) because it helped give them vigor. They would boil the stalks (large amounts of Vitamin A for the skin and eyes) and eat them regularly.

Cherries. All kinds of cherries were eaten either raw or boiled and then eaten as a dessert. This is a high Vitamin C food. The sweetness was considered the gift of the gods for making life joyfully sweet. Some would eat raw cherries. This is a top-notch source of skin rejuvenating and respiratory healing Vitamin C. Others would crush cherries and mix with maple syrup. Some even mixed such cherries with whole grain (Vitamin E) meal in baking. Indians throughout the American continent would eat all fruits, berries and cherries. The high Vitamin A and C content nourished them, kept them strong, gave them sleek skins, bright eyes, youthful alertness and vigor.

Kelp. Indians who lived in the Alaskan region, and many from the northeastern area would eat this wide-leaved algae that we today know as seaweed or kelp. This ocean plant is a prime source of Vitamins A, B-complex and C. The vitamins then activate the sea minerals to guard the body against goiter. A unique property of seaweed vitamins is that they help metabolize fats into an unsaturated form to protect the body against arteriosclerosis or heart distress.

Vegetables. The Indians prized vegetables with the same worshipful attitude as displayed toward fruits. The Indians felt that cantaloupes, watermelons, squashes, pumpkins, cucumbers, lettuce, asparagus and other vegetables were sources of vigor and strength. Their medicine men said that the mystical powers gave life to the soil and put life into all that was grown in the sacred soil. Therefore, eating the vegetables would give the people the same vitality from the soil. Today, we recognize that power as being vitamins and other nutrients that nurture the seed, cause it to grow into a vegetable plant brimming with vitamins that are needed by the body for youthful health. Cooked or raw, vegetables give you better health.

Yes, the American Indian looked to the fields, forests and streams for medicinal vitamin healers. Nature was his God. The vitamin foods of Nature were God's medicines. The Indian thrived, survived and flourished with these plant vitamins. With a revival in the search for natural healers, our modern civilization may well have to look to the American Indian for his vitamin healing secrets.

IN A NUTSHELL

1. The early American Indians worshipped vitamin plants for their mystical healing properties. Nearly all of these medicinal plants are available for your own vitaminization programs.
2. Indians used a variety of vitaminized herbs for healing of almost all known external and internal ailments.
3. The Indians also considered such medicinal vitamin foods as nuts, peas, beans, seeds, corn, wild rice, wheat, asparagus, cherries, kelp, vegetables. Foods were medicinal vitamins to the Indians. Modern science recognizes that the vitamins in such foods make them valuable for building and rebuilding youthful health from top to bottom, from the inside to the outside.

15

How Orientals Use Sprouts
As Youth Vitamins

The amazing health and vigor of the Orientals may well be traced to his secret of growing vitamins in a dish! Yes, the Oriental has long discovered that when seeds or beans are "planted" and nurtured at home, they sprout and become a veritable Fountain of Youth in vitamin value. The perpetual youthfulness of most Orientals even during times of privation or famine may well be traced to the traditional growing and eating of these seed sprouts. To many such Orientals, seed sprouts are so supercharged and chock full of vitamins (as well as minerals, proteins, enzymes, essential fatty acids, many trace elements), that they are miracles of life. Many even believe that in dire times, *seed sprouts are so nutritiously powerful, they can sustain life in the absence of other foods.*

The Total Vitamin Food Package

Orientals have long hailed seed sprouts as a total vitamin food package. It rivals meat for protein, has a wide assortment of minerals, and has unusual protein. The Orientals prize seed sprouts because their hardy soil and the constant threat of war, famine, pestilence, destruction, made farming impractical.

The Oriental needed a food that could be prepared with a minimum of utensils, little or no soil, in a short length of time. But more important, he needed an all-purpose food, one that could serve all of his nutritional needs. He discovered the technique of making *seed sprouts* to fill all of these requirements. Eating raw (or cooked) seed sprouts gave the Oriental nearly all known nutrients, and just about *all* vitamins required for life and health. So to the Oriental, seed sprouts were the source of life as a total vitamin food package.

Easy to Grow. Vitamin-rich and spray-free sprouts are very easy to grow. All you need is a container or a jar. You can grow these vitamin packages on your windowsill, on a table, at the edge of your sink or just about any spare space you have, even your shelf. No cumbersome equipment or plowing is required.

Vitamin Treasure. A sprouting grain is just about the only food you can consume that has *living vitamins.* While plants are picked, and vitamins are present, only sprouting seeds are *alive* with living vitamins. You eat the growing sprout with the life-giving vitamins. This makes sprouts a treasure of *living vitamins.*

Speedy Vitamin Growth. On an average, vitamins grow by leaps and bounds during the sprouting. For example, sprouted soybeans increase some 500 per cent in Vitamin C. Sprouting oats jump to 1350 per cent in Vitamin B_2. Sprouting wheat rises to 106 per cent of folic acid. Sprouting mungbeans have four times the value of niacin. Corn, barley and wheat veritably explode five times their amount of Vitamin B_2. The fat-soluble Vitamins A, E, K also soar in value during sprouting. Just about all seeds will undergo a fantastic vitamin boosting during sprouting.

Healthful Pattern. Sprouting appears to endow seeds with a healthful pattern of protein that can sustain life; sprouting also creates a compatible balance of minerals as well as needed essential fatty acids and carbohydrates. Folks who count calories will enjoy using sprouts for weight reduction since they are very low in carbohydrates. The sprouting process transforms starch into simple sugar which is more speedily and easily metabolized.

This protects against buildup of pound-building carbohydrates. Sprouting is about the speediest way to improve the nutritional content of foods. Sprouted seeds are a smorgasbord of nutrients that are delicately balanced by Nature.

Seeds to Sprout.   Select any whole natural seed. Popular seeds are alfalfa (considered the best), lentils, soybeans, wheat seeds, sunflower seeds, peas, rye, oats, wheat, corn, fenugreek, mung beans, radish seed, red clover. When purchasing seeds, select an organic seed outlet. The seed should be of good quality, free from insects. It should be spray-free, and it should be clean. Avoid any seeds that have been treated with harmful chemical sprays.

Hulled seeds or broken seeds do not sprout well. Therefore, select *whole* seeds with their shells. If any are shrivelled or broken, pick them out and remove. For super-vitamin potency, use *whole* seeds.

THE JAPANESE SECRET OF
VITAMINIZING SEED SPROUTS

Overworked, overtired Shirley V. was on a vacation in Japan where she hoped the serenity of the Far East would soothe her nerves and make her feel more energetic. As a buyer for a large furniture store, she was always under constant pressure. She felt edgy, tense, given to frequent outbursts. Shirley V. found her workday growing longer and longer, her energy growing shorter and shorter. So she marvelled when she noted how so many Japanese could work under arduous, crowded conditions with amazing vitality. When Shirley V. visited the home of a Japanese housewife who was a part-time furniture designer, and also devoted much time to charity work, she could not believe how such vitality was possible. Her hostess let her in on the secret.

Sprouts Offer Health.   The Japanese hostess was a bundle of energy, even though she was older than Shirley V. and had much more work to do. She said that she followed healthful programs but she ate sprouts almost daily. The hostess explained that in Japan, they have small land area and exploding population.

The Japanese have a problem of growing the most nourishing food in the smallest amount of space. One food — *sprouts* — offer this possibility. The hostess said that she grew sprouts and ate them daily, as did so many other millions of energy-alerted Japanese. It was their secret of limitless vitality.

How Japanese Grow Vitamin Sprouts

The Japanese hostess following this simple vitamin-exploding sprout program:

1. Use whole, untreated seeds. Prepare rectangular shaped wooden boxes. Ask your grocer for discarded cheese boxes. Even old berry cartons are good as they offer you good drainage.

2. First soak dry organic seeds overnight in triple their volume of water. This speeds up the seeds' vitamin metabolism and the germinating process has begun.

3. Next morning, place the seeds in the wooden boxes.

4. Four times a day, water the sprouting seeds carefully. This protects against formation of undesirable mold. Be sure to water seeds regularly for better sprout development.

5. Within three to four days, the sprouts are ready. The Japanese have discovered one secret of sprouts. *Longer sprouts have much, much more vitamin and nutritive value. For top-level vitamin value, they let seeds sprout up to five days.* Longer days are undesirable since the taste appears to grow rancid.

6. At the end of the fifth day, gather up the seed sprouts and eat as a wholesome food that is a powerhouse of potent vitamins.

New Vitality, Amazing Energy, Youthful Appearance

Shirley V. ate a bowl of these sprouts for lunch, then another bowl for dinner. In two days, she experienced a surge of new vitality and energy that made her look and feel youthful. She was grateful to her Japanese hostess for showing her how to grow sprouts. Back home, she grew them regularly in her kitchen and was able to enjoy unsurpassed youthful stamina.

Secret of Sprout Vitality

Why should sprouts offer such a treasure of vitality? They are the best source of vitamins. Sprouted seeds are enzyme catalysts for vitality. Vitamins in sprouts have certain *auxone* substances that boost the vital processes in the body's billions of tissues and cells. Furthermore, vitamin sprouts take up its own self-created essential fatty acids (known as Vitamin F) and use these to protect against age-causing cholesterol buildup. Furthermore, sprout vitamins change starch into easily digestible malt sugar that the body instantly uses for youthful energy. The seed vitamins are alive and bursting with vitality. . . that gives the body its healthful surge of amazing energy. The Japanese have this enviable stamina even in their crowded land and encroaching pressures of civilization. Yet they are perpetually alert, filled with youthful vitality. Sprouts may well be the Japanese secret of youthful energy at all ages!

HOW TO GROW VITAMINS
IN A GLASS JAR

You can grow vitaminized sprouts in a glass jar. It is the easy way to replenish your body and give you a feeling of youthful alertness. It works for Ronald E., a big city business consultant who has to keep alert, on his toes, and have a good memory. His thoughts had become fuzzy. There were times when he would even forget appointments. He also had problems of insomnia. He looked and felt haggard and worn. No doubt, his irregular eating also took its toll. His skin was wrinkled. He had dark circles under his eyes. He looked much older than his 46 years. He feared loss of his job if his condition worsened.

Uses Sprouts As Natural
Home-Grown Vitamin Supplements

Ronald E. had done some research on a farm project and that was when he learned that home-grown seed sprouts offer an unbelievable treasure of vitamins. In fact, *seed sprouts can be natural vitamin supplements!* Here is how Ronald E. grew vitamins in a glass jar:

1. Place clean whole and organic seeds in a clean quart jar. Cover with lukewarm water and let them soak overnight.

2. Next morning, drain seeds through a collander (or strainer) and rinse thoroughly. Pour off any excess water.

3. Rinse the quart jar clean. Now put the seeds back in the jar for sprouting. Cover the mouth of the jar with a double thickness of cheesecloth. Fasten with rubber bands. (You may also use a bit of wire screening secured with string or wire.)

4. Place the jar, mouth down, at about 45° angle. This helps spread the seeds in a single layer along the side of the jar. Remaining water will also drain out and the seeds will be moist and free of undesirable mold.

5. Put the jar in a warm (not hot) place such as your cupboard or shelf.

6. Water the seeds three times a day. Do NOT remove the jar covering but pour lukewarm water through this covering.

7. Within three to five days, sprouts will grow and you will have a supply of vitaminized seeds that rival the power and effectiveness of any synthetic pill. Most important is that the seed sprouts are food vitamins as created by Nature. This gives you the built-in rewards of vitaminization that you, a creation of Nature, require.

Boosts Vitality

Ronald E. would eat a bowl of such sprouts daily. He also improved his intake of lots of fresh raw fruits and vegetables. His regular meals included lean meat, fish, low-fat dairy products as well as beans, nuts and seeds. Results? In two weeks, Ronald E. felt a boost in his vitality. His memory became keen. He slept better. He awakened with vitality. His appearance was youthful. His skin firmed up. His eyes were alert and smooth. He soon received a promotion, winning out over a younger man. Ronald E. now eats sprouts daily. It's the natural way to take vitamin supplements as created by Nature.

THE CHINESE WAY TO GROW
VITAMIN-PACKED SPROUTS

Hundreds of centuries of wars, famine, pestilence, plagues, have taught the Chinese to "make do" with as little land as possible for sustenance. Even in the midst of poverty and apparent starvation, many Chinese were able to do more than survive. They *thrived* with amazing vigor and strength to overcome their enemies. A secret was in surviving on sprouts. Here is how the Chinese made sprouts which served as their *only* source of food during times of extreme privation.

1. Soak seeds in plenty of water overnight.
2. Next morning, spread seeds thinly and evenly on the bottom of a glass pan.
3. Cover with wet cheesecloth or any cloth that permits good ventilation and will permit water to go through.
4. Three times a day, sprinkle generously with water.
5. Within five days, you will discover a *green garden of vitamin sprouts growing in your glass pan.* Eat these sprouts for one of the most complete foods ever created by Nature.

The Chinese would survive on sprouts grown in their shacks or huts or even in hide out caves and became strong, healthy and vigorous enough to fight off enemies and regain and hold their freedom. Throughout the Orient, seed sprouts are revered as the supreme source of life.

THE RAG DOLL WAY OF SPROUTING SEEDS

In very hot areas of Asia, the Orientals have learned a "rag doll" way of sprouting seeds. Here is how they do it:
1. Spread clean but soaked seeds on a terry cloth.
2. Roll up and keep it well dampened and in a dark warm place.
3. Sprouts should appear within two days.

The Asiatics use this "rag doll" method because the climate may be very hot and very dry and seeds might not otherwise sprout. They also use the sprouts within two days since mildew may otherwise develop with a damp cloth.

Sprouts may also be stored. Just place in a closed jar in your refrigerator. Keeping quality is about as long as any fresh vegetable that is covered and kept refrigerated. You should plan on using sprouts as soon as possible since vitamins may deplete if the vegetables (and sprouts are vegetables) are left standing too long.

HOW TO ENJOY GOOD SPROUT EATING

Sprouts, for maximum vitamin vitality, should be eaten *raw*. You may mix in a raw vegetable salad. You may eat them by themselves. You may toss a handful of sprouts in soups. Use sprouts in fruit salads, or add to jelled salads just before setting occurs. Add wheat sprouts to home baked bread foods. Sprinkle sprouts over almost any dessert dish. Mix generously with omelets, sandwiches or just about anything. The Orientals have discovered that sprouts are delicious by themselves — or with just about anything else that is healthfully nourishing.

Egg Foo Yung

The Orientals add chopped sprouts to scrambled eggs and omelets; they sprinkle a bit of soy sauce. This is *egg foo yung* that you can make in a jiffy. It's a meal-in-itself, brimming with almost all vitamins that you need for good health.

Almost any seeds, peas or beans can be used. Make a variety and you'll enjoy creative taste with almost all known vitamins, minerals, enzymes, plant proteins, essential fatty acids. The Orientals have long ago discovered the complete food package available in sprouts. They thrive, survive and enjoy rejuvenated stamina with sprouts as their basic wholesome food.

NATURE'S PERFECT FOOD

The Orientals call seed sprouts "the perfect food of Nature." A sprout is *complete*. When you eat a sprout, you eat everything such as the roots, the seed, the stem and all else that goes with it. This gives you a perfect assortment of vitamins and other nutrients to make it a "perfect nourishment" according to the Orientals who should know since it served as their sole means of survival for so many centuries. The sprout is "perfect" because it is capable of growing, bearing roots, stocks, stems, a flower and seeds. This makes it a perfect food, capable of supporting its own life to the fullest. It can help give you nutrients that can support your own life to the fullest.

VITAMIN ENERGY BREAKFAST

You can begin the day with bursting energy by mixing 1 cup of seed sprouts with a handful of sun-dried figs or natural dates, and 1/2 cup of sun-dried raisins. Serve with milk and honey. This *Vitamin-Energy Breakfast* is a powerhouse of all known essential nutrients. It gives you that "get up and go" that keeps you going for hours and hours, well past noontime. It's the all-natural energizer you need.

Sprouts are chemical-free, can be enjoyed in wintertime when other plant foods are in scarce or costly supply. They can be grown in your kitchen in a glass jar or pan, or even with a wet towel, with a minimum of bother. They offer you a maximum of life-giving vigor. Do as the Orientals do. Use sprouts daily. You can vitaminize and supercharge your health with this simple food.

HIGHLIGHTS

1. Seed sprouts are revered in the Orient as being a total food package.
2. Sprouting increases vitamin content some hundred percent.
3. Shirley V. bounced back with youthful vitality by following the Japanese secrets of making seed sprouts.
4. Ronald E. was able to grow vitamins in a glass jar in seven easy steps. Sprouts boosted his vitality, refreshed his memory, made him look and feel youthfully alert.
5. In five easy steps, you can use the Chinese way of growing seed sprouts. Within five days, you will have a green garden of vitamin sprouts growing in a glass pan.

6. Enjoy good sprout eating in a variety of ways. Make simple but nutrition-packed *egg foo yung* in a few moments. Start your day off with amazing vigor with a Vitamin Energy Breakfast. Vitaminize and supercharge your body and mind with this simple but powerfully effective all-natural food. For a few pennies, you receive a million dollars of vigor!

16

Herbs—Nature's Garden
of Organic Vitamins

Nature has planted a garden of organic vitamins in the forests, the fields, the woods, the meadows and even the oceans. These organic vitamins are available in the form of *herbs,* the "fruit" of the soil, prepared under the perfect guidance of Nature. The miracle of herb vitamins is that they have helped heal people for thousands of years before the advent of chemicalized medicines. To the ancients and the moderns, herb vitamins are *pure* medicines from Nature. These botanicals were so revered by the ancients that they would hold sacred rites concerning their planting and harvesting and their use as Nature's own medicines. The ancients recognized that herbs contained magic-like ingredients (today we identify them as vitamins) which could produce healing of almost all known ailments. Herbs may well have helped the ancients survive in an age when chemical healers were unknown. Small wonder that they looked upon herb vitamins with awe and mystical worship.

Persians, Greeks, Egyptians, Israelites

The ancient peoples in the lands near the Mediterranean were all aware of the healing powers of herb vitamins. The Persians, Greeks, Egyptians and Israelites would all turn to their recognized herbal healing physicians for prescriptions to heal their ailments. Herbs were used as Nature's medicines as early as 2500 B.C. Discovered ancient clay tablets reveal that the ancient Sumerians used herbs for healing. As early as 1600 B.C., the ancient Egyptians had a vast knowledge of herbs to promote healing of almost all known health problems. The Persians, Greeks and Israelites all considered herbs to be holy medicines of Nature. Their writings all refer to man's search for health since being cast out of the Garden of Eden. It is said that the use of herbs for healing could, indeed, restore mankind to Eden-like health and eternal youthfulness.

Today, as in ancient times, herbs are being used to help prevent illness and also heal the body and the mind. Herb vitamins help restore a delicate biological balance within the system that then favors healing.

Herb Vitamins Are Miracles of Healing

Herb vitamins have the unique ability to help regulate and stabilize the process of metabolism; that is, the building up and breaking up of the billions of body cells and tissues. The use of herb vitamins helps regulate metabolism. This produces a wholesome benefit on the body's various processes, helps stabilize the glandular influence, and helps restore health and vitality to the ailing parts of the body. Since the body cannot retain all of the essential herbal vitamins, it is important to replenish them regularly. A balanced food program of healthful fruits, vegetables, meats, seeds, nuts, dairy products, will offer a foundation of organic vitamins. But the use of herb vitamins can help promote *specific* healing of *specific* body parts. This is the credo handed down from ancient days. Today, we have identified vitamins in herbs and know they are helpful in promoting effective healing. Herbs are plants of Nature. They are Nature's organic vitamins for healing.

Secret Healing Power of Herbs

Your body needs these herbal vitamins for miracle healing. Your body is a vital organism with a living electrical energy within the *bioplasm* of your cells. This is the important healing force. The *bioplasm* is able to select, dissolve, metabolize and transform to its own use the therapeutic ingredients of any remedial herb utilized. The *bioplasm* in your cells draws its material from your bloodstream. The *bioplasm* takes out essential nutrients from your bloodstream to be sent to your brain, your muscles, your heart, your skin, your bones, your hair, your organs, and just about every part of you from top to bottom. When your body has herb vitamins, the *bioplasm* can use these for a miracle secret healing power to help restore the body to living health and vitality.

How Nature Puts Vitamins in Herbs

A herbal plant grown in Nature's soil is a prime source of all the rich goodness endowed by Nature. The herbal root is the stomach of the plant. The herbal branches have mouths that suck up food from the soil. This food consists of the nutrients placed in the soil by Nature. This food is the "blood" that goes up in the stalk to nourish the herbal plant. The entire herbal plant (including the bark, wood, leaves, flowers, fruit) is made from this "blood" or sap of Nautre. This is the purest and most potent source of vitamins available by Nature.

This "blood" sap, carrying vitamins, goes up one set of plant pipes or arteries, and down to the roots through another set of plant arteries. The "blood" sap goes throughout the plant, to the leaves (lungs) which have breathing pores (respiratory tract and skin), and causes every part of the plant (Nature's body) to flourish and regenerate. This sap in the plant is comparable to the blood in your body. Nature put this "plant blood" for the life and health into the herb, just as Nature put blood for your life and health. The plants draw food from the earth for its own sustenance. When you partake of a herb, you are feeding yourself Nature's "blood" that helped nourish a plant. . . and can help nourish your body from top to bottom.

Herb vitamins are comparable to Nature's medicines. They are available to you to help create the *bioplasm* process that will promote effective healing for just about every part of your body. Just as your vitamin-carrying bloodstream nourishes you from head to toe, so does the vitamin-carrying plant bloodstream work to nourish you, thanks to this Miracle of Nature.

Today, herbal healing is becoming recognized as the natural way to give the body the working materials (vitamins) from which good health can be created; to help fortify yourself with more than just vitamins, but a tremendous life force of plant medicines, capable of building and rebuilding every part of your body so that you can enjoy life to the fullest. This is what Nature wants for you. All Nature asks is that you follow the organic way to better health through healthful living programs, wholesome foods and miracle herbs.

HOW TO PREPARE HERBS
FOR EASY HOME USE

How to Buy.   Seek out an organic herb dealer in your locality. To locate the dealer, look under "herbs" or "herb pharmacy" or "botanicals" in the classified pages of your telephone directory. Telephone or write them for your specific needs.

How to Use: Herbs should be organic. Avoid any that have been treated with chemical sprays or insecticides of any sort. Store herbs in clean, airtight containers in a cool, dry, dark place. Since these plants of Nature are delicate, you would do well to keep them in a glass bottle on a shelf, away from excess heat or cold. Remember that Nature creates everything in a cycle. Whatever you do will return to you. So treat your herbs with healthful care and they will return to you with the same healthful care.

Herb Tea: Steep herbs in a pot of boiled water for 5 to 10 minutes. Strain and use. For added nutrition and flavor, use a bit of lemon juice and honey.

Fomentation: Boil the selected herb in a minimum of water for 10 minutes. Then dip a clean cloth or heavy white towel in the warm liquid, wring out, and apply locally to the ailing region.

Salve or Ointment: Mix 1 part of the herb with 4 parts of oil. Heat and stir gently for 15 minutes. Cool and strain. You now have a vitamin-enriched natural salve or ointment.

Poultice: Dip a herb in boiling water long enough to soak it. Now apply this herb to the ailing region; cover with a clean cloth that has been dipped and wrung out in hot water. When this cloth cools, replace with another one.

Suggestion: Herbal vitamins are delicate and should be treated with care. Plan to use herbal healers as fresh as possible. If you must store any tea or ointment, then put in a small wide-mouthed glass jar. Cover tightly and keep in a cool place. But remember that herbal vitamins lose potency if stored for a long time. If you do store such concoctions and notice an "off" odor, then discard all the contents. Scour and sterilize the container and then start off fresh. To thoroughly sterilize glass jars, wash thoroughly with soap under hot water. Rinse several times under hot and gradually cooling water. Then rinse with alcohol or vinegar. Now fill with water, place in a water-filled pot, and boil for 15 minutes. Turn off heat. Let cool. Drain. Place bottles on a clean towel for upside down draining. This is the natural way to sterilize glass containers in which herbs are to be stored.

HERB VITAMIN HEALERS FOR COMMON AND UNCOMMON AILMENTS

Skin Bruises. Ordinary bruises, scratches, cuts, will respond to an ointment made out of any of these herbs (or a mixture for assorted vitamin content): alfalfa leaf, camomile flowers, dill seeds, lemon peel, marjoram, rosemary, sesame seeds, wintergreen.

Very Severe Blemishes. Mash yerba santa leaves and soak in boiled water for five minutes. Apply the comfortably hot leaves to the blemishes and cover with a clean towel.

Burns. Mix some marshmallow root, comfrey root in 1 cup of vegetable oil. Now pour into an enamel kettle. Cover. Let simmer 15 minutes. Strain. When comfortably cool, slather over the burned area and let the vitamins help promote natural soothing healing.

Warts. Squeeze a bunch of dandelions. The milky "sap" or "blood" that comes out should be applied to the warts and left dry. Keep applying regularly. NOTE: It is said that corns on the feet will also respond to this natural remedy. Just keep applying until you see results.

Bronchitis.   A playschool supervisor, Katy C. has to go out in all sorts of inclement weather. Her bronchitis appears to be relieved if she chews on licorice root lozenges or horehound lozenges. These are sold at many herbal pharmacies. Katy C. can make her own lozenges in this simple manner: Steep 1 cup dried horehound leaves in 1 cup of boiling water for 15 minutes. Steep and strain. To this liquid, add 1 cup honey and 1/2 teaspoon cream of tartar. Heat to 220° F. Remove from heat. Add 2 table-spoons lemon juice. Pour into hot, oiled muffin tins. These should be marked into squares. Let cool. Then do as Katy C. does, just remove the squares, wrap in wax paper, tuck into your handbag or brief case. Eat one when you feel a bronchial threat. A myriad of vitamins will go to work to soothe your system and help give you *natural* protection against infections. Katy C. is able to cope with her bronchitis with these horehound lozengers.

Sinus.   Steep one very large wintergreen leaf in one cup of boiling water for 10 minutes. Strain. Add lemon juice and honey. Sip slowly. The vitamins take up the herbal properties and help heal the feeling of fullness in the nose.

Sore Throat.   If troubled with a raspy, sore throat, sip fresh pineapple juice throughout the day. Or mix sage tea with lemon juice and honey and take as a natural herbal-fruit cough tonic.

Natural Sleeping Tonic.   Mix equal amounts of dandelion root and camomile. Now put 1 tablespoon of these herbs in a cup of boiling water. Let steep for 10 minutes. Strain. Flavor with lemon juice and honey. Sip slowly about one hour before bedtime. It is said to send soothing vitamins into the system to help relax the endocrine system and induce a feeling of natural euphoria and eventual contented sleep.

Headaches or Earaches.   Herborists feel that this ache may be traced to a vitamin deficiency causing constriction of the arterioles near the center of the head. This tightness causes the ache. Folklore herbalists suggest drinking comfortably hot winter-green tea, with lemon juice and honey. This helps provide needed vitamins to nourish and relax "starved" nerves and arteries.

Muscle Strain.   Make a salve of camomile flowers and mix with some vegetable oil. Then use a massage over the aching muscle. Helps send vitamins and soothing emollients into strained muscles to nourish the fibers and promote better healing.

Arthritis-Like Aches.   A folklore program calls for mixing equal portions of linseed oil with olive oil. Shake well. Then apply onto the aching part. It is believed that essential fatty acids and vitamins converge to nourish the starved tissues and soothe the ache.

Rheumatism.   American Indians would make a salve out of either stinging nettle or scrub pine, and rub into their aching body parts. Early pioneers said a compress made of either of these herbs would relieve discomfort of rheumatism.

Insect Bites.   Folklorists suggest mixing frankincense powder with bay rum oil and then anointing the portion of the body distressed by insect bites. It is said to relieve the sting and help facilitate better healing.

Poison Ivy.   Ocean herbs are said to be helpful. Add 1 cup sea salt (made from kelp, an ocean herb) with one cup of olive oil. Pour into a lukewarm bath. Immerse yourself for 30 minutes. This is said to help heal poison ivy and also help soothe other skin irritations.

Insect Repellent.   Early settlers who had to venture into an insect-infested region, would rub themselves with the whole onion plant. It is believed that this repelled insects. Onion juice may well be considered a modern natural insect repellent.

Athlete's Foot Powder.   This is good for general foot care and protection against irritations and scratches. Mix together 1 tablespoon of powdered gum benzoin with 1/2 cup of ordinary starch. Then sprinkle over the feet just as you would any foot powder. Many early folklore herbalists suggested a natural antiseptic in the form of *soap bark* which was said to disinfect the feet. Good for the entire body, too.

Oriental Aphrodisiac.   Korean ginseng, known as Panax Schinseng, is the Oriental herb that has reportedly been able to induce virility for its users of almost any age. Known as the "Divine Root" or "Root of Life" the Korean ginseng herb has been used to promote better health and to stimulate sluggish physio-sexological responses. Ginseng is basically a wild plant that thrives in moist, darkened, humus-filled earth. Above ground it shows a few leaves and a white-green blossom. The root (said to be a powerful source of vitamins that invigorate the libido) develops slowly in rich soil. The root is shaped like a man, with a thick body and straggly tentacles that look like arms and legs. The *main trunk* is said to possess the richest source of substances that can help boost sexual libido. Orientals chew the main trunk or the roots and report enjoying longer lives and extended virility. Herbalists sell ginseng as a tea, an extract, powder, capsule. You take it according to package directions. It is said to be an all-purpose rejuvenator. Helps improve strength and energy. It is a natural tonic. Specifically, ginseng vitamins increase the body's resistance to external strain. The ginseng vitamins help soothe the central nervous system, reportedly stabilize blood pressure, influence cholesterol metabolism to protect against arterio-sclerosis, send vitamins to the liver to enable it to function health-fully and to give a general feeling of well being and contentment. This induces a healthy libido. Ginseng is heralded in the Orient (for well over 5 to 6 thousand years) as being the elixir of life!

Ulcers.   Ancients praised alfalfa in any form as a means of healing peptic ulcers, acting as a natural diuretic for the kidneys. Alfalfa is a deep growing plant that takes out rich vitamins from the very core of Nature's earth. These same vitamins help soothe digestive unrest.

Natural Sedative.   Boil asparagus roots and eat the pulp, drink the juice. It is said its vitamins help create a feeling of contentment and natural relaxation. Ancient folklorists prescribed it as a natural sedative.

Inner Restorative.   Black currant leaves are prime sources of bioflavonoids and Vitamin C. When you drink a tea made of these leaves, you send vitamins to your system to help strengthen the walls of the capillaries. You will also feel a sooth-ing contentment from this herbal tea. It helps restore you to good health from the inside.

Stomach Tonic.   Eat raw celery. Ancients knew it was healing. Today we know that raw celery is alkaline, has a good supply of those vitamins that are used to help control acid-form-ing starches and to help dissolve this corrosive liquid. This helps neutralize body liquids and guard against acidosis. Eat the stalk and, if possible, celery seeds, for a healthful stomach tonic.

For better health, you would do well to enjoy herb teas throughout the day. All health stores and almost all large food outlets will have a wide variety of different herb teas. Drink different herb teas in place of caffeine-containing coffee or tannin-containing commercial teas. You'll be invigorating your body with nutrients in Nature's plants — the garden of organic vitamins.

IN REVIEW

1. Herbs have been hailed as healers since the ancient days. Herbs are considered pure medicine from Nature, prime sources of vitamins and many other life-health boosting substances.
2. The secret healing power of herbs is in the ability to stimulate the *bioplasm* (electrical energy) within your cells to promote regeneration and restoration.
3. It's easy to prepare herbs for home use. Follow simple instructions.
4. Enjoy natural healing with herbs for a variety of common and uncommon ailments. Katy C. made her own throat lozenges and experienced freedom from bronchitis, thanks to the healing elements in herbs.

17

Ten Everyday Foods with "MV" Youth-Building Power

Everyday foods, found at most food stores as well as the specialized health food stores, offer you a treasure of vitamins that have the unique "MV" Youth Building Power. That is, these foods are created by Nature with "Miracle Vitamins" to give you the essential ingredients for building the vigor and stamina of youth.

Nature endowed these foods with healthful vitamins so that they can nourish you, help protect you against distress. Most important, Nature nourished these foods so that they can nourish you! They are simple, everyday foods. But they carry a rich treasure of "MV" Youth Building Powers. When your body is thoroughly vitaminized, you now have the foundation for perpetual vigor and health. These food vitamins are Nature's own medicines. They help give you good health for your body, your mind, from the inside to the outside.

If you will include these 10 foods with "MV" Youth Building Power in your eating program, you will reap a harvest of nutritional goodness. You will be supercharging your body with healing vitamins. You can actually eat your way to better health and a forever young, always alert feeling that radiates youth. Here are the ten foods with their Miracle Vitamin youth building powers.

DAIRY PRODUCTS —
MIRACLE VITAMIN YOUTH FOOD #1

Wholesome milk and cheese are exceptionally good sources of vitamins that work with minerals to improve the condition of your skin, strengthen your skeletal structure, improve better digestion. Organic eggs are good dairy products because they contain vitamins and hormones that can help feed your glands. Yogurt is a healthful dairy food for folks who might otherwise be unable to digest milk. It is also a good source of vitamins for better intestinal health. Natural ice cream made with natural foods will use kelp (a sea plant or ocean herb) as a preservative which gives you more essential youth-building vitamins. Plan to use wholesome dairy foods regularly. If you are calorie-watching or cholesterol-counting, select skim milk dairy products.

WHOLE GRAINS —
MIRACLE VITAMIN YOUTH FOOD #2

Norah R. was troubled with irregularity. She knew she needed fibrin or roughage and ate grains, but she was still bothered with embarrassing irregularity. But then she realized she ate processed and refined grains. It called for a simple change. She now bought whole grain products. Just one or two days and regularity was established. But Norah R. enjoyed more benefits. The whole grain unbleached foods were prime sources of Vitamin E, which nourished her bloodstream, improved her heartbeat, gave her a supply of essential fatty acids (known unofficially as Vitamin F) and made her feel lighter and better. Now, Norah R. eats whole grains but they need to be natural.

Whole grains include wheat, oats, buckwheat, corn, rye, millet. They should be made without preservatives. Be sure to keep them refrigerated as they are highly perishable. Flour made from whole grains are prime sources of the precious skin-building B-complex vitamins, the nerve-feeding thiamine and riboflavin vitamins and also the valuable Vitamin E. Use these flours for baking. You may also want to enjoy stone-ground flour products such as cereals, breads, cookies; be sure to obtain steel-cut oatmeal. Mix cooked oatmeal with sun-dried raisins, sprinkle with wheat germ and you'll have a dynamic "MV" meal that gives you that get up and go you always wanted. Makes you feel young all over!

Brown rice is another wholesome grain food because it retains the outer husk which is one of the best sources of B-complex vitamins. Any meal made with natural brown rice has the essential vitamins you need to give you youth-power.

You will also feed yourself youth-building vitamins with whole wheat and buckwheat spaghetti and macaroni. Good taste with good nutrition.

PLANT FOODS —
MIRACLE VITAMIN YOUTH FOOD #3

Fruits and vegetables are prime sources of nearly all known vitamins. You should plan to eat these *raw* in order to obtain top level amounts of healthful vitamins.

Fruits give you good supplies of cell-tissue rebuilding Vitamin C that help strengthen blood vessel walls, resist infection and boost healing of wounds.

Vegetables give you valuable supplies of Vitamin A to help keep your skin smooth and youthful; vegetable vitamins also help improve your vision and help keep your mucous membranes (lining) of the mouth, nose, throat and digestive tract youthfully healthy with a youthful resistance to infection.

Simple Youth Program

Gladys I. had problems of a sallow, blotchy skin. She caught colds upon the slightest provocation. She was troubled with recurring bronchial disorders. Her skin frequently had blotchy bursts. She was "hung over" as she put it. Her problem was that she was always eating cooked foods. All she had to do was make this simple adjustment:

Eat lots of fresh raw fruits and vegetables as salads *before* and *after* her cooked meals. This meant she could savor the luscious enjoyment of cooked foods. She also discovered a highly exciting taste in juicy good fruits and succulent raw vegetables. This simple youth program gave Gladys I. the supercharging of health-building Vitamins A through K. Now her body bounced back with youthful vigor.

Gladys I. had a colorful "peaches and cream" skin complexion; her breathing improved and she resisted colds and respiratory attacks. She felt alert. She sparkled with good health, thanks to the miracle of youth-creating vitamins in plant foods. In her own words, Gladys I. now feels "glad all over," thanks to plant food vitamins.

Wherever possible, eat wholesome fresh raw fruits and vegetables. An easier program is to drink their raw juices as often as possible. It's the healthy way to drink your way to miracle youth!

MEAT, POULTRY, FISH — MIRACLE VITAMIN YOUTH FOOD #4

Good quality meat, poultry and fish are prime sources of the fat-soluble vitamins A, D and E as well as assorted trace elements and other nutrients.

Organ meats (liver, kidney, heart) are especially good because they give you vitamins needed to build, maintain and repair all body tissues and help form antibodies to fight infection. These foods also help supply energy in compact form and offer those fatty acids which help keep your skin smooth and healthy. For better blood clotting and stronger bones, meats are also healthful.

Poultry includes chicken and turkey. Both of these are low in cholesterol, yet amazingly high in vitamins and related minerals and proteins, which help improve the health of your heart, your nervous system, your internal organs. Vitamins in poultry combine with iron and protein to help make hemoglobin, the red substance in the blood that carries oxygen to all of your body cells. Poultry vitamins work with iron to help your cells use oxygen and give you youthful energy. Feature lean poultry regularly for good youth-building vitamin intake.

Fish is a prime source of the same vitamins found in the depths of the ocean. Fish will also have special essential fatty acids (Vitamin F) that will help control cholesterol buildup. Known as Vitamin F, such essential fatty acids can often help protect against arteriosclerosis and heart distress. Fish vitamins are speedily metabolized. They are considered to be very swift in body metabolism in contrast to the slower meat vitamins. Ocean vitamins are often favored by folks with sluggish digestion. Fish will give you these needed ocean vitamins.

To help give yourself youthful vitamins together with a harmonious blend of other nutrients, plan on eating meat once a week, poultry once a week, and fish at least two or more times a week. This is the balanced way to feed yourself miracle vitamins as created by Nature.

NATURAL SWEETS —
MIRACLE VITAMIN YOUTH FOOD #5

Satisfy your sweet tooth and vitaminize your body with speedy energy at the same time. This is possible with *natural* sweets such as honey, molasses, maple syrup, corn syrup, carob. These are sold at nearly all food markets as well as specialized health foods.

These natural sweets are excellent sources of the B-complex vitamins that you need for protecting yourself against anemia, for soothing your nervous system, for building up and maintaining body cells and tissues. These natural sweets do even more. They help maintain the health of the intestinal tract, help transform food into the energy you need to give yourself that youthful vitality you deserve.

Energy Elixir. Whenever Michael O. wants a speedy "pickup," he just brews a cup of herb tea which he laces liberally with honey. This gives him the vitalic energy he needs. He feels the heaviness leaving his shoulders. He can move about with the agility of a youngster. It's the sweet way to get sweet energy at any age!

Bounce Brew. As a nightworker at a large factory, Bill E. has always been tempted to doze off right on the job. Sometimes, he feels so overcome with sleep or fatigue that he has to sneak off and lie down in the locker room, right on the floor! His supervisor caught him, but instead of chastising him, suggested a simple change. He advised Bill E. to prepare a glass of fruit juice into which he stirs one-half tablespoon of blackstrap or unsulphured molasses. Sprinkle a bit of Brewer's yeast, if desired. Stir vigorously. Then drink. Bill E. tried it and after a few such Bounce Brew tonics, was able to experience youthful vigor. *Secret?* The fruit juice is a prime source of Vitamins A and C, and these are *activated-amplified* by the B-complex vitamins in the molasses and given even a better boost by the Brewer's yeast. The secret benefit here is that this *Bounce Brew* contains fructose which requires little metabolism. It offers "instant" energy. This fructose transports nerve nourishing vitamins throughout the system so speedily, that hardly long after the one glass is finished, the body "bounces" with vitality and youthful energy. Bill E. drinks just one glass a night, and he fairly speeds through the night shift with amazing vigor.

Select natural sweets and use them in moderation. They are highly concentrated in vitamins. A little goes a long way. They can help make a lazy person an energetic one. Use them whenever sweetening is desired and enjoy youthful energy of your body and mind.

NUTS —
MIRACLE VITAMIN YOUTH FOOD #6

In reality, nuts are dry stone fruits! They are prime sources of the B-complex vitamins needed for energy. Some nuts are also high in Vitamin A to help build better skin and eye health.

Almonds are good sources of the B-complex vitamins. Cashews, pecans and walnuts are prime sources of Vitamin A.

If you want to give yourself a highly-concentrated supply of these and other vitamins, plan to eat nuts regularly. Be sure to *chew thoroughly* since these are also high in minerals and protein; you need to completely chew them so mouth enzymes can send vitamins to the nuts and use them to transport minerals and protein throughout your body.

Many nuts are available. Examples include almonds, Brazil nuts, butternut, cashews, chestnuts, coconut, hazelnut, hickory nuts, macadamia nuts, peanuts, pecans, pistachio, walnuts.

Nuts are well-balanced products of Nature and contain a goodly assortment of healthful vitamins. They are Nature-created vitamins that are able to supercharge you with vitalic energy and youthful alertness. Plan to eat nuts regularly. A dish of nuts for a dessert is healthful. Or eat nuts for a snack. You might also use nut flours (they are sold in many stores) to use for baking to give you even more youthful vitamin fortification — the Nature way!

SEEDS —
MIRACLE VITAMIN YOUTH FOOD #7

Locked within its Nature created envelope, the seed contains the whole embryo of life! It is capable of sustaining itself without outside help. Nature created the seed as an all-purpose complete source of life.

When you eat a seed, you give this embryonic life a chance to flourish within your system and enter into your life and health building processes.

A seed is the very core of youth. Within its minute kernel, the seed has a miracle concentration of vitamins created by Nature to give it life. This same powerhouse is given to you, too.

Vitamin F

Raw, non-processed seeds are the most powerful source of Vitamin F, or those unsaturated and essential fatty acids needed to keep your bloodstream sparkling fresh and clean. Seeds also contain substances to protect against formation of stones in the system.

Seed vitamins help improve your resistance to infectious ailments because they help create strong cellular connective tissues. Seed vitamins also protect against the drying effects of winter as well as summer. A handful of raw seeds will give your body the needed Vitamin F to moisturize your skin and keep it soft and smooth.

Seeds are also high in the nerve-feeding B-complex vitamins, the healthful Vitamin E for your heart, as well as Vitamin A that helps improve your eyesight. *Seeds are one of the few plant foods that contain Vitamin D.* You need Vitamin D to help the formation and integrity of bone tissue. Sunflower seeds are prime source of Vitamin D, which they form in large amounts because they are exposed to the sun's ultraviolet rays for long amounts of time; their faces turn to the sun from dawn to dusk. Sunflower seeds may well be considered the one source of plant Vitamin D that your body needs to build strong bones. Seeds' Vitamin D also helps your body's calcium and phosphorous to nourish your system. Eat seeds daily.

Suggestions: For good vitaminization, eat sunflower and pumpkin seeds as the two that are highest in these needed nutrients. Also include other seeds such as alfalfa, barley, chia, chick peas, clover, fava, lentils, millet, oats, rye, sesame, wheat seeds. Because beans belong to the seed and nut family, include all of them. About 1/2 pound of seeds daily will give your body a treasure of just about all known vitamins that you need to have the throbbing vitality of youth.

BEANS —
MIRACLE VITAMIN YOUTH FOOD #8

Beans, also known as legumes, are one of the best meatless sources of vitamins. But more important, many beans (especially soybeans) contain complete proteins, nearly all known minerals, as well as miracle vitamins A, B and C and also lecithin.

Bean oil such as soybean oil is a very good way to feed yourself nearly all known nutrients, and the valuable Vitamin F, or the essential fatty acids. You may also combine bean flours — such as soybean flour with wheat flour to increase their nutritive potency. Roasted soybeans make excellent vitamin-empowered snacks. Be sure to obtain naturally roasted soybeans since excessive heating and chemicalization will reduce the potency of vitamins.

You will also be giving yourself a goodly amount of these needed vitamins in green beans, string beans, snap beans, lima beans, butter beans.

"Yahni" from Greece

The hardy Greeks must often survive on a minimum of food. They traditionally eat "Yahni" which reportedly contains just about *all* the vitamins as well as minerals and proteins you need for youthful vitality. Here is how you can make "Yahni" from Greece:

Combine 1 pound green beans, a sliced onion and 3 tomatoes. Cook cut-up beans in a very small amount of water for 10 to 15 minutes. Add the onion and tomatoes and season with vegetable oil, sea salt and desired herbs. Add a few pieces of cooked lamb or other meat, if desired, and cook slowly for 30 minutes.

This "Yahni" has a powerhouse of nutrition and miracle vitamins needed to give you the forever young strength of the hardy Greeks.

(Other countries have modified this recipe by adding a minced garlic clove, chopped green pepper, diced celery and chopped parsley. These ingredients may be cooked for a few minutes in soybean oil before adding beans.)

You can also further build up your vitamin intake by using cold-pressed and non-pressed soybean oil. Any vegetable or fruit or plant oil is healthful and beneficial because they contain Vitamin F, or essential fatty acids, that help wash away debris from your arteries and make your arteries and body feel young and alive with the flush of youth.

SUN-DRIED FRUITS —
MIRACLE VITAMIN YOUTH FOOD #9

Sun-dried fruits are excellent sources of Vitamins A, B-complex and C as well as some Vitamin E and K.

When apricots, peaches, plums, grapes, raisins, apples, pears, pineapples, etc., are dried in the sun, the removal of moisture means that the fruits are *naturally* preserved. The high vitamin content becomes very concentrated. So does the natural fruit sugar (fructose) as well as many minerals and enzymes.

This sun-dried fruit now becomes a *package of vitamins* that can give your body a dynamite reaction of youthful energy.

In effect, sun-dried fruits are concentrated vitamin potencies that send a treasure of nutrients streaming throughout your bloodstream, nourishing and invigorating you from head to toe.

You would help give your body the needed vitamin energizers if you will frequently eat these sun-dried fruits. Be sure the package label says that *no* chemicals have been used. Often, commercial products are sulphuric-acid dried and this is unhealthy and vitamin-destructive. Instead, see that the label says "organic" or sun-dried and made without any chemicals. This gives you Nature's most concentrated source of speedy vitamin-creating energy!

COLD-PRESSED OILS — MIRACLE VITAMIN YOUTH FOOD #10

Cold-pressed vegetable oils are believed to be higher in nutrional value than commercially processed oils. They are also said to be more healthful than "hard" fats such as butter or margarine. Many health specialists have suggested an increase in the use of cold-pressed oils and a subsequent reduction in the use of "hard" fats.

Cold-pressed oils contain polyunsaturated fatty acids or *essential fatty acids* (Vitamin F) which the body does *not* make. Therefore, you have to feed your body Vitamin F with cold-pressed oils. This healthful food also helps promote normal growth, guards you against infection and helps maintain a youthful and healthy blood vessel network.

To feed yourself cold-pressed oils, just use them as salad dressing, in marinating, for baking, or as a replacement for animal fats and hydrogenated fats. It is as simple as that.

Cold-pressed oils have the d-alpha-tocopherol form of Vitamin E which is one of the lipids, along with protein and other compounds, and make up the structure of living cells. This vitamin in cold-pressed oils is a natural anti-oxidant in that it helps prevent rancidity. It acts to protect your heart and your blood vessels against premature aging and deterioration.

Food Sources: Most food stores contain cold-pressed oils. Read the label to be sure you are getting the polyunsaturated kind that is highest in polyunsaturated linolenic acid (a member of Vitamin F) and other essential vitamins. Tasty oils available are almond oil, apricot oil, avocado oil, cod liver oil, corn oil, linseed oil, rice bran oil, safflower oil, sesame oil, soybean oil, walnut oil, wheat germ oil. You may use these singly or mix several of them together. Use as a salad dressing on raw vegetables and give yourself a tremendous supply of needed nutrients that help give you the ingredients that extend the life of your cells — and the life of your body, too.

Yes, it's easy and delicious to feed yourself the foods of youth. A few common sense corrections and you will embark upon a delicious way to enjoy the youthful vitality of good health at all ages.

IMPORTANT HIGHLIGHTS

1. Nature has created ten everyday foods with "MV" or Miracle Vitamin youth building power. You can eat your way to perpetual youth.

2. Norah R. eats natural whole grains and now has the digestive apparatus of a youngster.

3. Gladys I. uses fresh raw plant foods that supercharge her system with all known vitamins and now looks and feels "glad all over."

4. Michael O. uses an Energy Elixir to give himself the speedy pickup he needs.

5. Bill E. bounces back with youthful vitality on his night-working job by drinking a *Bounce Brew.*

6. Nuts, seeds, beans, a special "Yahni" dish from Greece, sun-dried fruits and cold-pressed oils are just a few of the vitamin-dynamite foods from Nature that give you "MV" or Miracle Vitamin vitality. Eat your way to perpetual youth!

18

Vitamins for Increased Virility

Vitamins in everyday foods help produce bio-electrical stimuli that activate your body's glands and prompts them to send forth a stream of youth-building hormones. Once your hormones flow abundantly throughout your body, your prime of life enjoys a healthful boost. Your glands hold the key to better health of your body and your mind. Both are needed to enjoy healthy virility with a forever young desire.

Glands: Gateway to Virility

Your endocrine glands are mysterious but powerful internal laboratories that control the secret of healthful virility. Your glands influence your emotional desire for lovemaking and also enter into your ability to reproduce. Your glands send forth hormones which are "spark plugs" that alert and then stimulate your natural capabilities for virility. Your glands need vitamins to be alerted. Once your glands are vitamin-nourished, they can send forth their secretions that will help invigorate your "rivers of virility" and help give you youthful desire for lovemaking.

Hormones: Messengers of Vigor

Hormones are secretions of your endocrine glands that have electrical impulses to prod your desire for consummation in marriage. These hormones also alert the mind as well as the body to create a wholesome and encompassing urge for lovemaking. A healthy stream of these "rivers of sex" flowing throughout your body will do much to give you the impetus to fulfill healthful desires. Hormones would remain lifeless rivers if vitamins were not available to prod them through glandular action so that they can alert your body's responses to perform as an adequate virile person.

Vitamins open the gland gateways to nourish the hormone messengers to flood throughout the body and fill the millions of cells, tissues and muscles with a healthy desire for consummation of the virile urge for fulfillment.

HOW VITAMINS HELP INVIGORATE YOUR "VIRILE THYROID" GLAND

The thyroid is a two-part endocrine gland resembling a butterfly. It rests against the front of your windpipe. The thyroid secretes a virile hormone, *thyroxin,* that stimulates the activity of the body cells. A vitamin shortage means a sluggish thyroid which leads to a weak cellular action. It also reduces the normal virile instinct. A weak or lazy thyroid may well turn a young and vital male into one who is prematurely aged or inept.

B-Complex Vitamins

The B-complex vitamins nourish the cellular and tissue construction of the thyroid. They perform as "energizers" to create a healthful hormone flow to boost virile vigor. The secret here is that the B-complex vitamins become an essential component of a coenzyme in carbon dioxide fixation which is a vital stimulus in intermediary metabolism. This action then helps boost healthful virile responses.

Food Sources: To help feed vitamins to your thyroid so it can secrete healthful virility-boosting thyroxin, you should obtain such wholesome foods as whole grain breads, whole grain cereals, Brewer's yeast, steer liver, nuts, beans and brown rice.

Hormone Energizer

To help vitaminize his glands, Mark K. uses a simple *Hormone Energizer.* In a glass of freshly prepared vegetable juice, he mixes two tablespoons of Brewer's yeast and two tablespoons of wheat germ. He mixes thoroughly. He drinks it with his evening meal. This *Hormone Energizer* is a delicious beverage. But more important, it is a tremendous treasure of the B-complex vitamins that Mark K. needs, because they speedily energize his thyroid and give his gland the working materials out of which the thyroxin hormone is made. Once this hormone flows throughout his body, he reports he feels a throbbing desire and a surge of virility that makes him look, act and consummate like a youngster. Mark V. uses this simple but effective vitamin food for his glands about once a night and enjoys perpetual youth.

How Iodine Boosts the Virile Thyroid Gland

As a mineral, iodine functions in the presence of vitamins. Iodine is needed by the body to help correct problems of tiredness, lethargy and the "cold" feeling that is typical of male or female inadequacy. It is a *combination* of iodine with vitamins that can help correct the problem of being "too tired for love."

Special Food Sources: A powerhouse of iodine is found in kelp, a sea salt. Seafood is another good source. Sun-dried fruits offer you a special combination of iodine with Vitamins A and C. If you will use kelp as a healthful sea salt seasoning, and then eat sun-dried fruits, you will be giving a needed thrust to your thyroid so that it can send virile hormones streaming throughout your body.

Thyroid Feeding Plan

A simple protein is needed to help awaken and alert your sleepy thyroid gland. But this protein, *tyrosine,* (an amino acid from which the thyroid hormone is made) will not function without the presence of Vitamins B_6 and C. Both of these vitamins work to put power into tyrosine, to give it the energizing reaction upon the thyroid and prompt an onrush of virile-alerting thyroxin. So you need a balance.

Natural Aphrodisiac

Loretta U. has found that if she mixes together certain vitamin and protein foods in a special potion, she reacts with exciting vigor. She calls it a *Natural Aphrodisiac*. Here is how she makes it:

In a glass of fruit juice, mix one tablespoon of Brewer's yeast, one tablespoon of wheat germ, one-half tablespoon of blackstrap molasses. Add one tablespoon desiccated liver (sold at health stores or large food outlets) and stir vigorously. Drink one glass in the morning, another glass at noon and a third glass in the evening.

Results: Loretta U. says she experiences such an invigoration, she is as youthful as a bride. She even prepares it for her husband. The two of them feel they are on a perpetual honeymoon, thanks to the gland regeneration of this *Natural Aphrodisiac*.

Effective Energizer

The secret of the *Natural Aphrodisiac* is that it contains Vitamins B_6 and C as well as tyrosine. The two vitamins whip up the tyrosine protein and it goes speedily to the thyroid. Within a brief time, the thyroid gland is alerted, sending forth thyroxin to give the body and the mind the youthful energy it needs to function adequately. This is Nature's miracle of helping to activate a sluggish thyroid — key to virile vigor.

THE PITUITARY — MASTER GLAND OF VIRILE POWER

This gland, about the size of a pea, hangs from a short stalk at the base of the brain. It is called the "master gland" because its three lobes secrete at least nine known hormones that help create a healthfully strong desire for virility.

Sex Hormones

The pituitary generates the function of the male sex hormone, *testosterone* and the female sex hormone, *estrogen*. These hormones influence stimuli and drive for the body as well as the mind. When vitamins are made available to the pituitary, it can send forth these sex hormones which can give the body and mind the vigor and power needed to consummate a healthful desire for lovemaking.

A vitamin-starved pituitary may mean a sex hormone deficiency or decline or deprivation. This may be responsible for premature inadequacy in the male and premature malfunctioning of response in the female.

How to Feed Your Master Gland

While all vitamins are helpful, two of them appear to be especially beneficial because these two vitamins use body stores of protein to feed the pituitary master gland. These are the B-complex vitamins, riboflavin and pantothenic acid.

Riboflavin Sources: Liver, leafy vegetables, eggs, organ meats, Brewer's yeast.

Pantothenic Acid Sources: Fresh fruits and vegetables, soybeans, nuts, egg yolk, desiccated liver and also Brewer's yeast.

Pituitary Potion: In one glass of tomato juice, mix one tablespoon of Brewer's yeast and one tablespoon of desiccated liver. Stir vigorously. Drink in the early evening. *Benefits:* The vitamins in this all-natural potion use the protein to help prod the pituitary gland into youthful alertness. These vitamins also join with the protein to nourish this master gland so that it can then send forth a healthful river of sex hormones that invigorate your entire body and help make you feel as youthful as a honeymooner!

Feed Vitamin E to Your Pituitary

This vitamin is more concentrated in your pituitary gland than in any other part of your body. It helps nourish your hormones and boosts their activity to give you a healthful urge for fulfillment. *Food Sources of Vitamin E:* Wheat germ and wheat germ oil. Cold-pressed polyunsaturated plant oils such as corn, safflower, sunflower, sesame seed oil. *TIP:* Serve broiled liver coated with wheat germ and sesame seeds to give your sex hormones a healthful and vigorous boost.

THE PLANT VITAMIN THAT CREATES
HEALTHFUL POTENCY

Vitamin C, found in many citrus fruits and vegetables, known as a "plant vitamin" may be recognized as a "potency vitamin" because it has a recognized influence on promoting the health of the sexual glands.

There appears to be a unique relationship between the ability of the sex glands to produce hormones and the body's levels of Vitamin C.

Prostatic and reproductive fluids are normally high in Vitamin C. It is reported that the fluids of folks who complained of reduced marital interest, contained a deficiency of Vitamin C. When corrective measures were taken, the virile response was boosted. This gave rise to calling Vitamin C a "potency vitamin" because of its influence on glandular secretions.

Food Sources of the Potency Vitamin

Fresh citrus fruits and their freshly squeezed juices are your best sources of organic Vitamin C. *Note:* Because Vitamin C evaporates rapidly when exposed to air and sunshine, it is advised that you eat or drink fruits or fruit juices speedily upon preparing. Try not to store them. The fresher the fruit juice, the more potent the Vitamin C supply.

HOW VITAMIN E CAN GIVE YOUR GLANDS
A YOUTHFUL "GO" POWER

Many have hailed Vitamin E as a reproductive or "virile" vitamin. In many parts of Europe, it is called a "sex vitamin." It has already been noted that Vitamin E can supercharge the glands with vigor and give "go" power to the hormones so that folks enjoy extended vigor at an extended age.

Vitamin E Helps Improve Fertility

The male reproductive fluid undergoes a qualitative improvement when nourished by Vitamin E, thus enabling it to unite with the female ova to produce a healthy offspring. Vitamin E reportedly also helps regenerate new fluid in the ducts of the male which may otherwise be empty. Vitamin E alerts the glands to create more reproductive fluid and protect against inadequacy.

Secret Benefit: Vitamin E nourishes the sex-generating cells. They alert the glands to create spermatozoa within the reproductive fluids and nourish the semi-niferous tubules of the testes. They also influence the female glands so that response and desire retain youthful vigor. Vitamin E is more concentrated in the pituitary gland which influences the creation of hormones in the reproductive organs.

Since Vitamin E protects both the pituitary and adrenal glands to prevent their destruction by conserving oxygen, you should obtain it daily.

A simple program is to use wheat germ oil in a salad dressing. Use polyunsaturated cold-pressed oils wherever a fat is called for in a recipe. This will give you a healthful supply of this needed gland vitamin that helps give you fertility and virility.

HOW TO USE VITAMINS TO GET YOUR
GLANDS TO WAKE UP AND LIVE
. . . AND LOVE

To keep your glands healthy, full of life and love, here are some vitaminization suggestions:

1. Nourish your thyroid and other glands with B-complex vitamins. Season foods with kelp as well as Brewer's yeast. Also use natural brown rice and whole grain breads and grains.

2. Include lots of seeds and nuts and non-processed nut butters, in your food program. This gives you a natural balance of vitamins, minerals and proteins that are needed by your glands for healthful nourishment.

3. Because seeds contain all the elements necessary to launch and sustain a new life, they are rich in prime nutrients that make up the hormones of your body. Serve a dish of mixed seeds for dessert or a TV snack. Munch on pumpkin seeds, sesame seeds, sunflower seeds. Use cold-pressed seed oils, too.

4. Meats should be fresh and as non-processed as possible. Many preserved meats such as frankfurters are saturated with

nitrates and nitrites. These two chemical preservatives destroy vitamins. Furthermore, another name for potassium nitrate (found in preserved meats) is saltpeter, the substance that is known for stifling sexual desire. Your meats should be fresh-killed for better vitaminization of your glands and better health of your body.

5. Do your baking with whole grain flours. A suggestion is to add a tablespoon of rose hips powder to your baking for a natural vitamin enrichment. This powder is sold in many health stores. (Rose hips are the red berries left after the rose petals have fallen. They are some 60 times higher in Vitamin C than most citrus fruits.) Also sprinkle rose hips powder on cereals, on toast, or in a hot herb beverage. For any use of flour, it should be unbleached and natural.

6. For a healthful salad dressing, mix a little honey with a fruit juice. The benefit here is that honey contains *aspartic acid,* a protein that is taken up by the vitamins in the fruit juice and sent to your glands for replenishment and nourishment. Without vitamins, this protein substance might be inactive. So just combine honey and fruit juice in a salad dressing, and you have a healthful gland food.

7. Omit tobacco. There have been cases in which potency was restored when the cigarette habit was given up. Tobacco destroys Vitamin C and other nutrients so when you kick this habit, you help give your glands the needed vitamins for nourishment.

8. Wherever possible, select wholesome and chemical-free foods that are prime sources of nutrients.

9. Daily, eat a large fresh fruit salad or abundant fresh fruit or their juices.

10. Daily, eat a large fresh vegetable salad. Munch on raw vegetables. Drink vegetable juices.

Your glands are the fountainhead of your love life. Give them nourishment and they will send forth the fountains of hormones that will help you wake up and live . . . and love.

SPECIAL POINTS

1. Vitamins nourish your glands and prompt them to send forth virile-activating hormones.

2. Mark K. experiences a thyroid activation with an easy *Hormone Energizer* beverage.

3. For folks "too tired to love," a *Natural Aphrodisiac,* as used by Loretta U. can help make them feel as if they are on a perpetual honeymoon.

4. Use B-complex vitamins and a *Pituitary Potion* for an all-natural life that gives you "go power."

5. Vitamin C is being hailed as a "potency vitamin" and is readily available in most citrus fruits and juices.

6. Vitamin E has a secret sex-generating benefit. It's recognized as a youth vitamin.

7. Your gland-energizing program is easy with the simple ten-step outlined system. Organic vitamins can help give a miracle of youthfulness to your glands, your hormones and your love life.

19

How to Plan Your Personal "MOV" Program for Youthful Health

An amazingly simple schedule can help fortify your body with natural vitamins and other nutrients for better and more youthful health. Here is how you can plan your own personal "MOV" (Miracle Organic Vitamin) Program to help enjoy good food and better health.

FOR EFFECTIVE "MOV" BENEFITS, USE WHOLESOME FOODS

To get the most out of your "MOV" Program, select wholesome foods. Basically, there are *three* types of wholesome or better foods.

1. *Organic Food.* Refers to the growing stages of food in which the soil was treated solely with natural fertilizers (such as compost and humus) and not with any chemicals. Plants have not been treated with chemical pesticides, neither have they been doused with polluted waters. Organic meats have been fed with organic feed. They have not been given antibiotics, or chemicalized synthetic hormones.

2. *Natural Food.* Refers to food after the growing stage. That is, such food made available to you is non-processed, not treated with preservatives, is free of artificial flavorings or color-

ings. The simple rule of thumb is "nothing added — nothing taken away." An example would be fresh fruits as being all-natural. This is in opposition to processed applesauce or prepared apple foods that may have been processed or otherwise treated.

3. *Health Food.*   A more generic meaning includes all that is organic, natural or whole-grain. Also refers to stores of this type which will stock wholesome foods that may be organic from growth, natural after growth, and non-processed. It is healthful to eat wholesome foods that are free from vitamin-destroying chemicals. So, be sure to read the labels of any item packaged as a "health food" to determine if it is as pure as you desire it to be.

Wherever possible, the first "MOV" law is that purchased foods should be as natural as possible. This means it has organic vitamins that are needed by your body to help give you youthful health. If your food is healthy — you will be healthy, too. Now, here is how to plan your personal "MOV" program for youthful health.

1. *Milk.*   Plan to drink at least two glasses of whole milk daily to give you a balance of vitamins, minerals and protein. It is a *natural* combination that helps fortify your body with healthful elements. You may also use fat-free or skim milk or yogurt for your daily quota of vitamins.

2. *Whole Grains.*   Breads, cereals, rice should be whole grain and unbleached. Use whole grain wheat germ in cooking or added to whole grain cereals. Brewer's yeast as well as lecithin will give you needed B-complex vitamins with the whole grains. Granola cereals as well as any unbleached natural cereals made with wheat germ, yeast and fresh fruit slices give you healthful and natural vitamin fortification.

3. *Vegetables.*   Essential for Vitamin A, select dark-colored raw vegetables. Eat them raw. Cook *only* those vegetables which must be cooked. Use a simple salad dressing of some fruit juice and honey, or a dollop of yogurt for a natural balance of organic vitamins.

4. *Fruits.*   Eat fresh raw fruits daily. For good Vitamin C buildup, eat the white of the rind. Avoid cooking fruits, except as an occasional treat. With so many fruits available throughout the year, you can enjoy luscious juicy plants regularly with a different taste thrill for each.

5. *Fish Oils.* Concentrated fish liver oils are good sources of Vitamins A and D and other essential nutrients. Just one tablespoon daily is healthful. A simple *Vitamin Tonic* that is brimming with goodness is one enjoyed by a schoolteacher from the cold Northeast where Louise B. is deprived adequate sunshine and Vitamin D. Louise B. puts a tablespoon of a fish liver tonic in a glass of tomato juice. She adds a bit of Brewer's yeast, a half teaspoon of desiccated liver. She stirs vigorously. Just one glass a day of this *Vitamin Tonic* helps nourish Louise B. so that her skin is healthy and clear, her bones are strong, her eyesight is good, and she is able to resist winter infections more readily. This is a power-packed natural *Vitamin Tonic* that is helpful to all.

6. *Plant Oils.* Use polyunsaturated cold-pressed vegetable oils daily in cooking, as seasoning or in salad dressings. Keep these oils refrigerated. They are prime sources of Vitamin E and the essential fatty acids of Vitamin F.

7. *Raw Juices.* For quickly assimilated vitamins, drink raw fruit and vegetable juices daily. They quench your thirst and also drench your billions of body cells and tissue with rejuvenating vitamins.

8. *Meats.* Healthful meat that is as organic as possible will send a high quality vitamin supply into your system. Select glandular meats such as kidneys, liver, heart and plan to serve at least once or twice a week.

9. *Poultry.* Chicken and turkey are high in vitamins and low in calories and cholesterol in comparison to other meats. Eat them regularly.

10. *Fish.* All that is in the fish has come from the ocean, one of Nature's richest source of vitamins, minerals, proteins. Fish is a good source of many vitamins and also Vitamin F which helps protect against cholesterol. If possible, serve fish several times a week.

11. *Eggs.* Use once or twice a week. Boil, poach or scramble gently in small amounts of polyunsaturated oils at a moderate temprature. Eggs are good sources of Vitamin A with a balanced amount of protein.

12. *Soups.* Any simple soup can be transformed into a treasure of vitamins. John W. reportedly had frequent bronchial

attacks; he was nervous and ill-tempered. He also had dimming vision. He ate irregularly. When his wife gave him soups, she fortified it *naturally* with vitamins. She included powdered milk for Vitamins A and D. She added yeast for the B-complex vitamins. She added vegetable slices for more vitamins. Results? John W. was improved. The vitamins helped soothe his respiratory tract; his nervous system was nourished. His eyes were fed, too. Now, John W. eats soup daily. It's the delicious and natural way to build better health with tasty vitamins from Nature.

13. *Salads.*   A salad can be a vitamin meal in itself. By just combining raw or some cooked vegetables, sprinkling with yeast, you have a vitamin meal that is succulent and deliciously tasty. Fruit salads are also brimming with Vitamins A and C. A tossed salad is always welcome when appetites are sluggish. No need to be malnourished or vitamin-starved when you have fresh raw salads available. For a powerhouse of tasty vitamins, just serve a raw fruit salad with cottage cheese and sun-dried raisins and apricots. You'll be giving yourself almost all known vitamins. . . in one plate!

14. *Nuts.*   These are Nature's own seed-bearing fruits, in the form of nuts. Rich in Vitamins A through K and also the essential fatty acids known as Vitamin F. Plan to eat nuts regularly. You may also mash nuts and mix with casseroles, add to baked goods, for a natural triple fortification of vitamins.

15. *Seeds.*   Nature's perfect food. Seeds are self-perpetuating. Seeds carry within their enclosures the means for survival without any outside help and can so survive for thousands of years. Plan to partake of this perfect food. Eat raw seeds as snacks. Use them for baking, too. Seed flour (and nut flour, too) can be used in baking for even greater "MOV" health buildup. Tasty and healthy.

16. *Fresh Foods.*   For top notch vitamin power, your foods should be as fresh as possible. If you must buy canned foods, then do so sparingly. Eat your canned food with some fresh or raw foods to maintain a balance so that you will be giving your body an assortment of healthful vitamins.

17. *Frozen Foods.*   These are preferable to canned foods. Frozen foods do contain a large amount of vitamins

(canned foods are low in natural organic vitamins) and can be used if you are unable to avail yourself of fresh foods.

18. *Herbs.*   These are Nature's own vitamins and considered all-purpose natural supplements. Use herbs as flavorings and also for sprinkling over salads. They are highly concentrated sources of miracle vitamins as grown by Nature.

19. *Combinations.*   A happy stomach means happy health. Put a smile in your stomach with visual and taste appeal combinations. Arrange foods so that they look flavorful. If they look good, they will taste better and give you better health, too.

20. *Controlled Fasting.*   On an occasional day, treat your body to a controlled fasting. On that day, enjoy either fruits *or* vegetables for your meals. No other foods to be taken. You will be able to give these vitamins an opportunity to help scrub away body debris and toxemia and make you feel fresh and alert.

With some common-sense suggestions as outlined above, you can enjoy good "MOV" replenishment of your body and emerge much the better for it.

SUMMARY

1. It's easy to plan your personal "MOV" (Miracle Organic Vitamin) program using wholesome foods. For top notch vitamin content, foods should be as natural and non-processed as possible.

2. Louise B. uses an easily made *Vitamin Tonic* to vitaminize her skin, strengthen her bones, eyesight and resist winter infections.

3. John W. uses vitamin-enriched soups to nutritionally resist bronchitis and to soothe his nervous system and improve his eyesight.

4. In just 20 easy steps, you can supercharge your system with healthful vitamins in foods.

20

A Treasury of Organic Vitamin Home Healers

Help Nature nourish your body's needs to keep it looking and feeling young. A balanced food program that emphasizes healthful vitamins will do much to protect you against distress and also give you the substances out of which youthful health is created. Organic vitamins in foods are the "missing links" in a jigsaw puzzle. Put them in place, in the puzzle that is your body, and you have a complete picture of healthful living.

Here is a treasury of organic vitamin home healers using simple, everyday foods, yet with a rich goldmine of miracle rejuvenation. These are Nature's very own secrets as found in wholesome and delicious foods. Now, Nature shares those secrets of healing with you. Now you can use Nature's food to help enjoy happy good health. Nature always meant you to have that reward for good vitaminization of your body and mind.

A GOLDEN DOZEN SECRETS OF VITAMIN CELLULAR REJUVENATION

Vitamin C is the magic-like ingredient in citrus fruits, (especially oranges) that prompts the creation of collagen, the cellular rejuvenation substance your body needs in order to keep your billions of cells in healthful working order.

Here are a reported[1] golden dozen secrets of using orange vitamins to help rebuild your cells and tissues:

1. Float an unpeeled slice of orange in a glass of eggnog or any other health drink.
2. Baste your turkey or chicken with freshly squeezed orange juice, a grated peel and honey.
3. For a refreshing reward to any meal, tuck tender, flaky coconut between slices of juicy oranges—and munch away.
4. Soak dried mint leaves in freshly squeezed orange juice and add a little honey. This is especially good on lamb.
5. If you're shy of dessert dishes, serve fresh fruit slices in scooped out orange shells left over from the breakfast orange juice.
6. Try cooking natural brown rice in orange juice. Be sure to add the grated peel for extra flavor.
7. Stuff chicken or hen with quartered oranges.
8. Cut large oranges in half and serve them like grapefruit.
9. Try an orange omelet. Beat a little of the fresh, grated peel and juice in with the eggs.
10. Slice orange sections into tossed green salad.
11. Use freshly squeezed orange juice instead of water to make any kind of gravy. Add the grated peel, too.
12. Break a raw egg into a glass of freshly squeezed orange juice. Shake to a froth and sip a vitaminized "orangenog."

Also: Just one cup of fresh orange juice gives you about 125 milligrams of Vitamin C, nearly double the basic minimum. Since this water-soluble vitamin is not stored in the body, you need it every single day to enjoy good cellular rebuilding and better health. Plan to enjoy fresh citrus fruits and juices daily. Your cells will love you for it.

Acidosis. An overworked and tension-driven executive, Floyd L. has frequent bouts of acid unrest and "sour stomach." He finds that if he begins his meal with a fresh vegetable juice, it helps soothe his burning and lessens discomforts. Vegetables contain soothing Vitamins A and E and help promote a natural tranquility in the digestive system, especially before a meal.

[1]*Parker Natural Health Bulletin,* West Nyack, New York 10994. Available by subscription at $15.00 per year. Vol. 3, No. 5. March 5, 1973.

Skin Blemishes.   Lots of fresh fruits and vegetables with many vitamins help rebuild skin tissues to protect against acne or other blemishes. After washing your face, splash on some lemon juice for the Vitamin C invigorated acid to restore the natural acid mantle, a protective coating against blemishes.

Addison's Disease.   Skin blemishes traced to underactivity of the adrenal (endocrine) glands. Nourish the glands with vitamins in whole grains, lean meats, seeds and nuts. Cold-pressed oils with Vitamin E and the essential fatty acids (Vitamin F) are helpful in alerting and invigorating the sleepy adrenal glands.

Allergies.   Rebuild fragile skin tissues and also nourish the epithelial linings of the nose and throat with fresh fruits and vegetables. Emphasize whole grains and natural brown rice, lean meats, fish, wholesome cheeses. These give the needed vitamins to help invigorate respiratory tract to guard against virus and allergen attacks.

"Tired Blood."   Whether poor blood or anemia, your billions of blood cells and corpuscles need nourishment. Broiled liver, poultry, soybeans, onions, garlic, tomatoes, will give you the needed organic vitamins out of which rich red blood corpuscles are made. An "always cold" commercial artist, Vivian T., had a pale skin with bluish lips. Even when working in a warm office, she had to wear a sweater. She was given to frequent chills that made her hands and feet feel "like ice." She was able to warm up her "cold blood" by a simple vitamin *Blood Building Tonic.* In a glass of tomato juice, stir a tablespoon of desiccated liver. Then add a spoon of shredded or mashed onion rings. She would drink one or two glasses of this *Blood Building Tonic* daily. She would also eat broiled liver twice weekly and emphasize garlic and onions as well as cooked soybeans in her program. Results? The vitamins used the iron in these foods to replenish her blood cells. She let Nature rebuild the corpuscles in her bone marrow and now she has a bright warm skin, bright lips. She no longer wears sweaters indoors. Her hands and feet and body feel "as warm as sunshine," thanks to the vitamin rebuilding in the natural tonic. Let Nature do the healing!

Heart Care.   Protect against oxygen deficiency with a low "hard" fat program. Increase intake of Vitamin E in cold-pressed polyunsaturated plant oils. Use whole grain foods and natural brown rice. These offer oxygen-sparing vitamins to protect your heart.

Arteriosclerosis. To protect against cholesterol clogging, use whole grain foods and polyunsaturated oils for Vitamin E and the essential fatty acids (Vitamin F) to wash away internal deposits. These vitamins help wash the blood vessel walls and keep your arteries nice and clean.

Arthritis. Plant vitamins are able to metabolize deposits in and around the cartilage of the joints. Often, excessive carbohydrates predispose to stiffening of the limbs because they cannot be metabolized. Reduce intake of starches and sugars. Substitue with wholesome foods, lean meats, poultry, and fish. Ocean fish are good for their Vitamin F content that helps to wash away carbohydrate sludge and protect against arthritic-like joint stiffness.

Better Breathing. Allergies such as asthma call for the cleansing away of mucus buildup. Mucus is usually caused by excessive intake of concentrated carbohydrates. Eat lots of fresh raw fruits and vegetables. The vitamins help scrub away carbohydrate grime in the respiratory tract. Lean meats, poultry, fish, also offer good amounts of Vitamins A and D that help cleanse the system and prompt better breathing.

Eyesight. Most essential are Vitamins A and D which are found in yellow and dark green plant foods and also in fish, especially fish liver oils. A tablespoon of cod liver oil taken daily will send a stream of eyesight-nourishing Vitamins A and D. Also eat fish several times a week for more eyesight and body vitaminization.

Biliousness. This bloated or "gas" feeling is often traced to incomplete digestion of fats and excessive fermentation in the digestive tract; this causes improper flow of bile from the liver. To correct, *begin* a meal with vitamin-rich raw vegetables. The vitamins in the vegetables will alert digestive enzymes to begin metabolizing foods that will be introduced. The vitamin-powered enzymes will help digestive juices metabolize the fats and guard against fermentation. This protects against gas bloating.

Bladder. Distress of the bladder may be traced to insufficiently metabolized protein foods. Protect against acid end products (from incompletely digested meat foods) by increasing your intake of vitamin-high raw fruits and vegetables. These vitamins will help cleanse away acid crystals from the system and soothe the bladder so it can function contentedly.

Hypertension. Control a "runaway blood pressure" by cutting down on excessively high fatty foods and eliminating table salt from foods. Use the needed Vitamin F (essential fatty acids) in cold-pressed oils to soothe the blood pressure. Increase intake of whole grains for nerve-nourishing B-complex vitamins. Fish and poultry should replace excessive meat intake. Fresh plant juices are soothing.

Bronchitis. Wash away debris from your bronchial tubes with vitamins in raw fruits and vegetables. Fresh fruits also help scrub the excessive mucus clinging to the bronchial tubes. Cleanse away inner waste and detoxify bacteria with vitamins in fruits and vegetables. Ease up on excessive carbohydrate intake.

Bursitis. Caused by the drying up of the moisturizing oil (synovial lubrication) in the joints. The avocado is a plant food high in oils that should help make up for a deficiency. The use of any polyunsaturated cold-pressed oils daily will do much to give your body and joints the needed oils to guard against symptomatic reactions of bursitis. Reduce intake of "hard" fats and replace with "soft" or plant oil fats. The latter have high natural oil content needed by your body and joints, too.

Colds. Fortify yourself with Vitamin C from citrus fruits, and a balance of wholesome grains, lean meats, fish, poultry, cheeses, nuts and seeds to give you a *variety* of nutrients that work in *harmony* to help guard against infections of a virus source.

Colitis. Send healthful vitamins into your fluttery colon by drinking a glass of buttermilk. Its vitamins soothe the burning tissues of the colon. Eat more raw fruits and vegetables since these nourish your digestive system and content your colon. Ease up on cooked foods which are vitamin deficient.

Regularity. To help correct problems of constipation, eat vitamin-high bulk foods such as fibrous vegetables. Also eat whole grain foods which contain the B-complex vitamins needed to prod the act of peristalsis and correct constipation.

Throat Cough. Nourish the parched respiratory tissues of

the throat with Vitamins A and C. Lean meats, turkey, cheese, plant foods and their juices will give you good amounts of needed cellular rebuilding vitamins. Seed oils offer needed moisture to lubricate the throat tissues.

Tired Feeling.   Call it fatigue or mid-day slump, that tired feeling can be a symptom of malnourishment of body cells and tissues. Nourish and clean them by lots of fresh fruits and vegetables. The citrus fruits offer Vitamin C which speedily send energy-building fructose to your body glands and prompt them to issue forth vitalic hormones. Drink a glass of fruit juice and supercharge your organism with vitaminized hormones.

Gall Bladder.   Biliousness and distress may often be caused by improperly digested fatty and fried foods. Begin by cutting down on animal fats. Use Vitamin F foods such as seeds, nuts and their plant oils. A folk remedy is to take the juice of a lemon in a glass of hot water and drink several times a day. The vitamin content helps wash away improperly metabolized fats. An occasional raw juice fast in which nothing but fresh juices are consumed throughout the day, is soothing to the gall bladder and also helps improve liver health.

Gastritis.   Often traced to end products of hot condiments such as ketchup, mustard, harsh vinegar, tobacco, alcohol and also chemicalized soft drinks. To soothe your system, protect against the formation of gas by eliminating harsh and unnatural seasonings. Use healthful herbs in a natural form. Eat more raw foods with important vitamins that weaken and dilute these harsh volatile end debris and help wash them out of your system.

Sleeplessness.   Help soothe your nervous system and protect against insomnia by drinking a glass of warm milk. Vitamins in the milk use its minerals to help soothe the nerves and promote an overall relaxation. Milk vitamins also guard against excessive acidity in the system which churns and keeps you awake. Soybean milk is healthful, too. Just warm slightly for a feeling of relaxation all over your body and your mind, too.

Neuritis.   For problems of nervousness or symptoms of an undernourished nervous system, a self-cleansing program is healthful. Frequently, accumulated uric acid crystals press against raw nerves and cause unpleasant side effects. Use wholesome and non-processed foods. Whole grains, natural brown rice, are prime sources of nerve-feeding B-complex vitamins. Replace meat foods (causes of uric acid buildup) with a brief vegetarian fasting program. For several days, enjoy raw vegetables as well as fruits, nuts, seeds, and use soybeans for a nearly-complete protein food. It helps vitaminize your nervous system and wash out acid buildup. Soothes the body and nervous system.

Heartburn. Also known as *pyrosis.* Use vegetable vitamins because these plants contain minerals that can soothe and relax that burning sensation in the digestive tract. Vegetable vitamins use these minerals to cool and dilute the acid buildup and help weaken its burning sensations. Eat raw vegetable salads. Drink vegetable juices. To help insulate your system against corrosion, begin each meal with a well-chewed raw vegetable salad. Replace acid-causing coffee or tea or chemicalized soft drinks with fresh raw vegetable juices.

Sciatica. This is an inflammation of the sciatic nerve or surrounding muscle. It is often traced to deterioration of the nerve covering or myalin sheath. Vitamin B-complex in whole grains, also natural brown rice, unbleached cereals, natural bread goods, Brewer's yeast, will help build up this protective covering of the nerve and protect against sciatica.

Yes, Nature has placed a goldmine of vitamins in foods. These vitamins are nuggets of health that can give you the feeling of golden youth from top to bottom. The key is in maintaining a *balance.* Obtain a balanced food program using wholesome foods and you will reap the rewards of the miracle of organic vitamins for better. . . and everlasting health.

FINAL SUMMARY

1. Organic vitamins in everyday foods can rebuild your body and offer you hope for youthful health.
2. Rejuvenate your billions of body cells with citrus fruits. You have 12 delicious ways to feed your cells the needed Vitamin C.
3. Floyd L. was able to control his acidosis or "sour stomach"

with a simple program. Just begin each meal with a vitamin-soothing plant juice.

4. Vivian T. was able to wake up and warm up her "cold blood" with a simple vitaminized *Blood Building Tonic*.

5. Use Nature's organic vitamins in tasty foods to help give your body the working materials with which to help heal and correct many described disorders.

Organ-O-Matic Vitamin Finder Index

need

cod liver oil
Brewer's Yeast